Studying School Effectiveness

Edited by

David Reynolds

(on behalf of the
School Differences Research Group)

The Falmer Press

(A member of the Taylor & Francis Group)
London and Philadelphia

UK   The Falmer Press, Falmer House, Barcombe, Lewes, East Sussex,
          BN8 5DL

USA   The Falmer Press, Taylor & Francis Inc., 242 Cherry Street,
          Philadelphia, PA 19106-1906

Copyright © School Differences Research Group 1985

First published 1985

Library of Congress Cataloging in Publication Data

Main entry under title:

Studying school effectiveness.

   Papers originally presented at the British Educational
Research Association Annual Conference held at the
University of London Institute of Education on
2 September 1983.
   Includes bibliographies and indexes.
   1. Schools—Great Britain—Evaluation—Congresses.
2. Education—Research—Great Britain—Congresses.
I. Reynolds, David, 1949–   . II. British Educational
Research Association. Conference (1983: University of
London Institute of Education).
LA632.S825   1985   379.1′56   85-1592
ISBN 1-85000-023-9
ISBN 1-85000-024-7 (pbk.)

Typeset in 11/13 Garamond by
Imago Publishing Ltd, Thame, Oxon

*Printed in Great Britain by Taylor & Francis (Printers) Ltd,
Basingstoke*

Contents

Preface   *vii*

Introduction: Ten Years On — A Decade of School Effectiveness   1
Research Reviewed
David Reynolds

1   Frameworks for Research on the Effectiveness of
Schooling.
Peter Cuttance   13

2   Issues in the Assessment of School Outcomes
Janet Ouston and Barbara Maughan   29

3   School Climate: A Review of a Problematic
Concept
Janet Strivens   45

4   Conceptualizing Curriculum Differences for
Studies of Secondary School Effectiveness
Brian Wilcox   59

5   Pastoral Care and School Effectiveness
David Galloway   75

6   Examination Results in Mixed and Single-Sex Secondary
Schools
Jane Steedman   87

7   Combining Quantitative and Qualitative Approaches
to Studies of School and Teacher Effectiveness.
John Gray and Ben Jones   103

8   The ILEA Junior School Study: An
Introduction
Peter Mortimore and Team   117

Contents

9   The Theoretical Underpinnings of School
    Change Strategies
    Jill Lewis   137

10 Pathways to Institutional Development in
    Secondary Schools
    Derek Phillips, Ron Davie and Eileen Callely   155

11 Schools Make a Difference: Implications for
    Management in Education
    Pamela Young   177

12 The Second Stage: Towards a Reconceptualization
    of Theory and Methodology in School Effectiveness
    Research
    David Reynolds and Ken Reid   191

13 Studying School Effectiveness: A Postscript
    Anne Jones   205

Contributors   211

Indexes   213

Preface

The papers included in this collection were originally presented at the British Educational Research Association Annual Conference held at the University of London Institute of Education on 2 September 1983. The seminar was chaired by Anne Jones, Head of Cranford Community School and a past chairman of the Association for Child Psychology and Psychiatry.

The School Differences Study Group receives a grant from the Association for Child Psychology and Psychiatry which covers the travelling costs of participants. It started in 1979 and has been meeting regularly since then. We meet for a whole day once a term with papers being presented either by members of the study group or visitors. The group is quite informal, and has a central core of about fifteen members from universities throughout England and Wales. As will be seen from the papers included here, our interests and backgrounds cover a wide range of social science disciplines including education, sociology, psychology and educational administration.

Each of the conference participants was asked to review briefly three questions:

> Why are you interested in this problem?
> What has (or will) come out of research in this area?
> What are the unresolved issues?

The papers included in this volume are extended versions of the conference presentations.

Introduction: Ten Years On — A Decade of Research and Activity in School Effectiveness Research Reviewed

David Reynolds

A decade ago there were very few people engaged in the study of schools as institutions for learning. Now — ten years on — the number of those involved in research in this field has grown and the literature available on the school and its internal processes has begun to reach a considerably more respectable level.

Our aim in this book is to present the substantive findings of school effectiveness research over the last decade, and also to discuss the areas where this first stage of research has indicated we need to concentrate our efforts. This task, though, cannot really be accomplished without an understanding of the social and educational climate within which this body of research has been situated, since this professional climate and 'paradigm' that has been dominant within the educational research community in Britain and abroad has itself affected the nature of the past decade's work on schools. Since school effectiveness research has arisen in part as a reaction and a challenge to the allegations that schools are not important determinants of pupil characteristics, it is with the traditional paradigm that we must start our review of our field's accomplishments and limitations to date.

A variety of factors outside the educational research discipline were influential in generating a belief in the unimportance of schooling. The failure of post-1960s 'social engineering' to improve either the overall quantity of educational talent or its historically unequal distribution between social classes, racial groups and sexual groupings led many within the discipline to echo Bernstein's (1970) call that 'education cannot compensate for society'. The overwhelming majority of studies conducted in the United States into the determinants of pupil learning — represented by Coleman (1966) and Jencks (1972) in particular — reinforced this view by showing that knowledge of certain characteristics of pupils' schools did not enable one to predict with any degree of accuracy the attainment of individual pupils on leaving school. Knowledge of the pupils' individual characteristics or the characteristics of their family environment, by contrast, had high predictive value.

In Britain, too, the great majority of research indicated that home background was the important determining variable. The Plowden Report (1967) found little relationship between outcomes and school characteristics, with the great majority of variance in attainment explicable by family background and parental attitudes. Ainsworth's (1972) follow-up of the Plowden children found a remarkably high correlation of 0.8 between children's verbal reasoning scores at age 10 and age 15 at the end of compulsory secondary schooling.

The great majority of research studies took as a given base that family factors were determinant and proceeded to 'reinforce' this paradigm. Any cursory glance at educational research journals of the 1960s and the early to mid-1970s, at lists of higher degree titles or at reviews of the literature shows that they are concerned to 'individualize' as due to individual or family background characteristics the various pupil school outcomes, whether these are educational problems, affective characteristics or cognitive outcomes. Authors were able to claim school influence to be minimal even though in many cases the school was never measured or assessed — Cooper (1966), for example, argued that 'the role of the school seemed to be minimal' in explaining truancy but had absolutely no data on schools to justify such a statement. Tyerman (1968) argued for the importance of the home in determining levels of non-attendance, but when some of his sample of truants gave school-based explanations for their actions he considered them as mere 'rationalizations' and ignored them. Even if data were not available to support exclusively family-based explanations and even if there were conflicting evidence, research studies were reported in ways that made them 'fit' with existing dominant paradigms.

The National Children's Bureau cohort study, *From Birth to Seven* (Davie *et al.*, 1972), of children born in a defined period in 1958 is also notable in its early phases for its concentration upon the home and personal variables of its sample and neglect of the characteristics of their schools. The study itself, its accompanying publicity and the associated publications linked with it (Donnison, 1972) all substantially emphasized that the evidence from the study showed the importance of the home, yet the neglect to gather anything other than the most basic data upon the schools that the sample were attending made such findings highly likely. It seems extraordinary that studies went into such detail on the quality of the plumbing in people's houses and on their sanitary amenities but measured so very little about their children's schooling. Given the independence of some cohort children from their family background, as evidenced by the Scottish children's high reading scores in poor housing conditions (Burgess, 1975), the absence of investigation into the schools is even more remarkable.

What factors can explain this past neglect within educational research of the school characteristics of children? The predominance of former teachers within the educational research community may be one explanation, given the well documented tradition of such practitioners to blame external forces as the source of their problems within schools. Perhaps the social pathology model or medical models have had an effect in moulding the individualistic paradigm and perhaps even governmental funding policy for social scientific and educational research — which has been notably favourable to certain institutions which have generated individualistic explanations — has encouraged a proliferation of home-based explanations, given the latter's tendency to represent less threat to 'the state apparatus' than school-based or institutionalized ones. Perhaps the psychiatric paradigm — with its belief that there are home-based explanations for problems such as truancy which may otherwise be school related — has influenced educational research through its influence upon educational psychologists, with whom child psychiatrists have close professional links. Perhaps concentration upon the homes of children rather than upon their schools simply reflects the fact that it is considerably easier to harass the parents of the socially deprived than it is to harass their schools.

The most likely explanations, however, seem threefold, reflecting the intellectual insecurity of the early British educational research enterprise, the specific nature of British sociology of education since the late 1960s and the sheer volume of practical problems that have dogged work in this field.

If one looks at these factors in sequence, it seems likely that the existence of a paradigm which 'individualizes' the explanation of child behaviour reflects the way in which educational research, conscious of its youth, its intellectual insecurity and its very recent intellectual origins, grasped at educational psychology as its source discipline of methodology and theory. Given the number of educational researchers who are also educational psychologists, this seems highly understandable — in one survey (Thomas, 1980), of eighty-three professors of education in Britain, twenty-seven were psychologists as listed in the British Psychological Society membership list. Psychological beliefs or paradigms as to, for example, the importance of early experience and early family life in general and the importance of family factors in the work of the 'abnormal' psychologists are highly likely to have had an effect upon a wider intellectual tradition. Interestingly, whilst psychology has increasingly begun to turn against the importance of early family experience (Clarke and Clarke, 1976) and has begun to see behaviour as more and more situationally determined (Rutter, 1980), the new concentration upon those characteristics or 'coping strategies' that enable individuals to *avoid* family influences (in stressful families for example) is not in evidence within the educational research community.

The second major factor affecting the nature of the 'individualizing' paradigm that has dominated educational research thinking is the widespread assumption within sociology of education, our other source discipline, that schools were merely *confirmed* by the capitalist economy into child processing institutions that faithfully reproduced their family and home-based inequalities. Whilst in the 1960s it was assumed that the school was independent of the nature of its intakes inasmuch as it had its own effects upon outcomes (as in the work of Hargreaves, 1967 and Lacey, 1970), the rise of neo-Marxism in the 1970s as seen in the work of Bowles and Gintis (1976) and others popularized the 'correspondence' theory of educational system/ society interrelationship. What went on in the school was now simply *determined* by outside school factors such as the social class system. It was the political, economic and wider social systems not the school that became the focus of interest for many sociologists of education. Research using the school as the unit of analysis all but ceased.

The third set of factors influencing the adoption of the individualistic paradigm was the sheer practical difficulty of undertaking school-based research. There was major difficulty for researchers who wanted to gain access to schools for comparative work, as the unhappy experience of Michael Power in Tower Hamlets showed. In the absence of any well developed sociology or social psychology of the school, the consequent lack of clear guidelines as to what to measure within schools meant that everything about the internal life of a school was a potential area for investigation, which made research a laborious and time consuming task. The demise of the 11+ meant that standardized data on pupil intake quality were no longer available and the absence of any centrally, routinely collected data on output variables such as school delinquency rates, child guidance referral rates or attendance rates necessitated the need for further laborious work. Also — and perhaps most important of all — the necessity of measuring all the outside school factors (such as family and neighbourhood characteristics) to test the hypothesis that it was the schools that had an effect made any research enterprise of even greater proportions.

The intellectual policy climate within which school differences work has grown up, then, has not been conducive to its rapid popularity or growth. Interestingly, whilst American research in the area grew very rapidly in the early and mid-1970s, it was not until the late 1970s that results of comparable British work began to appear. The reanalysis of the Coleman data suggesting large school effects on some outcomes (see the review in Reynolds, 1982), the appearance of the IEA studies showing substantial system effects and the publicity in British literature given to some of the early American school differences research by workers such as McDill, Brookover and Edmunds certainly began to prepare the way for a change in intellectual climate as regards the power of the school. The somewhat hostile and critical academic reception given to the Rutter (1979) study and the doubts voiced about the Reynolds (1976; 1979) work (which, for example, Musgrove, 1981, called 'weak' and 'implausible') came as something of a surprise. Certainly in the Rutter work, for example, the limited range of data about intakes may have underestimated the amount that school differences actually reflected *school* process and operation, yet it seems highly likely that individual URQ scores would be highly inter-correlated with any other (not chosen) intake variables. It seems highly *unlikely* that the school differences merely reflect unknown, unused intake factors.

Whilst there may be a genuine doubt as to how far these early studies have accurately discovered those factors within schools that actually affect outcomes, and whilst there must remain even more doubt as to whether we have discovered *how* these factors have their effects, the fact that schools have effects has been confirmed by much recent American research (see Rutter, 1983, and Reynolds, 1982, for reviews) and by the recent British work of Gray *et al.* (1983) and Galloway *et al.* (1983), both of whom show substantial school effects even after controlling for the effects of intake variables such as social class of school catchment area.

School differences research is, then, a sort of fledgling, still seeking the intellectual status that has been associated with the dominant individualizing paradigm and still not completely convincing the wider educational research community that it has the potential to make a major contribution to knowledge.

As befits an intellectual infant, it is not sure about the directions in which it should move in the future, an uncertainty that shows itself in the very differing views on theory and methodology that are evident in this collection of papers.

The first paper by Cuttance usefully outlines the frameworks which the existing body of research has utilized. Early work utilized an input/output model whereby attention was focussed upon the resource inputs available to the school attended by pupils together with the social background of the pupils, as determinants of 'outcomes'. The organizational model which became of later popularity saw the social actions of individuals as being constrained by the organizational structure of the school, which was increasingly seen as a set of nested administrative levels. The institutional model, by contrast, looks at variables which cut across individual schools such as streaming systems, curriculum placements, age differentiation or denominational differentiation for example. The most recently fashionable model — that concentrating on identifying unusually effective schools — is also described, together with a consideration of the rather large number of methodological shortcomings that exist in the studies conducted within this framework. Cuttance concludes by arguing for the reanalysis of existing data bases using these theoretical frameworks.

The next two papers — by Ouston and Maughan and by Strivens — outline the difficulties involved in conceptualizing and measuring two out of three of the central planks in school differences work of intake, process and outcome. On the latter, Ouston and Maughan outline the difficulties involved in the selection of which outcomes to measure, especially when different societal interest groups may attach differing importance to each of them.

Outcomes are used in five ways, they argue: as measures of individuals, of groups, of single schools, of several schools within an LEA and across LEAs or school systems. At an individual level, exam results, attendance, delinquency, behaviour, participation in sports and clubs, and attitudes are argued to be important, of which examination results appear to be viewed by many as the most important school outcome measure. They have the advantages of also being available for most pupils and schools, they are based on national standards and they can be combined to give a single overall score for each pupil.

There are difficulties in using them, however, which Ouston and Maughan usefully explore — only some children in fact sit exams, children can increase their passes after the original sitting in the fifth year, 'points' systems for different types of examination have comparability problems and their use by researchers may actually change the goals of schooling towards a more narrow concentration on cognitive outcomes. Various strategies — such as use of graded tests and the development of measures covering the 'affective' areas — are suggested as remedies for this situation.

Strivens deals with the other important area of school 'climate', a concept much talked about but rather elusive in practice. Observers seem to have low reliability in their assessments of climate or 'tone', and often school climate research has concentrated merely on the ratings of the teachers and not upon those of the pupils. Strivens outlines the American research of Epstein and McPartland, Halpin and Croft, and McDill, together with the British work of Finlayson and King, who attempted to collect more 'objective' organizational indicators of school climate. Whilst all these studies assume the existence of rationally conceived and defined goals, recent organizational work suggests by contrast that schools may be more anarchic, heterogeneous and loosely coupled than had been formerly thought. Whatever the problems in the conceptualization and measurement may be though, Strivens argues that school climate as a variable is too important to be ignored.

The next two papers — by Wilcox and Galloway — focus on two areas of within-school life that have been surprisingly under-researched in the early British research tradition — curriculum and pastoral care organization. Wilcox agrees that the 'curriculum' is an 'elusive, slippery and complex conception' but argues it is important and must be measured at the three levels of organization, content and the learning transaction in school. A curriculum notation system is outlined which systematizes information on curriculum balance and, interestingly, huge variation is seen to exist between schools in the proportion of time given to the different subjects. Links between this variation and pupil examination results could usefully be explored, Wilcox argues, together with the possible consequent variation in pupil behaviour. Whatever is done with such curricula data, however, the value of such data to the researcher must clearly be recognized.

Galloway documents the increasing importance of pastoral care systems within comprehensive schools, the differing conceptions of their purposes that already exist and the difference between schools in how they are organized. Certain pastoral care characteristics seem in his work to be associated with low levels of disruptive behaviour — teachers dealing with problems themselves rather than referring to middle management seems to be associated with low disruption, for instance. Interestingly, school behaviour, disruption or suspension levels seem to bear little relationship to intake quality *or* to relate with other outcome measures like attendance or academic success. Ways forward for study in this area — involving a concentration on the ways some schools manage to excel in their outputs because of their ability to project themselves and a concentration on curriculum variation — are suggested in conclusion.

The next two papers — by Steedman and by Gray and Jones — give a very clear assessment of some of the problems and unresolved issues which school effectiveness researchers are continuing to face. Steedman presents data from the National Children's Bureau 1958 cohort study which suggest that, after controlling for intake, very little of the difference in examination results between schools is explained by whether schools are mixed or single-sex. Though there were hints of a 'school type' effect in French, science and in general examination performance (favouring girls in girls' schools), the effect of substantial differences in the pupil peer group structure and probably of substantial variations in the teaching group structure and school 'ethos' also seems to have been remarkably small.

To doubt, then, about the size of school effects upon examination attainments which Steedman's study raises, Gray and Jones add further doubts about the assumptions of existing work in the field. Existing American work in the 'effective schools' tradition they regard as highly tentative, often showing inadequate assessment of intake variables. Using their own work, it seems that individual teachers are not *consistent* in their effectiveness from year to year, neither are individual effective teachers necessarily effective across subjects. At school level also, schools appear to be performing above the level to be expected from the quality of their catchment area in one year and *not* necessarily in another. A strategy that combines the strengths of quantitative approaches with the 'detective work' of the qualitative ethnographer is argued to be appropriate to wrestle with these sorts of problems.

The next paper, describing the ongoing ILEA Junior School Study, suggests that the answers to some of these unanswered questions that litter the field may soon be available. The study is based on an age cohort of nearly 2000 pupils over the four years of their junior school experience. Information has been obtained on pupils' backgrounds and, once allowance has been made for this, the study aims to outline which within-school factors appear to be associated with 'successful' development, defined in cognitive, affective and behavioural terms. These within-school factors are measured in areas such as school organization, home/school liaison, school physical structure and school equipment levels. A detailed description of this impressive study is given, together with extensive information about new methods of statistical analysis which the authors are employing.

The next two papers are both produced by a project which aims to translate some of the research findings produced to date into actual school practice. These papers — by Lewis and by Phillips, Davie and Callely — outline the philosophy behind and the results of a project to change within-school functioning by means of developing certain teachers as change agents within their schools. Lewis outlines the existing models of school change strategies which are derived from other societies and which have influenced the content of the Cardiff course — mostly informed by the doctrines of OD (organizational development). These include the Swedish Programme of School Leader Education, the American Programme for Principals of Elementary Schools and an 'experiential' programme for educational leaders developed at the Centre for Urban Education at the University of Nebraska. The Cardiff programme for change agents draws on all those schemes, involving utilizing teachers in the collection of data about schools, contextualizing those data against other research data on school differences and school processes, and lastly feeding back to schools information that may hopefully lead to school change.

Some of the results of this ambitious programme are described by Phillips, Davie and Callely. Using a mixed strategy of quantitative and qualitative data collection, the authors outline the characteristics of course members, the pathways of development that were followed in schools where change occurred, the amount of change that was generated by teachers of different levels of seniority and the importance of close colleague consultation within school in determining the levels of institutional development. Of particular importance are the findings that headteachers seem to have generated more within-school changes than other teachers, and that deputy heads on the course were unable to go straight to the heart of the school system and directly 'action' any school change themselves.

The implications of the research literature for school management are the subject of Young's paper. She reviews findings on the importance of 'ethos' and the unimportance of resources in determining effectiveness and argues that the input/output, systems theory model so popular within educational management circles has now outlived its usefulness. The contributions of primary school and secondary school 'case' studies are outlined, and 'leadership' (defined in a dynamic, interactional sense rather than in terms of leader attributes) is seen as a key variable which change strategies should attempt to influence. Evaluation too is seen as important in providing the data needed to inform effective managerial strategies.

The final paper by Reynolds and Reid attempts to outline those directions in which research should be moving. Larger samples are needed, together with more intake variables. Further outcomes need to be developed in the 'social' areas of schooling, they argue, and the pupil group needs to be disaggregated to see if different types of pupil are differentially affected by their schools. A reorientation towards theory generation also seems important, given the atheoretical nature of much of the work to date. The authors conclude that their strategy can be enabled by raiding school change programmes for process data, by utilizing existing LEA data bases and by utilizing teachers on certain in-service courses as data collectors of school process material.

Conclusions

We hope that the papers presented here give an indication of the progress that British school differences research has made in the last decade, together with indications of our continued awareness of the numerous problems of theory, methodology and research practice that still face researchers in this field. The last ten years have shown what many of these problems are and, whilst as a body of researchers we are not necessarily much nearer resolving them, we are now more clear about their nature at least.

Because of its direct policy relevance and its general interest to parents and others, there is no doubt that people undertaking school differences research have raised very high expectations of themselves in the wider community. Many have hoped — and are still hoping — for blueprints of the 'effective' or 'high achieving' school or for clear visions of what makes the effective teacher, so that practice can be directly improved. The pressure on people working in this field is therefore not just to make intellectual progress in solving the problems outlined in this volume but also to satisfy public demands for clear answers to their questions. As a group, we suspect it may take us all at least another decade of research and collective activity to provide such answers.

References

AINSWORTH, M. (1972) *The Plowden Children Four Years Later*, Manchester, Manchester University Press.

BERNSTEIN, B. (1970) 'Education cannot compensate for Society', *New Society*, 387, pp. 344–7.

BOWLES, S. and GINTIS, H. (1976) *Schooling in Capitalist America*, London, Routledge and Kegan Paul.

CLARKE, A.D.B. and CLARKE, M. (1976) *Early Experience*, London, Open Books.

COLEMAN, J. (1966) *Equality of Educational Opportunity*, Washington, D.C., US Government Printing Office.

COOPER, M.G. (1966) 'School refusal: An inquiry into the part played by school and home', *Educational Research*, 8, 3, pp. 233–9.

DAVIE, R. et al. (1972) *From Birth to Seven*, London, Longmans.

DONNISON, D. (1972) *A Pattern of Disadvantage*, Slough, NFER.

GALLOWAY, D. et al. (1983) *Schools and Disruptive Pupils*, London, Longmans.

GRAY, J., McPHERSON, A. and RAFFE, D. (1983) *Reconstructions of Secondary Education*, London, Routledge and Kegan Paul.

HARGREAVES, D. (1967) *Social Relations in a Secondary School*, London, Routledge and Kegan Paul.

JENCKS, C. et al. (1971) *Inequality*, London, Allen Lane.

LACEY, C. (1970) *Hightown Grammar*, Manchester, Manchester University Press.

MUSGROVE, F. (1981) *School and the Social Order*, Chichester, John Wiley.

PLOWDEN COMMITTEE (1967) *Children and Their Primary Schools*, London, HMSO.

REYNOLDS, D. (1976) 'The delinquent school', in WOODS, P. (Ed.), *The Process of Schooling*, London, Routledge and Kegan Paul.

REYNOLDS, D. (1982) 'The search for effective schools', in *School Organization*, 2, 3, pp. 215–37.

REYNOLDS, D., and SULLIVAN, M. (1979) 'Bringing schools back in', in BARTON, L. (Ed.), *Schools, Pupils and Deviance*, Driffield, Nafferton.

RUTTER, M. et al. (1979) *Fifteen Thousand Hours*, London, Open Books.

RUTTER, M. (1980) *Changing Youth in a Changing Society*, Oxford, Nuffield Provincial Hospital Trust.

RUTTER, M. (1983) 'School effects on pupils progress — findings and policy implications', in *Child Development*, 54, 1, pp. 1–29.

THOMAS, J.B. (1980) 'Scholarly productivity in psychology: A criticism of citation count research', *British Educational Research Journal*, 6, 1, pp. 91–5.

TYERMAN, M. (1968) *Truancy*, London, University of London Press.

I   *Frameworks for Research on the Effectiveness of Schooling*[1]

Peter Cuttance

In the decade after the Coleman *et al* (1966) study, research on the influence of schools on pupil outcomes found that less than one quarter of the variation in pupil outcomes lay between schools, hence it concluded that school effects must be small. Further, school resource inputs were found to explain little of the variation in pupil outcomes which did lie between schools. These studies, which I characterize as belonging to an *input-output* framework, employed the term *school effects* to describe the influence of schools on individual pupil outcomes.

During the last decade three alternative frameworks for the study of the effects of schools have achieved some prominence in the literature. These I characterize as: (a) the organizational framework, (b) the institutional framework and, (c) the exemplary schools framework. The essential difference between the first two of these and the earlier input-output model is in their conceptualization of the way in which schools may differentially affect the various groups of pupils within them. The exemplary schools framework can be viewed as a truncated version of the input-output model which is combined with case study or other exploratory methods to study selected schools in greater detail.

These more recent developments have coined new terms to describe the types of effect which individual schools may exhibit, however, the umbrella terms *school effectiveness* or *effectiveness of schools* are now widely associated with these frameworks. An important aspect of these studies is their focus on comparisons between schools, in particular, schools are described as *effective* if their pupils perform at a higher average level than the average school, and *ineffective* if their pupils perform at a lower average level than the average school. The *average school* is usually taken to refer to schools in the system which perform at about the mean average level, in a statistical sense, for all schools in the school system under consideration.

Studies which are carried out in either the institutional or organizational frameworks aim to explain the differential effects of schools in terms of their influence on pupil outcomes for various subgroups within schools. For example, the organizational framework incorporates the possibility of differential effects at the various levels of school organization: between subgroups within classes, between classes, between year levels. The institutional framework suggests that the differential effects of schools will be associated with variation in pupil performance between various institutional groups within schools, for example, between working class and middle class pupils, between fifth and sixth forms, between boys and girls. Thus, unlike the input-output model, these newer frameworks do not assume that the effect of a school is constant for all subgroups within it. The term *effectiveness* may thus be used with reference to particular subgroups within schools. For example, we may speak of a school as being particularly ineffective for working class pupils, or, particularly effective for sixth form pupils. The term *effectiveness of schooling* is also used in the literature as an omnibus description to cover the effects of schools in all the various senses in which the terms *effectiveness* and *effects* are outlined above.

In the sections which follow I review the features of the four frameworks which can be used to describe the orientations of research on the effects of schools over the last two decades. To recapitulate, these frameworks are: (i) the input-output framework (ii) the organizational framework, (iii) the institutional framework and, (iv) the exemplary schools framework.

The Input-Output Framework

The early focus in school effects research was on differential effects between schools. The studies typically attempted to account for differences in between-school outcomes using economic and policy oriented resource variables, such as the average level of teacher training, average expenditure on text books, etc, after controlling for influences attributable to the racial and social background of individual pupils in the school. Economic resources which were found to have little influence on pupil outcomes included those associated with teacher-pupil ratios, teacher education, teacher experience, teacher salaries, average expenditure per pupil, quality of facilities and quality of administrators (Hanushek, 1981).

It has been evident all along that there are large differences in schooling outcomes between individual pupils. In the input-output model most of the variation was attributed to causally prior home background influences, with a maximum of one quarter of the variation being attributable to differences between schools (Coleman, 1976). As evidence accumulated that school inputs, at least as they were then measured, seemed to have little impact on the variation in outcomes between schools, the validity of the model began to be questioned. It was argued that the school related factors responsible for the differential effects that schools were believed to have on individual outcomes had not shown-up because of the methodological and conceptual inadequacies of the input-output model. This led to two significant developments in research on school effects: first, there was a shift toward the view that schooling was not a uniform experience for all, even after taking account of differences in the social and cultural background of pupils and, secondly, there was the emergence of new frameworks which viewed schools not as production units, but as organizations or institutions which were linked closely into the wider educational system and other social institutions or as small administrative and social systems in themselves.

The basic formulation of the input-output model specified that the average level of resource inputs available to the school attended by each individual pupil, plus the social, racial and ability background characteristics of a pupil were the essential policy manipulable factors in determining individual pupil outcomes. Some of the developments which arose from the criticism of the model have been taken on board in later research. For instance the change of view about the non-uniformity of the effects of schooling led to a respecification of the functional form of the relationship between individual pupils and the resource inputs to schooling. In particular, the resources of schooling were respecified to reflect their differential input to each individual, as for example, in the Harnischfeger-Wiley model (Wiley, 1976).

Another adaptation of this model was to include factors which measured the average compositional characteristics of the intake of schools. In particular, the social background, race and ability of pupils in schools were found to vary systematically with the between school outcomes of pupils, even after control for individual level measures of these characteristics. This effect of composition was labelled a *contextual effect* and it was assumed that social psychological processes of social comparison and identification with group norms were the reason for this finding. These findings were a major influence in social policies in the USA, culminating in the *bussing* of large numbers of pupils in major cities.

Erbring and Young (1979) have argued that many of the theoretical models which are suggested as the basis of contextual effects are sociologically and social psychologically vacuous and that meaningful models of inter-individual interaction require a reconceptualization of the role of *context* in school effectiveness research. There has also been much argument as to whether contextual variables such as the mean socio-economic composition of schools are valid indicators of social psychological processes or whether they are artefactual representations of the processes through which pupils of like social characteristics are selected into schools, that is, whether their association with school effects are really due to *contextual* or *compositional* aspects of school intakes (Hauser, 1970; 1974; Alexander *et al*, 1979). Some degree of systematic selection from the range of social and racial groups in society is to be expected given the social differentiation of residential areas and the practice of many educational systems of zoning school catchments on the basis of residential criteria. Even without a formal policy of school catchment zoning, as in the non-state sector of schooling, we expect to find selection effects due to economic and social factors, since parents would not normally be expected to choose their children's school on a purely random basis. The selection of pupils into denominational schools is one such example. Given that one of the known factors for selecting a school is the expected performance of the pupil, and that this is related to social background, there will be an inevitable confounding of influence between the selection effect and any subsequent contextual effects on performance. Even if we were to directly measure the social psychological processes which these contextual variables are purported to represent in terms of their comparative and normative group processes (Erbring and Young, 1979) we should still expect to find severe statistical confounding between the two effects (Alexander *et al*, 1979).

It is my view, however, that the objective of separating the effects of schools' intake compositions exclusively into either contextual or selection effects is mistaken. The types of social processes which may derive from the particular socio-economic, racial or ability composition of schools are of a categorical nature. The processes and criteria on which pupils compare themselves with the average pupil in a school are, I suggest, categorically different in working class and middle class schools. Both the cultural form of this comparison and the criteria on which pupils compare themselves to others will be different in schools of different social compositions. Erbring and Young (*op. cit*) also describe a form of contextual effect in which the value orientations of the pupils in a schools' intake may allow it to adopt particular educational practices. For example, a school with a middle class intake from homes where education is valued as a means of social and career advancement may be able to adopt teaching methods which result in increased breadth of curriculum coverage. Particular educational practices may thus be founded upon the selection processes which give schools their various intake compositions. Pupils in schools with working class intakes may not exhibit the above value orientations, hence those schools may be unable to implement particular educational practices. Employing the same measure of intake composition across all schools may thus confound the different contextual effects emanating from different intake compositions. Contextual effects reflect both the selection processes which give schools their particular intakes and group level manifestations of processes of comparison, educational practices, etc. Within schools, however, the nature of the contextual effect may vary from school to school.

Over the last decade the main question behind school effects research has shifted away from that of asking which economic and direct policy related variables could be manipulated to equalize or raise outputs, to one of asking what would explain the pattern of differences in the effects of schooling, in terms of the social processes and educational practices which take place in the process of schooling. This redirection has emphasized a different set of educational resources to those viewed as important in the earlier input-output framework. In particular, the new frameworks count instructional variables and social psychological inputs, such as pupil motivation, attitudes and behaviours, among the resource inputs to schooling, and more emphasis is placed on the social, organizational and historical context of schools (Rutter *et al*, 1979; Gray, McPherson & Raffe, 1983, Mortimore *et al*, this volume).

These frameworks view schools, not as an autonomously managed production unit in which all pupils receive a uniform input of resources which then have the same productive effect, net of social background, across all pupils, but rather as a unit which is constrained by the organizational and institutional structure in which it is set and by its own internal social organization and structure. The question asked in these frameworks is, *where in the schooling system should we expect to find the most significant differences?*

The Organizational Framework

In this model the social actions of individuals are viewed as being constrained by the organizational structure of schooling. Schools consist of a set of administrative levels of organization, each of which is hierarchically nested within the one above it (e.g. pupils within teaching-groups, teaching-groups within classes, classes within year-groups, year-groups within schools) (Barr and Dreeben, 1983; Dreeben, 1983; Bidwell and Kasarda, 1975; 1980; Bidwell, 1983). The description of this model given by Bidwell and Kasarda (1975) also includes levels of organization which are beyond that of the school (e.g. local authority administrative divisions). For Bidwell and Kasarda the main features of the organization of schools are those relating to the production processes of schooling, such as: materials and technology and their configuration, decision-making structures and administrative processes of production management. School effects are thus attributable to the effect of the form and operation of the organizational structure of schools on individual outcomes. Failure to maintain the conceptual distinction of levels within the structure has, it is argued, resulted in a narrowly individual and social psychological approach to the study of school effects (Bidwell & Kasarda, 1980). Further, the conflation of organizational structure to a single level as in the input-output model is suggested as one of the reasons for the finding that school effects are small in magnitude, because the model has failed to take account of the main source of school effects, those within and between the various levels of the structure. Positive effects at one level may be offset by negative effects at other levels, therefore the net effect when organizational structure is left out of the model is to find only small overall school effects, particularly when the average performance of pupils across all levels within schools is employed as the measure of school outcomes. Further, this model posits that the outcomes at one level, and hence the inputs at the next level, may differ between levels. Thus it is argued that the input-output model fails to capture both the form and complexity of the relationships between levels. If the organizational model does locate significant schooling effects at the different levels and find that net school effects are zero-sum, as is suggested by these arguments against the input-output model, then that would be a most important finding.

Each school is seen as having an organizational structure of its own, hence such structures may vary across schools. Thus, the question of what the main features of the organization of schools are, is of some considerable importance if we are to compare schools. For if it is not possible to find organizational features which are effective within particular schools and to compare these across schools, then it seems impossible to see how these features could be built into other schools so as to change their performance also. It would seem important to try and formulate a model of the range of variation in organizational structures across schools.

In the organizational model of schooling, resource stocks comprise: (i) the instructional and managerial resources of teachers and school administrators, (ii) materials, and (iii) time (length of school day/year). This tripartite formulation of resource inputs to schooling rejects the distinction that they should be viewed as either school inputs or extra-school inputs since it also treats the compositional attributes of schools relating to family, neighbourhood and peer groups as a resource input to the process of schooling. Differential school effects are thus the result of differences in the contingent covariation between pupil and school resource inputs under differing conditions of unit organizational structure.

Resource distribution decisions are made at all levels of the organization of schools and the school system, but I shall restrict my discussion here to the school and lower levels of organization within the school. At the school level, decisions about the allocation of resources are made with respect to such inputs as teaching skills to be allocated to different classes or subject areas, curriculum resources in relation to the time allocated to each subject, material resources in the form of teaching aids and curriculum materials, and the assignment of individual pupils to classes and curriculum tracks.

At the class level, teachers make decisions about the variation in and level of instructional input available for individual pupils in the class (Barr and Dreeben, 1983). For example, formal teaching methods based on lectures or copying notes allow for less variation in the distribution of teacher inputs to individual pupils, than group and task orientated teaching methods, although the former may allow a higher average level of input to all pupils (*c.f.* the argument often made for ability streaming). However, even within formal teaching methods, some variation in the total resource input to learning will occur, due to variation in the resources input from the pupils themselves, as a result of differing abilities to interact with the compositional and contextual *milieu* of the classroom. The more precocious and socially skilled pupils may be able to demand, and obtain, more teacher inputs than other pupils, even in a situation where the teacher attempts to provide an equal or compensatory level of input across pupils in the class. Pupils are expected to be differentially affected by teaching practices which influence the degree of public visibility of performance levels across pupils in the class. High achievers receive strong positive confirmation of their abilities and low achievers may feel inadequate in a classroom where the teaching methods employed produce a high degree of public visibility of the range of achievement and progress of individual pupils in the class. Thus different teaching methods may produce different rates of progress in pupils of different entry ability. The learning which takes place in a classroom is dependent on the interaction of teacher and pupil inputs within an emergent framework conditioned by the social context (climate, ethos) and organization of the school and classroom.

An analytical model which incorporates these conditioning effects needs to include variables which measure the organizational properties of schools which influence pupils' access to or use of resources, both directly and through the structure of interpersonal interactions within instructional units. The principal properties of organizations which may effect the process of schooling are those relating to policies and administrative actions with respect to the distribution of resources. Thus the analytical model needs to include both relationships among the variables which comprise the process of schooling and statements describing how conditions at a particular level in the organization may vary as conditions at other levels change.

This model goes some way toward offering an alternative which avoids the principal criticisms levelled against input-output models. In particular, it recognizes the role of organizational structures in conditioning the social actions of individuals.

British research by Rutter *et al* (1979) and Reynolds *et al* (forthcoming) can be located within the framework of the organizational model, although it has usually focussed on just the two levels of schooling: classrooms and schools. This research has, however, taken seriously the idea that organizational and managerial processes within the school are significant determinants of pupil outcomes.

The Institutional Framework

The institutional model of schooling takes the social institutions which cut across schools to be the principal units between which the effects of schooling are to be found. Different institutions within the system are thus seen as the categories of schooling which have differential effects across schools. The institutional categories appeal to system-wide criteria for their definition. Examples of categories include: each grade level of schooling, different curriculum tracks, denominational education. Since each institutional category is not bound by the individual school, but rather by the system as a whole, schools may have differential effects across institutional categories. The development of this model of schooling has been principally associated with Meyer (1970; 1977; 1980; Meyer and Rowan, 1977; 1978). Meyer argues that schooling is essentially the institutional process by which individuals from particular institutional social (background) categories are sponsored to take-up particular adult institutional positions. Institutional categories of education are defined by more or less consensual views of the roles, rules and definitions of each category in society at large. The institutional categories so defined control definitions of what it means to be a pupil and the frameworks within which pupils make decisions and take actions with respect to their social futures. Thus, for instance, the role of and the educational future of a pupil in the sixth form is defined by the institutional and accreditation processes which demarcate the sixth form as an institutional category, different from all other forms. The accreditation processes condition their future by indicating that graduation from the sixth form is required before they can move to the next institutional category.

In this model the pupil is viewed as a rational actor who is cognisant of the institutional structure of schooling and who, more or less, consents to the authority of that structure. Continued success and participation in the system are necessary for survival and for gaining the credentials which give access to valued social positions as an adult. Meyer (1980) portrays the pupil as rational and informed by a variety of consultants (peers, teachers, parents, counsellors, etc). In order to achieve their goals, pupils must also develop a commitment to the pupil role in a situation which presents a conflicting variety of options with respect to how to proceed and of the actual range of social and educational futures available.

Variations in pupil behaviour in this model may arise from the accuracy of and amount of information that pupils have about the system, the degree of their commitment to the pupil role and differences in their perceptions of the linkages between their educational present and social futures. Individual level factors such as ability and social background provide the pupil with extra-system inputs. Further, the structure and status of the institutional categories and pupil behaviours within the system feed back into it as one of the sets of factors which (re)define and legitimate it. Thus, the institution of schooling is conceptualized as a weakly-bounded locus of contested and partly legitimated action. Each party (pupils, teachers, parents, administrators) contests the others' purposes and practices and formulates its own practice partly in the light of its own understanding of the other parties' purposes and practices. The process of schooling thus represents a *truce* between the various parties, but the nature of the truce may vary across pupils because of their membership of different institutional categories. Pupil outcomes with respect to participation/non-participation and what and how much they choose to learn are thus determined by a range of factors which influence the interaction of individual pupils' characteristics with institutional categories based on a consensual, although contested, view of how society should be structured.

Correspondence theories of education (Collins, 1971; Bourdieu, 1974; Bowles and Gintis, 1976) employ an institutional model with similar features to those above, but one which has more direct linkages between family background (social class) and the attainment of valued social positions. Also, they view the pupil as being much more constrained with respect to choice within the system of schooling; pupils are given a particular socialization in their schooling, according to their social class. By contrast, the institutional model outlined above constrains pupils' actions by organizing learning and participation in a sequenced set of institutional categories and by making success in each of these categories vital to future prospects. Unlike reproduction theories it does not constrain what individual pupils *choose* to learn at each level, and the contested nature of the institutional categories means that they are continually open to a degree of revision and redefinition by the participants within the system.

The institutional model recognizes the qualitative nature of differences within the school system, although quantitative differences are also important in determining the variation in pupil responses. Qualitative differences are to be found in the different institutions across schools but quantitative variation may occur in pupils' responses within each institution.

The Exemplary Schools Framework

Largely due to the failure of earlier research to provide a satisfactory explanation of the effects of schools there has developed a literature on effective schools based on exploratory empirical studies of effective and ineffective schools. Essentially, these studies have employed the analytical model of the input-output approach to locate exceptional schools by removing variation in individual-level schooling outcomes which could be attributable to social and family background, and ability, to produce adjusted measures of outcomes. Schools which have high or low adjusted outcomes are described as being particularly effective or ineffective schools, respectively. A measure of the (in)effectiveness of schools is usually calculated as the difference between the actual and the predicted outcome for pupils in a school. The predicted outcome is computed from a regression model across all schools, thus the effectiveness score is the deviation of pupils in a school from the regression line through all schools. The relationships between the effectiveness scores and other information on the schools are then explored or, a small number of schools are chosen for closer study by ethnographic methods of investigation.

This method of seaching for effective schools is premissed on the assumption that the marginal effect of social and family background, and ability, is the same for all pupils in all schools and that within schools all pupils are affected in the same (constant) way by the factors omitted from the model. The organizational and institutional models outlined above suggest that the main effects of schools are to be found in their effects for different subgroups of pupils. That is, they explicitly allow for a variation in effects across groups within the school. This means that they can conceive of defining the effects of schools as the differential effects for groups who are drawn from different organizational levels within schools or, who belong to different institutional categories in the education system. Thus, the model described above for locating effective and ineffective schools may not be appropriate. The designation of a school as an *outlier* (i.e. particularly effective or ineffective) is critically dependent upon the specification of the model. As indicated above, the methodology for choosing the outlier schools is based on a statistical model which specifies that within-school relationships are constant across schools. Further, the regression slopes representing these relationships are estimated from the data for all schools in the analysis, but the effects of the non-random clustering of pupils within schools is not taken into account in the interpretation of the residuals in the regression model. Hence the estimates of residuals in the model may be unreliable, and since the estimates of the effectiveness scores are computed from the residuals, they may also be unreliable. Thus, schools chosen as effective may be an artefact of the model and data employed in a particular situation. If the model is not correctly specified, further intensive study of schools so chosen may be misleading (see Cuttance, 1984 for a more detailed discussion of these issues).

Studies which have employed case study methods to explore the characteristics of schools which had high effectiveness scores on the basis of the above methodology have suggested that an effective school is one which has strong instructional leadership, a high degree of control or discipline, and high staff expectations for pupil performance. However, in their reviews of these studies Purkey and Smith (1983) and Ralf and Fennessy (1983) concluded that they have some critical weaknesses when assessed on methodological grounds. The studies have usually failed to provide adequate information on the magnitude of differences between effective and ineffective schools; most are based on elementary schools using standardized achievement in reading and mathematics as the criteria of achievement, thus, the findings may not be generalizable to secondary schools; many of the most often cited studies have serious methodological flaws due to a failure to use adequate control variables for ability, and, social and family background characteristics, and the number of schools studied is generally very few. A further methodological weakness noted in these studies is that they frequently compare schools identified as being either positive or negative outliers, instead of comparing each of these groups with the average school. There will probably be some schools which occur as outliers in any sample from the population of schools, on the basis of sampling probabilities alone. Thus comparing positive and negative outlier schools increases the possibility that one is merely studying a chance artefact in the data. In order for a given school to be designated as exceptional it is first necessary to show that it is consistently exceptional across a range of outcome criteria and/ or over time or grades. Exceptional schools, so defined, are then assumed to be in some way systematically different to the average school. Thus a comparison which aims to provide information on exceptional schools, *vis a vis* schools in general, needs to compare the exceptional schools with average schools, rather than those which are at the other end of the performance spectrum.

As noted previously these studies should also be extended to take into account a broader definition of the effect of a school, consonant with the institutional and organizational models of schooling. In particular, they need to consider alternative dimensions of the effects of schools, such as the effects for pupils in vocational versus academic curriculum tracks, and for schools drawing their pupils from catchments with qualitatively different social characteristics. These suggested changes all centre on the probable existence of differential effects for different subgroups of pupils within and between schools. The basis of both the institutional and organizational models of schooling is the proposition that such differential effects do exist and to ignore them is to seriously misspecify a model of schooling.

Recent research by Rutter *et al* (1979), Madaus *et al,* (1979), Steedman (1983), and Gray, McPherson and Raffe (1983) has explored the relationship between the effectiveness of schools and aspects of the organization of schools. Rutter *et al* focussed on the social organization of schools and investigated the way in which school *ethos* was related to schooling outcomes. Gray, McPherson and Raffe investigated the influence of schools' organizational histories (the organizational forms which the school passed through in the decade prior to and during comprehensive reorganization) on pupil outcomes. These studies go some way toward addressing the features of the organizational and institutional frameworks in their discussions of the effects of schools, although this was not one of their main objectives. Evaluations of the performance of pupils in selective and comprehensive schools (Gray, McPherson and Raffe, 1983; Steedman, 1983) also provide evidence that the organizational features of schooling have an influence on pupil outcomes.

Towards an Evaluation of the Effects of Schools from Different Perspectives

The evaluation of and explication of models of the effects of schools based on the input-output, organizational, institutional and exemplary schools frameworks ideally requires the development of data bases in which the observed variables are framed within the specific conceptual schema of each. However, we may obtain an initial evaluation of the likely pay-off of alternative model formulations by analyzing extant data which contains measures for which we can assume reasonable validity with respect to the theoretical concepts concerned. The data base used in the Rutter *et al* (1979) research; the Scottish Education Data Archive data on Scottish school leavers; longitudinal data from the National Children's Bureau cohorts

(Fogelman, 1984); the data collected by Reynolds *et al* (Reynolds and Reid, this volume); and the ILEA data on London primary schools (Mortimore *et al*, this volume); and the data for twenty English secondary schools collected under the DES-funded project on multi-ethnic education, combine to form a large amount of recent information on British schooling and the way in which schools influence both cognitive and non-cognitive outcomes of pupils. Obviously, we will encounter many instances where we can find only partial coverage for the matrix of theoretical variables in a particular model, but this is a problem faced to a greater or lesser degree in most non-experimental research. The ability to model the structure of theories and to incorporate empirical information about different parts of that structure from different data sources means that a strategy of partial evaluation on the basis of extant data is feasible. There are quite severe technical constraints on the analysis of such models but, nevertheless, they do present an opportunity to assess a range of possible interpretations of extant data.

The brief outlines of the organizational and institutional models presented in this chapter provide a general conceptual framework for research on the effectiveness of schools and they suggest that school effects may be most evident for particular subgroups of pupils between different levels of organization within and between schools and, between different institutions (in Meyer's sense) which cut across schools in an education system.

Notes

1 This chapter was prepared as part of the programme of research 'effectiveness of schooling' funded under ESRC grant number C0022003.

References

ALEXANDER, K.L. FENNESSEY J., McDILL E.L. and D'AMICO R.J. (1979) *School SES Influences in Composition or Context.* Report No 280, Centre for Social Organization of Schools, Johns Hopkins University, Baltimore.

BARR, R. and DREEBEN R. (1983) *How Schools Work.* Chicago, University of Chicago Press.

BIDWELL, C.E. (1983) 'Discussion of papers'. Symposium on School Effects Research, Annual Meeting of the American Educational Research Association, Montreal, 11–15 April.

BIDWELL, C.E. and KASARDA J.D. (1975) 'School district organization and student achievement', *American Sociological Review*, 40, pp. 55–70.

BIDWELL, C.E. and KASARDA, J.D. (1980) 'Conceptualizing and measuring the effects of school and schooling,' *American Journal of Education*, 88, pp. 401–430.

BOURDIEU, P. (1974) 'Cultural reproduction and social reproduction,' in BROWN R., (Ed) *Knowledge, Education and Cultural Change*. London, Tavistock.

BOWLES, S. and GINTIS, H. (1976) *Schooling in Capitalist America: Educational Reform and the Contradictions of Economic Life*. Basic Books, New York.

COLEMAN, J.S. (1966) *Equality of Educational Opportunity*, US Government Printing Office.

COLEMAN, J.S. (1976) 'Regression analysis for the comparison of school and home effects', *Social Science Research*, 5, pp. 1–20.

COLLINS, R. (1971) 'Functional and conflict theories of educational stratification', *American Sociological Review*, 36, pp. 1002–1019.

CUTTANCE, P. (1984) 'Strategies for modelling the effects of schools'. Working paper, Centre for Educational Sociology, University of Edinburgh.

DREEBEN, R. (1983) 'School production and school effects'. Paper presented at a Symposium on School Effects Research, American Educational Research Association, Montreal, 11–15 April.

ERBRING, L. and YOUNG, A.A. (1979) 'Individuals and social structure: contextual effects as endogenous feedback', *Sociological Methods and Research*, 7, pp. 396–430.

FOGELMAN, K. (1984) 'Problems in comparing examination attainment in selective and comprehensive secondary schools', *Oxford Review Of Education*, 10(1), pp. 33–43.

GRAY, J., McPHERSON, A. and RAFFE, D. (1983) *Reconstructions of Secondary Education: Theory, Myth and Practice since the War*. London, Routledge and Kegan Paul.

HANUSHEK, E.A., (1981) 'Throwing money at schools', *Journal of Policy Analysis and Management*, 1(1), pp. 19–41.

HAUSER, R.M. (1970) 'Context and consex: a cautionary tale'. *American Journal of Sociology*, 75, pp. 645–64.

HAUSER, R.M. (1974) 'Contextual analysis revisited', *Sociological Methods and Research*, 2, pp. 365–375.

MADAUS, G.F., KELLAGHAN, T. RAKOW, E.A. and KING, D.J. (1979) 'The sensitivity of measures of school effectiveness', *Harvard Educational Review*, 49, pp. 207–230.

MEYER, J. (1970) 'High school effects on college intentions', *American Sociological Review*, 76.

MEYER, J. (1977) 'The effects of education as an institution', *American Journal of Sociology*, 83.

MEYER, J. (1980) 'Levels of the educational system and schooling effects'. Paper prepared for the Educational Finance and Productivity Centre, University of Chicago, Chicago.

MEYER, J., and ROWAN, B. (1977) 'Institutionalized organizations: formal structure as myth and ceremony', *American Journal of Sociology*, 83.

MEYER, J., and ROWAN, B. (1978) 'The structure of educational organizations'. In MEYER, M. *et al.*, *Environment and Organizations*, San Francisco, Jossey-Bass.

PURKEY, S.C. and SMITH, M.S. (1983) 'Effective schools: a review', *The Elementary School Journal*, 83, pp. 427–452.

RALF, J.H., and FENNESSY, J. (1983): 'Science or reform: some questions about the effective schools model', *Phi Delta Kappan*, 64(10), pp. 689–694.

REYNOLDS, D., JONES, D. ST LEDGER, S. MURGATROYD, S. (forthcoming) *Bringing Schools Back In*.

RUTTER, M., MAUGHAN, B. MORTIMORE P. and OUSTON, J. (1979) *Fifteen Thousand Hours*, London, Open Books.

STEEDMAN, J. (1983) *Examination Results in Selective and Nonselective Schools*, National Childrens Bureau.

WILEY, D.E. (1976) 'Another hour another day: quantity of schooling, a potent path for policy', in SEWELL, W.H., HAUSER, R.M. and FEATHERMAN, D.L. (Eds), *Schooling and Achievement in American Society*, New York, Academic Press.

2   *Issues in the Assessment of School Outcomes*

Janet Ouston and Barbara Maughan

Amongst the types of 'difference' investigated by school differences research, issues of pupil progress and school outcome are of central importance. If we are to assess the extent to which schooling can indeed 'make a difference' for children, our choice and use of indicators of outcome are crucial, and, as we shall argue here, by no means straightforward. Complex conceptual and methodological problems arise, and we make no apology for raising more questions than we are at present able to answer. The need for a full appreciation of these problems is, however, far from academic. Many of the issues involved must be faced in one form or another in any educational evaluation, whether by teachers in school or classroom-based assessments, LEA staff considering policy and practice across an authority, or parents attempting to make sense of publicly available education statistics. One of the main aims of the present chapter is to outline issues common to each of these differing types of outcome assessment, as well as problems more particular to one or other separate approach.

To begin with some definitions: we shall use the term 'outcomes' to refer to any effects which schooling may have, or be assumed to have, on children's development. Such a definition would exclude purely maturational factors, but not be confined in any other sense: the areas to be studied might be cognitive, behavioural or attitudinal, and assessed either concurrently with schooling or only at some later stage. We shall also assume that assessments of outcome will rarely take place in isolation: they will usually form part of some wider enquiry, whether into the relative progress of boys and girls, the implications of mixed ability teaching, or the effectiveness of a new policy to reduce non-attendance. Outcome measures are not ends in themselves, but rather one of the means necessary to achieve a wider end, a better understanding of the influences on children's progress at school, and the extent to which schooling is achieving its desired aims. Questions of values are thus inevitably involved: our choice of outcome measures will reflect what we take the 'desired aims' of schooling to be, and any discussions of school effects will turn on the criteria for effectiveness which we have chosen to employ. Our discussions will also inevitably reflect their historical context: as society's expectations of education change, so assessments of outcome must keep pace with these altered expectations, and indeed work in some areas to promote them. We shall focus, in the main, on the issues as we see them at the beginning of the 1980s. We will conclude with some thoughts on likely future developments, and begin, to set the discussion in context, with a brief look backwards at the questions educational researchers have pursued in recent years, and the influences which have shaped the types of outcome questions we are attempting to address today.

In the 1950s and 1960s, against a background of liberal optimism about the effects of education, and a predominant concern with equality of opportunity, much British research focused on inequalities of *access* to the different stages of secondary schooling. At a time when eventual school outcomes depended heavily on selection at 11+, or continuance in education beyond 16+, much concern centred on decisions at these critical turning points. Research showed that children from middle-class homes were much more likely to gain grammar school places than working-class children of similar ability, and subsequently more likely to stay on at school to sit public examinations; this in turn enabled them to move on to further education and higher status jobs. During the 1960s, researchers began more detailed explorations of the relationships between family and social factors and attainment. Douglas (1964) studied children's performance in the context of family attitudes and circumstances, while Hargreaves (1967) and Ford (1969) considered the interrelationships between social class, school organization and pupils' attitudes and attainments. These studies moved on from a general delineation of social class links with attainment to more detailed work attempting to explain *why* working-class children were less successful at school.

In the USA similar concerns were being expressed. Coleman *et al.* (1966) carried out a nationwide study of schools, relating differing school resource levels to the educational outcomes of children from different ethnic groups. They found that, above a certain point, additional expenditure showed no relationship with achievement. Jencks (1972), in his reassessment of Coleman's work, argued that schooling could do little to reduce inequalities in American society, and that much of the inequality in job status and income was a direct result of the economic institutions of society.

In more recent years, comprehensive reorganization and the raising of the school-leaving age in Britain have combined with changing educational expectations to provide a somewhat different focus for research and policy debate. The decline of the belief in a fixed IQ, together with concerns over 'standards' and 'accountability' in education, have all converged to shift the focus away from equality of opportunity, and towards equality (or perhaps equity) of experience and results. At a time when the majority of children attend similar types of school, and for a similar period, there has inevitably been a resurgence of interest in the quality of the schooling they experience. While concerns for underachievement amongst particular groups of pupils — girls, ethnic minorities, and the working class — remain very much alive, a further element has been introduced in comparative studies between *schools*. Although education may be able to do little, at least in the short term, to affect class and other divisions in society, there is nevertheless evidence of persisting variations in the education and progress of children from *similar* social backgrounds, and this seems at least partially attributable to the schools they attend. Studies such as those of Reynolds *et al.* (1976) and Rutter *et al.* (1979) have moved away from a focus on social class and expenditure, and turned instead to examine variations in outcome between individual schools. Here, social class and other differences in attainment are taken as givens, and used as controlling, rather than explanatory, variables. In these studies, the notion of school outcomes has been somewhat extended: measures which in earlier research might principally have been viewed as indicators of *pupil* progress are here seen as also, at least potentially, reflecting the effects and effectiveness of *schools*.

In parallel with these developments in research, school and LEA-based evaluations of practice have also become more widespread in recent years. Here, the aim in studying outcomes is to illuminate areas of practice within schools which may be in need of review or change. The uses and utility of outcome evaluation at the school level are thus of increasing interest to teachers, inspectors and advisers. With the requirement since 1982 that schools publish some details of their public exam results, some at least of the issues in debates on school outcomes have had even wider currency. If each of these various developments is to be used constructively, and to contribute to the improvement of the school experience and achievements of pupils, future research and assessments must attempt to learn from the lessons of the past. In the sections which follow, we shall attempt to outline what we see some of those lessons to be.

Definition and Measurement

The first problems facing the researcher or practitioner concerned to assess educational outcomes are those of definition. Factors selected as indicators of outcome must relate to the aims of schooling: there is little point in using performance on a Latin test as a measure of outcome if a school does not teach Latin. But the question is never as simple as this: it is often difficult to agree what the aims of schooling should be. They are rightly many and diverse and will result from the history of the school, the values of the staff and their perceptions of both present performance and future aims. Different interest groups may also have quite different expectations of schooling. Parents and teachers, for example, may lay emphasis on different areas and there may be as much variation within each group as there is between them. Each group will also have a range of expectations; parents may want their children to be happy, academically successful *and* to develop into responsible adults. Any rounded assessment of school outcomes must aim to take all these factors into account.

Just as parents and teachers vary in their expectations of schooling, so do pupils. They also differ in their talents, interests and needs. O-level and CSE results are, perhaps, an acceptable measure of attainment for 16-year-olds, but there is no comparable measure for children at primary school. The usual approach here, focusing on standardized tests of English and maths, ignores much of the work of a good primary school. Within the same school, too, there will be a wide range of needs and achievements — the slow learning child's progress in basic skills may be a greater achievement than the eight O-levels obtained by an able child. The notion of common, easily measured, generally accepted, educational outcome measures appropriate to all children clearly does not reflect the real work of schools.

The problem of definition is, however, complicated by the need to consider in addition possible *negative* responses to experiences at school. Outcomes may be seen either as the desired effects of certain types of school practice, or as unintended consequences of the ways in which schools are run. Hargreaves (1967), for example, argued that the boys he studied were seriously disadvantaged by being placed in the bottom class of a streamed school; the case study literature includes many other graphic examples of this kind. Disaffection, disruptive behaviour and truancy may be as much 'outcomes' of the school process as are examination attainments or success in gaining a job. These examples illustrate the importance of what has been called the 'hidden curriculum': the assumptions, values, attitudes and behaviour of pupils and teachers which are not evident in the formal curriculum. These are, almost by definition, difficult to measure, yet they seem likely to play a major part in explaining why some schools are more successful than others.

The language of outcomes may seem to imply once-and-for-all assessments of progress made only at the end of schooling. Such a view seems to us unduly restrictive, and likely to yield only very limited insights. If outcome assessments are to be of practical value to schools, highlighting areas of strength and weakness, they must not only include a wide range of factors, but also be made at a series of points in children's school careers, not simply when the race has been run or the horse fled. Disaffection from school, which may crystallize into truancy in later years, may have its roots in experiences of failure or frustration at a much earlier stage. Fourth or fifth year attendance figures alone can do nothing to uncover processes of this kind, and indeed may, if viewed in isolation, result in quite inappropriate types of response.

Examples of this kind could be multiplied in many areas; they emphasize the essentially cumulative nature of school experience, the dangers of viewing individual measures of outcome in isolation, and the difficulties inherent in applying any simple input-process-outcome model of evaluation in relation to schooling. A more complex and dynamic concept is required, where many of the elements are likely to interact, and where questions of definition are thus complicated further. 'Process' may vary depending upon 'in-take': each child's experience of school will depend on his or her own personality and abilities, as well as on what the school actually provides. In a similar way, 'outcomes' at any one stage of schooling may well affect the nature of the 'inputs' and the 'process' at the next. The eager 11-year-old may become the not-so-eager 15-year-old; assessments of outcome must aim to take into account such changes, and chart the stages in their development, as well as their final results. Some of these results may, of course, only be evident after pupils have left school. Although assessments at these later stages may be impractical for individual schools, they are clearly important for any general discussion of outcomes. We need to know, for example, how far qualifications gained at school do indeed influence later educational and career opportunities, and to what extent learning or behavioural difficulties in the school years affect young people's development as they approach adulthood. Most schools would include preparation for adult life amongst their aims, but few at present probably have any clear notion of how well or to what extent these are being realized. Our ideal agenda for the study of outcomes must clearly extend beyond the bounds of schooling itself, and take account of these longer-term implications, as well as those apparent during the school year.

Attempts to extend the range of outcomes, and to assess schools on a variety of criteria, raise a second set of issues which centre on the problem of measurement. Even if we are able, either as researchers or practitioners, to develop some agreed set of objectives, many of these will not be easily measurable. For research purposes, it might be possible to develop a wider range of indicators of both cognitive and non-cognitive outcomes, but it is difficult to see how this could be done across large numbers of schools or LEAs.

Many other types of outcome could, however, be explored; some possible approaches to the assessment of attitudinal and behavioural outcomes are discussed by David Reynolds in Chapter 12. In our own work (Rutter *et al.*, 1979) we have used four: exam results, attendance rates, delinquency rates and a school behaviour measure. As researchers we defined our own indicators, arguing that these were generally acceptable to both teachers and parents. A school which was performing poorly in all four areas would not, probably, be thought of as successful. The assumption here, as in most studies of school outcomes, is that schooling *may* affect all four of these indicators, and that some of these effects may be unintentional.

Controlling for Differences in Intake

So far, the issue of controlling for intake has not been discussed. It is, however, a central issue whenever school outcomes are to be compared, either within one school over several years or across a number of schools. In secondary schools, for example, it seems likely that the overall level of attainment in exams will reflect both the ability, aptitudes and needs of the intake *and* the quality of teaching provided. There is little point in comparing the performance in exams of, say, a selective grammar school and a non-selective comprehensive school, or even a highly regarded comprehensive school in a suburb with an inner-city 'restricted range' comprehensive. Almost inevitably the school with a more favoured intake will appear to do better.

There are two approaches which can be taken to the problem of controlling for differences in intake; each depends on having measures of children prior to school entry. The simplest method is to compare only similar children, so, for example, pupils might be allocated to groups according to earlier test scores and then subsequent results compared within these groups. This approach is taken by Steedman (1983). The second approach demands more elaborate statistical techniques so that the performance of schools is adjusted to take account of intake differences. Here each school's results are then presented *as if* each had the same intake.

Each of these approaches raises similar problematic issues. The first relates to the choice of intake (or controlling) variables. In analyzing exam results, for example, primary school test scores, and measures of social class and family income might be used. Ideally, parental interest and encouragement, and the child's own ambitions, would also be included. Previous research can suggest a wide range of factors likely to be involved, and the constraints in any individual enquiry are likely to be practical rather than theoretical. But with other measures of outcome, such as attendance, there is the additional problem of deciding what might be appropriate measures of intake to collect, since there are few obvious predictors of attendance. If important factors are omitted from the analyses, however, the results obtained are likely to be biased and potentially misleading.

Even if there were no difficulties about choosing controlling variables, it is never possible to assess the relative importance of intake factors and school influences, since the proportions in each case depend upon the range of variation in intakes and between schools (see Rutter, 1983, for a discussion of this point). The apparent size of relationships between variables will also depend on their reliability (Goldstein, 1979) and on a functionally complete specification of the casual model involved (Cook and Campbell, 1979). All of these issues require careful attention in comparisons between schools. At the level of the individual school, however, controlling for intake is only important when intakes change. If a school continues to serve the same catchment area and section of the child population there is probably little need for elaborate statistical controls. But if the intake changes, as has happened over recent years as selective schools have been phased out, it is clearly necessary for individual schools to be aware of such trends and of their possible effects.

Uses of Outcome Measures

As noted earlier, educational outcome measures have become a central feature in the monitoring and evaluation of educational progress. They are, however, used in rather different ways, each of which has its own particular set of demands. Broadly, outcomes are used in five ways: as measures of individuals, of particular groups (e.g., girls), of single schools, of several schools within an LEA, and across LEAs or school systems. At the *individual* level, exam results (either public or school-based), attendance, participation in sports and clubs, and general behaviour and attitude, have long been seen as appropriate areas of assessment of the individual pupil. Recently there has been interest in developing pupil profiles, covering a wider range of cognitive and non-cognitive outcomes. (See Scottish Council for Research in Education, 1977, and Goacher, 1983, for details.) These developments emerged as a response to the relatively narrow traditional criteria of exams and were originally seen as being most appropriate for less able pupils. More recently, however, it has been felt that completing profiles for the less able only devalues their worth, and that they should be available for all pupils. New examinations, too, have been developed as more appropriate measures of outcome than the traditional O-levels and CSE. Mode 3 CSEs have allowed teachers to be directly involved in assessment; the 16+ exam and the graded-test approach still remain experimental.

Assessments of individual pupils can be aggregated to give a picture of the performance of groups of pupils either across schools or within one school. The headteacher's annual report usually served exactly this purpose, summarizing the achievements of the school during the previous year. Research assessing the performance of girls, or children from ethnic minorities, for example, usually takes this approach.

Outcomes at the individual level are not, however, the only way of evaluating individual schools. Although they will doubtless form part of a school's regular monitoring of its own performance, it is important that schools also attempt to evaluate their own practices. Studying the most recent set of exam results may offer little guidance to future action: what is needed here is a critical appraisal of school process as well as an assessment of outcome. Much of what has been called 'in-school evaluation' may actually be descriptions of current practice, useful to the school as a way of highlighting areas of strength and weakness. The ILEA, in *Keeping the School under Review* (ILEA, 1977), suggest many of the topics which might be included:

these focus on areas such as the formal curriculum; the informal or hidden curriculum which is revealed in styles of interaction between teachers, and between teachers, pupils and parents; and the use of resources and the organization of classroom teaching. In each area specific questions are proposed, the wording being appropriate for either primary or secondary schools, with the purpose of focusing teachers' attention on the issues rather than on providing quantitative measures. Shipman (1979) was also concerned with in-school evaluation. He discussed some of the ways that schools can use both internally and externally referenced data to assess their own progress. HMI, in their descriptions of ten successful schools (DES, 1977), used a similar, qualitative approach to delineating good practice.

Moving beyond the purview of the individual school, outcome measures are increasingly used by parents and LEAs, as well as researchers, in comparisons *between* schools. Schools are now required to publish their exam results, although the details of how this is to be done have been left to individual authorities. Inevitably this leads to comparisons between schools and permits the construction of league tables of more and less successful schools. Plewis *et al.* (1981) review the implications of this development, and in particular the need to control for intake differences, while keeping the presentation of results as uncomplicated as possible so that they are easily understood by parents and governors. Both methods of allowing for differences in intake outlined above are used by some LEAs; the simple method of presenting average exam results for similar groups of children is probably the best approach for the publication of results for parents, whereas adjusted scores (using regression techniques) are perhaps more useful for LEA monitoring.

Linking these various approaches, there are further questions concerning the progress of different groups of pupils in different types of school setting. Does the school which is successful for its most able pupils achieve equally well for its less able? Are there particular types of setting which foster the progress of children from ethnic minorities? Do apparently favourable overall results mask consistent pockets of underachievement for identifiable groups of pupils? Such questions require a more detailed assessment of outcomes, and may in their turn suggest the need for a reappraisal of priorities, a shift in the balance of the curriculum or resource provision, or a closer study of the needs of particular pupils.

These differing uses of outcome measures — to assess the progress of individual pupils or to compare the performance of groups of pupils or whole schools — raise many issues. If the focus is on the assessment of either individual pupils or single schools almost any measures of outcome can be used; these will doubtless reflect parents', teachers' and pupils' expectations of school, and the effects that the school is thought to have on its pupils. But once comparisons are made between schools the choice of measures becomes more constrained. It is necessary here both to allow for differences in intake *and* to use measures of outcome which are common across schools. At present, these requirements can only be satisfied in relation to exam results. As these figure increasingly prominently in both research and LEA assessment documents, we will discuss in some detail some of the particular issues raised in the use of exam results as outcomes.

The Problematic Case of Exam Results

One of the attractions of exam results as a measure of outcome is that they appear to be much better indicators, statistically, than other measures: they are available for most pupils and most schools, are based on national standards and can be combined to give a single score for each pupil. In reality, however, there are many difficulties which are not easily overcome.

The O-level and CSE examinations were originally designed for the top 60 per cent of the ability range only, leaving 40 per cent of pupils excluded from the examination system. In practice more pupils enter at least one public exam. In London, for example, 81 per cent of fifth year pupils sat an exam in summer 1981; the remaining 19 per cent included non-candidates who were still on roll, Easter leavers, and pupils who were entered for exams but did not actually sit them. Problems immediately arise in the treatment of these pupils in any analysis of exam results. Is it really justifiable to give them an exam score of zero? Should the Easter leavers be included or excluded from the calculations? If they are included, they are assigned a zero score for exams they could not sit. If they are excluded, the number of pupils included depends, to some extent, on their dates of birth.

A related problem concerns schools' entry policy: should we attempt to assess the achievements of all pupils or only those of candidates? If the focus is on candidates only, then schools which enter most pupils may appear to perform less well than those with more restrictive policies, even though the restrictive school achieves fewer grades. Most researchers assume that *all* fifth year pupils are potential candidates for exams: this may be quite unjustified in some schools. Parents and others reading examination statistics must be alert to the implications of these issues, and the sometimes very different picture which can emerge if figures are presented in one way rather than another.

Other presentational issues concern the groups of pupils to be included in any summary of results. The DES exam statistics refer to the highest level of exam pass achieved by all school leavers, so aggregating results for pupils from three different school year groups in each year's summaries. In contrast, the ILEA focuses on summer exam results only, and keeps fifth and sixth year pupils separate. As has been shown by Rutter *et al.* (1982), these two approaches may give different results. In that analysis it was found that although black pupils did worse than white pupils in exams at each chronological stage, because many more black pupils stayed on at school their final exam qualifications, as a group, were better than those of white pupils. ILEA's cross-sectional approach also excludes the achievements of pupils who take exams before the summer of their fifth year.

Creating an exam results scale is also more difficult than it might appear. The major problem relates to the comparability of O-level and CSE grades. The weighted score developed by ILEA, and most less detailed systems, equates an O-level grade C and CSE grade 1, but Steedman (1983) considers the equivalent to be a grade B, since the official definition of the CSE grade 1 is that it is of *at least* the standard of an O-level grade C. Any scoring system builds in quite idiosyncratic equalities. In the ILEA score, two grade E O-levels, two grade 3 CSEs and one O-level grade B are all considered equivalent (i.e., 6 points). Other exams, such as RSA and City and Guilds, are not included in any exam scoring scheme. Another problem of comparability results from combining subjects together. We are forced to equate an O-level grade B in maths with a grade B in French or music. In order to get over this problem some researchers (e.g., Steedman, 1983) have restricted their analyses to particular subjects such as English and maths. But this in itself is no real solution since there are many different English and maths syllabuses which may not strictly be comparable with one another.

On the statistical side, exam results are also difficult to handle. A simple categorization of results into DES-type categories (five or more O-levels, one to four O-levels, etc.) is easy to understand but difficult to analyze statistically. Even a scoring system, such as that developed by ILEA, seems unlikely to be normally distributed as demanded by many statistical techniques. Typically, about 20 per cent of pupils have a zero score, and the remainder are distributed across a wide range with no obvious peak in the middle of the distribution.

The use of exam results for monitoring LEA performance raises the additional issue of the level of analysis to be used. The ILEA reports (e.g., ILEA, 1982) relate average examination performance for a whole school to intake measures at the school level such as the percentage of pupils in the top ability band, or the percentage receiving free meals. If the data were available, similar statistical analyses could be undertaken at the level of the individual child. The implications of using the school, rather than the child, as the unit of analysis are discussed in detail by Hannan *et al.* (1976) and Alexander and Griffin (1976) in their comments on Bidwell and Kasarda's (1975) paper on the differences in effectiveness between school districts. School-level analyses of intake and outcome variables may identify *schools* which are under or overachieving for their intakes but they give no information about within-school differences. These can only be examined by analyses at the level of the individual child.

Researchers, too, have been concerned with outcomes at all levels of analysis. Our own work in London schools (Rutter *et al.*, 1979) was concerned with comparisons between schools, and more recent studies undertaken by Steedman (1983) and Marks *et al.* (1983) have focused on comparisons between selective and non-selective school systems. These large-scale studies of educational systems raise many controversial issues — the two most important being the lack of clearcut boundaries between different systems, and the need for adequate statistical control for differences in intake to schools within different systems. Steedman's work was based on the National Child Development Study, so that data on intake *and* outcome are available at the level of the individual child. Here children with similar test performance can be compared across types of schools. Marks and his colleagues attempted to control for differences in intake by grouping LEAs into three categories according to the overall percentage of children from families in social classes 4 and 5. This clearly takes no account of differences between schools *within* an authority and cannot provide an adequate control for social class differences in intake. Marks *et al.* (1983, p. 46), show that in two of the three LEA groups the relationship between social class and outcome is almost as strong as it was before these 'homogeneous' groups were created.

An additional problem in the analysis of large data sets is the choice of intake variables. Often the researcher has to rely on data collected for quite different purposes. The ILEA, in their annual examination analyses, relate the average performance of schools to indicators of social *dis*advantage, such as the proportion of children receiving free meals or coming from large families. It is clear, however, that children who do well in exams, and thus contribute most to the school's overall average attainment score, are likely to come from favoured homes.

Do all these objections mean that exam results should not be used for assessing school performance? There are certainly educational reasons to be cautious about overemphasizing their importance, but even at the statistical level it also appears that they should be used with care. Both schools and researchers need to keep in mind the limitations of the data, and to be clear about the implications of decisions which are made about methods of analysis. Including or excluding certain groups of pupils, and the methods of combining results, for example, can have a marked effect on the apparent patterns of attainment which emerge.

The major problem with the use of exam results to assess school performance is not, however, the rather technical points discussed above, but the risk that education itself will be changed by the methods used to assess it. Most teachers, parents and pupils expect more from schools than merely good exam results, but in a period of falling rolls and diminishing educational expenditure all these other valued activities may be seen as less important and be allowed to decline. Yet these are the very activities and skills which will be of particular value to adults who are likely to spend much less time in paid employment than has been the case for previous generations of school leavers. It is obviously not acceptable to ignore the fact that a minority of schools may be failing to give their pupils the chance of achieving good examination results, but, at the same time, it would be an immeasurable loss if the broader aims of education became only secondary to paper qualifications.

Researchers are in a strong position to help schools use published figures wisely. Teachers may often not be clear about the status of such data. Some reject them entirely either because of limitations or because they find them too threatening to their professional esteem, whereas others seem far too uncritical and accept 'hard' numbers as having far more value than the experience and judgment of teachers and advisers. We should be able to help teachers take a critical but constructive approach to what is offered to children in our schools, encouraging them to use whatever information and resources are available as a starting point for more informed discussion, rather than as a final verdict to be mistrusted or ignored.

Looking Forward

The present use of outcome measures, particularly exam results, has arisen from three sources. The availability of secondary schooling for all to the age of 16 and the widespread entry for public exams have already been discussed. The third pressure has arisen from the demand for more accountability in education. Looking to the future, it is difficult to anticipate possible developments in these and other areas. It does, however, seem likely that the changing patterns of employment for young people will have a marked impact on the objectives of secondary schools. If the fifth year at school is no longer the final year in education for most young people, and the majority either continue their studies at school or college, or join a YTS-type scheme, the pressure for 16+ exams as we have them at present seems likely to decline. This might be accompanied by a more flexible approach to education so that many more young (and not so young) people could study on a part-time basis as suited to their needs at the time. What have been seen as appropriate measures of educational outcome would then change, possibly in two rather distinct directions. Attainments might be assessed in more discrete units, along the lines discussed for graded tests. At the same time much wider educational outcomes would be valued as a preparation for the demands of an adult life which will be much less secure than has been the case for the majority until recently. But these developments will depend on the willingness of government to finance them and on the enthusiasm of teachers and LEAs for educational change. The role of advisers and inspectors will be crucial here, both in helping schools to respond to these new demands and in providing in-service training.

If schools do become more flexible in what is offered to the community, it seems unlikely that they would wish to become less accountable. There seems to be little active opposition to the publication of exam results or HMI reports, and little to be gained from going back to the secrecy which existed ten years ago. The need to assess 'outcomes', and to make such assessments publicly available, seems likely to remain, although the content and timing of those assessments may change radically in the next few years.

Conclusions

It has been widely assumed that education makes a difference to children's lives. Gray *et al.* (1983) have called this belief 'the flickering light of the liberal love-affair with the Victorian ideal of progress'. Recently, however, the love-affair has entered a more critical stage — when all such relationships have to be evaluated. In this paper we have proposed that different approaches to the outcomes of education need to be taken for different purposes. Within schools, progress in a wide range of areas should be regularly assessed. The details of such reviews will depend on the established values of the head and staff, on the expectations of parents and on pressures from the outside world.

Assessing the *relative* effectiveness of schools creates rather different demands which may be *partly* met by the publication of exam results. It has, however, been proposed that this should only be part of the assessment of a school, and that the traditional role of inspectors and advisers in evaluating the important but less tangible aspects of schooling should not be undervalued.

Acknowledgement

This paper was written while the authors were financially supported by a grant from the Department of Education and Science.

References

ALEXANDER, K.L. and GRIFFIN, L.J. (1976) 'School district effects on academic achievement: A reconsideration', in *American Sociological Review*, 41, pp. 144–51.

BIDWELL, C.E. and KASARDA, J.D. (1975) 'School district organization and student achievement', in *American Sociological Review*, 40, pp. 55–70.

COLEMAN, J.S., *et al.* (1966) *Equality of Educational Opportunity*, Washington, D.C., Government Printing Office.

COOK, T.D. and CAMPBELL, D.T. (1979) *Quasi-Experimentation: Design and Analysis for Field Settings*, Chicago, Rand McNally Publishing Co.

DEPARTMENT OF EDUCATION AND SCIENCE (1977) *Ten Good Schools: A Secondary School Enquiry*, HMI Series: Matters for Discussion 1, London, HMSO.

DOUGLAS, J.W.B. (1964) *The Home and the School*, London, MacGibbon and Kee.

FORD, J. (1969) *Social Class and the Comprehensive School*, London, Routledge and Kegan Paul.

GOACHER, B. (1983) *Recording Achievement at 16+*, York, Longman for the School's Council.

GOLDSTEIN, H. (1979) *The Design and Analysis of Longitudinal Studies*, New York, Academic Press.

GRAY, J. MCPHERSON, A.F. and RAFFE, D. (1983) *Reconstructions of*

Secondary Education, London, Routledge and Kegan Paul.

HANNAN, M.T., FREEMAN, J.H. and MEYER, J.W. (1976) 'Specification of models for organizational effectiveness', in *American Sociological Review*, 41, pp. 136–43.

HARGREAVES, D.H. (1967) *Social Relations in a Secondary School*, London, Routledge and Kegan Paul.

INNER LONDON EDUCATION AUTHORITY (1977) *Keeping the School Under Review*, London, ILEA.

INNER LONDON EDUCATION AUTHORITY (1982) *School Examination Results in the ILEA, 1981*, Research and Statistics Group Paper No. RS 826/82.

JENCKS, C., et al. (1972) *Inequality: A Reassessment of the Effect of Family and Schooling America*, New York, Basic Books.

MARKS, J., COX, C. and POMIAN-SRZEDNICKI, M. (1983) *Standards in English Schools*, London, National Council for Educational Standards.

PLEWIS, I., GRAY, J., FOGELMAN, K., MORTIMORE, P. and BYFORD, D. (1981) *Publishing School Examination Results*, Bedford Way Papers No. 5, University of London, Institute of Education.

REYNOLDS, D., JONES, D. and ST. LEGER, S. (1976) 'Schools do make a difference', in *New Society*, 37, pp. 321–3.

RUTTER, M. (1983) 'School effects on pupil progress: Research findings and policy implications', in *Child Development*, 54, pp. 1–29.

RUTTER, M., GRAY, G., MAUGHAN, B. and SMITH, A. (1982) *School Experiences and Achievements and the First Year of Employment*, Report to the Department of Education and Science, London, University of London, Institute of Psychiatry.

RUTTER, M., MAUGHAN, B., MORTIMORE, P. and OUSTON, J. (1979) *Fifteen Thousand Hours*, London, Open Books.

SCOTTISH COUNCIL FOR RESEARCH IN EDUCATION (1977) *Pupils in Profile*, London, Hodder and Stoughton.

SHIPMAN, M. (1979) *In-School Evaluation*, London, Heinemann Educational.

STEEDMAN, J. (1983) *Examination Results in Selective and Non-Selective and Non-Selective Schools*, London, National Children's Bureau.

3   *School Climate: A Review of a Problematic Concept*

Janet Strivens

For whom is school climate a problematic concept and why? Chiefly, it seems, for the educational research establishment. Most of those who visit, live and work in schools seem happy to accept the idea that a particular institution has its own 'atmosphere', that it feels like a friendly, happy community or perhaps an uncaring, impersonal or even hostile environment. They are also likely to regard these differences between schools in their general atmosphere as important and significant, especially if they are considering whether they want to accept a job in one, or trying to decide where they should send their children. Of course, many parents and teachers also want to know whether a particular school has 'high academic standards' and how good its examination results are. However evidence of a school's achievement in terms of examination results has not until recently been readily available, and such information is not easily interpreted. In the absence of clearer guidelines, many parents and teachers set considerable store by their first impressions of a school, and are likely to assume that a seemingly happy and well regulated atmosphere is preferable to one of apparent disorder and hostility.

There are however a number of problems with this assumption that worry the educational researcher. In the first place there is no guarantee that this initial evaluation would command a high degree of consensus. What appears to one observer to be a friendly, open atmosphere where staff and pupils enjoy good relations and pupils are confident and articulate might strike another as disorderly, noisy and lacking in the proper respect owed by pupils to the teachers' authority. Educational values are affected by other more general beliefs and values we hold, for example, about human society, child development and institutional behaviour. These beliefs and values differ widely, and an immediately visible aspect of the school environment like the presence or absence of school uniform is likely to create a very different impression according to the observer's own educational viewpoint.

Researchers are also likely to be concerned to test out the assumption that a happy atmosphere leads to better results. Again, a lack of consensus bedevils attempts to relate differences between schools to desired educational outcomes. Most people, even the Black Paper writers, will pay lip service to the idea that schools should pursue a whole range of educational objectives. Academic achievements may be (at least superficially) the most readily assessed, but schools are also supposed to develop social skills and to impart 'values' to their pupils. Despite the fact that social-emotional and moral development are notoriously difficult to assess, British educational rhetoric has characteristically placed greater emphasis on this dimension of schooling than most other European educational traditions. Currently the bleak prospects for many school leavers have added a new urgency to this debate about educational objectives. Whether a relationship exists, and if so, of what kind, between maximal academic achievement and the full development of other dimensions of the person is not at all clear. Since these various aspects of a child's development may be differentially affected by features of the school environment, the researcher's task is correspondingly more complex.

It is useful to make a distinction between research into *school effectiveness*[1] which has taken as its main problem area the assessment of educational outcomes, and research into *school climate*. While there are clearly strong connections and overlapping interests, research on school climate has concentrated on exploring the first problem area referred to above: the definition of a good work environment, how it may be described and most importantly, how it is created.

This interest in the antecedents of a current situation carries with it its own research problems. However one chooses to describe and classify different environments, we may be fairly certain that they are not created overnight. Institutions have histories, but these are rarely available with any degree of completeness to the researcher. Changes which apparently followed from particular decisions, experiences or changes of staff are usually only available to the researcher as (and if) reported through the perceptions of members of the institution. In the absence of these important clues, researchers may decide to use assumptions drawn from other bodies of research and theory on what are likely to be important factors; or they may construct a story about the institution which is coherent but sometimes fails to make their own values and assumptions entirely clear; or they observe and record everything in sight in the hope that something significant will emerge. Thus we have a range of discrete research findings, where what has been seen as the central issue to one researcher fails to appear in the work of another, and the assumptions of one are taken to be the problems of another.

While all the questions outlined above are clearly interrelated, the particular interest of this chapter is to ask how, why and with what effects the concept of climate has been used in this context. What connotations and assumptions does the word carry from common usage? The most crucial seems to this writer to be the assumption that it has an objective existence irrespective of the perceptions of those experiencing it. Some people may feel the cold more, others have a greater tendency to bronchitis or rheumatism, but these differing experiences are the consequences of the same real conditions, which can be described and classified, and will have a predictable effect.

If this analogy is used to describe the effects of institutional environments on people working in them, the immediate consequence is to encourage a dualistic mode of thought separating the 'reality' of the organization from the perceptions of its members. This mode of thought has been challenged in many different guises within the social sciences, and some of the implications of this challenge will be considered at the end of this chapter. First, however, let us look at the effects of using the concept of climate in the research studies themselves, bearing in mind the tensions that are likely to occur; what is the status as data of members' perceptions? What is the relationship between these and the 'product'? What *is* the product? Inevitably much of the discussion will stray into ongoing debates within organization theory, and its own search for more effective conceptualizations.

Early Studies

Early work on school climate was inspired by 'classical' organization theory, in particular by studies of leadership and group behaviour. Halpin and Croft, in their pioneering work in the US in the early sixties, assumed that climate was a relatively stable if elusive property of an organization, which could in principle be classified and assessed. The typology thus developed would enable the researcher to explore both the conditions creating a particular climate and its effects. They justified the limitation of their research to teacher-principal (headteacher) relations by reference to existing research which identified leadership as likely to be the most important factor affecting organizational climate. Their study explores the effects of the leadership qualities of the principal on the sense of task accomplishment and social needs satisfaction of the teachers. Scales were devised to assess teachers' perceptions of their schools as working environments and the leadership characteristics of their heads, and a typology of climate was developed solely on the basis of internal statistical and conceptual consistency of responses. No account was taken of 'educational outcomes' in this research; whilst in principle this could follow on from the development of the scales, one senses that for these researchers the question of a school's effectiveness is relatively unproblematic:

> we have been supported by the central finding that pervades all research on leadership and group behaviour: an 'effective' group must provide satisfaction to group members in two major respects: it must give a sense of task accomplishment, and it must provide members with the social satisfaction of being part of a group. (Halpin and Croft, 1963, p. 10)

In presenting this view, Halpin and Croft acknowledge the major influence of Barnard's (1938) book, *The Functions of the Executive*. They apparently saw no reason to regard schools as different from other types of organization, and their study shows little curiosity about the process of education. References to the nature of the teaching task are virtually absent, but when they do comment, they reveal a certain naivety: 'we know that children interiorise their value-system through a process of identifying with those adults in their immediate environment who provide ego-ideals that the children can respect' (*ibid.*, p. 158). Children in general seem to be assigned a status as organizational products rather than as important members of the organization in their own right. This is a problem in the use of models from organization theory to understand schools to which the discussion will return.

In an extensive review, Thomas (1976) demonstrates the rise and fall in the popularity of Halpin and Croft's Organizational Climate Development Questionnaires (OCDQ). A large number of doctoral theses and some funded research made use of the scales to explore a bewildering variety of preconditions and outcomes. However, results have generally been highly contradictory and, in particular, attempts to link school climate with aspects of academic achievement have been almost entirely unsatisfactory.

Later Studies

Later research in the same tradition has been more sensitive to the peculiarities of schools as organizations, and, in particular, to the status of pupils. It has been more ready to accept that the perceptions of pupils should not be ignored; they do form the majority of the institution's members and their behaviour patterns, while clearly differentiated from those of the adult members, are probably the major influence on the attitudes of those adults towards the school, and also one of the most strikingly obvious features of the institution to any outsider. An approach similar to Halpin and Croft's in terms of its methodology, but taking the perceptions and attitudes of students as its key variable, is the body of research generated around Epstein and McPartland's Quality of School Life (QSL) Scales (Epstein and McPartland, 1976). In research using the QSL scales, student attitudes may be treated as either educational objectives in their own right or as indicators of organizational climate: 'at a group level aggregated attitudes may be interpreted as the affective context or climate of a school or class — the way in which average achievement scores can be used to characterize the academic content' (Epstein, 1981, p. 3). This work both recognizes the narrow emphasis of much school effectiveness research on academic outcomes, and moves beyond quantifiable material criteria such as school size or resource allocation in exploring organizational differences. One important dimension explored with the help of the QSL scales is the effect on student attitudes of participation in school decision-making. Research by Epstein (1981), Scheerer (1981) and McPartland *et al.* (1971) suggests a positive correlation between student participation (of some sort) and improved attitudes in terms of greater reported satisfaction and decreased hostility towards school staff.[2] A second factor to which this research draws attention, but with more tentativeness, is the importance of social distance between teacher and student life, with attitudes of students being more favourable when the degree of separateness is reduced.

Some developments of the OCDQ have also attempted to take into account this missing dimension of pupils' attitudes. Finlayson (1973) included a Pupil Questionnaire investigating pupils' perceptions of their peers and teachers when developing the measures used in the Comprehensive Schools Feasibility Study. Four factors emerged as important from pupils' responses, which were labelled as follows:

	Behaviour of:	
	Pupils	Teachers
Social and Emotional Needs	Emotional Tone	Concern
Exercise of Authority	Task Orientation	Social Control

The first two reflect the degree to which pupils see their peers deriving satisfaction from participating in school activities, and accepting the tasks set them by the school. The third factor reflects the pupils' sense of teachers' concern and sensitivity towards them, the fourth their perception of the imposition of expectations and exercise of power by teachers.

The factors describing pupils' views of their own behaviour reveal the influence of traditional organization theory in emphasizing the twin organizational tasks of social needs satisfaction and task accomplishment, as seen through the eyes of the junior members of the organization. This dual emphasis suggests a balance in school climate research in recognizing academic and social-emotional goals of schooling. However, this can be misleading, since it confuses 'sense of task accomplishment', a perception of the individual teacher or pupil, with objectively assessed achievement. This is an artefact of the research methodology, which uses teacher and pupil report as its prime source of data. There is a danger in assuming a high correlation between indicators of actual achievement and sense of accomplishment simply because common sense suggests some sort of link. It has already been observed that research using the OCDQ was not able to establish clear correlations between types of organizational climate and academic achievement. On the other hand, it is difficult to envisage the development of social skills and the acquisition of values other than in the context of good interpersonal relations, which reside in the perceptions teachers and pupils have of their own experience. This may reflect the difficulties of objective assessment in these areas, or suggest that we are even less clear-sighted about the precise values, attitudes and social skills we wish our children to acquire than we are about academic expectations. It is significant that some school climate researchers, including Finlayson, have stressed the importance of non-cognitive educational objectives, and have regarded a concern for climate as a means of fostering their development.

Finlayson's own use of the School Climate Scales (Finlayson, 1970; Banks and Finlayson, 1973; Finlayson and Loughran, 1976) reflects a sensitivity to the differing educational objectives which schools feel impelled to adopt, both for the institution as a whole and for different groups of pupils within that institution. The addition of pupils' perceptions to other measures, particularly when used with an awareness of the problematic nature of schools' goals, promised a more powerful tool for exploring the dimensions of school climate in relation to a variety of educational outcomes than was the OCDQ. Unfortunately the School Climate Scales have not been widely used.

A different approach to the problem is to dispense with self-report measures and to seek more 'objective' descriptors of organizational climate. However, it seems that the dimensions of organizational variety that are available to an outside observer are somewhat limited. The problem can be observed in King's (1973) study, *School Organization and Pupil Involvement*. Data on school organization were drawn from questionnaires completed by heads, some direct observation of school routines and a lengthy interview with the head, with some short supplementary interviews with senior teachers in the larger schools. King admits that occasionally the researchers found a wide divergence between what the head maintained and what was actually observed, and that in many cases checking the head's statements was impossible. Four 'structural' dimensions of organization (standardization, formalization, specialization by age, sex and ability, and ritualization) were suggested, but little information is offered about the creation of these categories. One is left with the feeling that the research team was overwhelmed with both the richness and the incompleteness of the data they collected, and was unable in consequence to generate or test any really useful hypotheses linking school organization and pupil involvement.

There has been virtually no follow-up work to Finlayson's study or to King's in the UK, and more significantly perhaps, no indication that the thinking behind these studies has been incorporated into the 'applied' world of administration and policy-making. While considerable energy has been invested in the development of school self-evaluation and accountability and the encouragement of innovation, the concept of climate has not played an important role in this work. In contrast it has maintained a steady popularity in the US, particularly in programmes designed to assess and improve 'school effectiveness'.[3] Such usage has not had the effect of clarifying conceptual problems. Kelley (1981) points out a number of confusions stemming mainly from the 'seductive' assumption of a relationship between satisfaction (morale) and productivity (achievement) which 'research has consistently shown to be neither predictive nor causal.' This assumption has led to researchers focusing on one or other of these two areas. In consequence, while there is general agreement that educational environments have significant effects, we are no nearer specifying what these are and how they are created.

However, Kelley himself in his proposals for 'auditing' climate is open to criticism for avoiding conceptual problems and thus increasing the confusion. He refers to the need for the auditing team to develop an 'acceptable' definition of climate, taking both satisfaction and productivity into account, to establish purposes, formulate indicators and prepare a status report. The only suggestion that any of these steps is problematic is the comment 'on occasion, the status report will need to include the statement that data are not available to permit decisions about how well purposes are being met.' This kind of directive, where the conceptual difficulties are disguised by the apparent clarity of the task instructions, is not helpful. 'Climate' is stretched here to mean whatever the school wants to look at.

Throughout all the approaches reviewed so far, there have been commonalities in both the conceptualization of school life and the methodology regarded as appropriate for its investigation. Schools are seen as a type of organization, implying the existence of rationally conceived and defined goals, and an equally rationally developed and adopted 'technology' for achieving them. Such a conceptualization suggests, among other things, that when a low degree of social needs satisfaction and sense of task accomplishment is experienced by the members of an organization, as detected through responses to well designed questionnaires, the situation can be rectified and the climate improved by better managerial skills on the part of the head. These include careful analysis of the appropriateness of the technology and the social aspects of the members' working conditions and more sensitive interpersonal skills in conveying decisions and extracting agreement.

There is little evidence in these studies of a critical reflection on the genesis of such assumptions in traditional approaches to understanding bureaucratic organizations, and their appropriateness to school life. However, as Bell (1980) suggests, such an approach tends to neglect 'the essentially problematic nature of goals in the organizational structure of the school', the ambiguous status of pupils as members of the organization and the fact that the technology for achieving desired goals is far from thoroughly understood. Not only do educational goals differ, whether through varying perceptions of pupils' needs or differing educational philosophies, but they tend to be stated at a fairly high level of abstraction. It is extremely unclear in consequence which aims actually conflict in practice and whether consensus ever could be obtained.

Bell points out that organization theory has itself come to question and reanalyze the view of rationality and orderliness based on commonly held goals as an adequate description of people's behaviour in organizations. He suggests as an alternative a concept of schools as 'anarchic organizations' (Cohen *et al.*, 1972); that is, where 'much organizational activity can best be understood as being characterised by unclear goals, unclear technology and fluid membership.' Among the factors which encourage this view is the recognition that schools 'operate in a complex and unstable environment over which they exert only modest control'; and the ideology of professionalism among teachers which encourages semi-autonomous decision-making which may lead not only 'to a modification of the overall goal but in certain circumstances, to an almost complete reversal of policy.'

This is not a new notion in the study of organizational behaviour. Corwin (1981), reflecting on the theoretical continuities in the idea of 'loose coupling' (Weick, 1976) as an organizational model, points to a long history of interest in the autonomy or independence of various parts or individual members of organizations, and in the phenomenon of 'slippage', the distortions occurring in policy as it filters down to the 'chalkface'. In loosely coupled organizations, processes are not really understood by members, practices arise on the basis of trial and error and tend to become habitual, decision-making is highly problematic because of the unpredictability of factors affecting the decision. This is not to suggest that such organizations have no identifiable structure, simply that the structure does not inhere in the formal characteristics of the decision-making process.

In this reconceptualization of organizational behaviour it becomes less easy to talk about climate in the terms of the preceding discussion. Staff morale would be likely to be a fluid and variable phenomenon depending on any one member's perspective of the current organizational processes and the degree of consensuality which holds for any set of joint actions. It would still be perfectly possible and acceptable to research this through seeking access to members' experiences of the organization and through direct observation of organizational events, but it is likely that standard questionnaires and scales would be found constricting for this purpose. Researchers in the field of understanding educational innovations and the blocks to achieving them are increasingly finding that 'ethnographic' methods are needed to allow an understanding to develop of members' experiences of institutional life. The conditions under which consensuality is increased are highly unpredictable. No doubt they include many of the areas to which traditional studies have drawn attention: the way in which headteachers exercise their authority, the degree of participation teachers feel they have in decisions which affect them, the support which they get for facing up to problems rather than shelving them and the balances of stress in this process.

Purkey and Smith support a move towards this kind of reconceptualization in their review of research on school effectiveness. They argue the need for a better understanding of school processes, 'the nature and style of political and social relationships and the flow of information within the school'. The linking of process to content ('roles, norms, values and instructional techniques of the school, and the information taught in the curriculum') provides the notion of *culture*, a more powerful descriptive concept than climate:

> the appropriateness of the school culture notion is supported by ideas derived from organizational theory and from research on the implementation of educational innovation ... schools by their nature may not prove amenable to command structure approaches, especially given the vested interests of the various groups of relatively autonomous professionals ... the school culture model begins to resolve the dilemma posed by loose coupling ... it assumes that consensus among the staff of a school is more powerful than overt control, without ignoring the need for leadership. (Purkey and Smith, 1982)

'Climate' seems to be used loosely by these writers as an aspect of culture, encompassing attitudes, behaviour and organizational structures influencing school effectiveness. It appears to carry no special significance, in which case its use in this context could be seen as a relic from an abandoned theoretical framework. An alternative is to see it as the 'static' aspect of a dynamic concept, a means of 'freezing' the flow of school life while recognizing that this inevitably fails to represent reality adequately. Something of this flavour is captured in Sagor's (1981) use of the term, describing a technique he calls 'A Day in the Life' for assessing school climate and effectiveness. His is the viewpoint of a practitioner, the principal of a school which is aware of dissatisfied students and staff and concerned to improve its educational practice. The process involves teachers 'shadowing' a number of students and experiencing a typical day from their perspective. Sagor is aware of the research literature and somewhat defensive about the 'lack of scientific precision' in this technique, but his report suggests that it can be a powerful tool for school self-appraisal. What he does not offer is an explanation of how this particular staff came to feel that 'tough, emotional, delicate and educationally valid issues' could be raised and examined.

Conclusions

This discussion has brought us back to our original question about the usage of the term 'climate'. It seems that there has been a tendency for its use to be associated with particular models of school life and research approaches which have been subject to some criticism but which still enjoy considerable influence particularly within the US. It is an open question whether the use of the term necessarily implies the dualistic mode of thought criticized by Greenfield (1975), but it does seem to encourage confusion and the avoidance of important value-laden conceptual problems raised at the start of this chapter. The substitution of culture may well not help in this respect, but it carries interesting methodological implications, suggesting the need for the skills of the ethnographer in exploring the elusive nature of a school's 'atmosphere'. There is at least a measure of agreement here; whatever it is called, it is too important to be ignored.

Notes

1 See REYNOLDS (1982) and PURKEY and SMITH (1982) for reviews of school effectiveness research.
2 See also SCHONFELD (1971) and MOOS (1978) for supporting evidence of the positive effects of student participation in decision-making.
3 See ANDERSON (1982) for a recent and comprehensive review of research with particular reference to the United States.

References

ANDERSON, C.S. (1982) 'The search for school climate: A review of research', *Review of Educational Research*, 52, pp. 368–420.

BANKS, O. and FINLAYSON, D.S. (1973) *Success and Failure in the Secondary School*, London, Methuen.

BARNARD, C.I. (1938) *The Functions of the Executive*, Cambridge, Mass., Harvard University Press.

BELL, L.A. (1980) 'The school as an organisation: A reappraisal', *British Journal of Sociology of Education*, 1, pp. 183–92.

COHEN, M.D., MARCH, J.G. and OLSEN, J.P. (1972) 'A garbage can model of organisational choice', *Administrative Science Quarterly*, 17, pp. 1–25.

CORWIN, R.G. (1981) 'Patterns of organisational control and teacher militancy: Theoretical continuities in the idea of "loose coupling"', *Research in Sociology of Education and Socialization*, 2, pp. 261–91.

EPSTEIN, J.L. (Ed.) (1981) *The Quality of School Life*, Toronto, Lexington Books.

EPSTEIN, J.L. and McPARTLAND, J.M. (1976) 'The concept and measurement of Quality of School Life', *American Educational Research Journal*, 50, pp. 13–30.

FINLAYSON, D.S. (1970) 'How high and low achievers see teachers' and pupils' role behaviour', *Research in Education*, 3.

FINLAYSON, D.S. (1973) 'Measuring 'school climate'', *Trends in Education*, 30, pp. 19–27.

FINLAYSON, D.S. and LOUGHRAN, J.L. (1976) 'Pupils' perceptions in high and low delinquency schools', *Educational Research*, 18, pp. 138–45.

GREENFIELD, T. BARR (1975) 'Theory about organization: A new perspective and its implications for schools', in HOUGHTON, V.P., McHUGH, G.A.R. and MORGAN, C. (Eds), *Management in Education Reader 1: The Management of Organizations and Individuals*, London, Ward Lock Education/Open University Press.

HALPIN, A.W. and CROFT, D.B. (1963) *Organizational Climate of Schools*, Chicago, Midwest Administrative Centre, University of Chicago.

KELLEY, E.A. (1981) 'Auditing school climate', *Educational Leadership*, 39, pp. 180–3.

KING, R. (1973) *School Organization and Pupil Involvement*, London, Routledge and Kegan Paul.

McPARTLAND, J.M., McDILL, E.L., LACEY, C., HARRIS, R.J. and NOVEY, L.B. (1971) *Student Participation in High School Decisions: A Study of 14 Urban High Schools*, Report 95, Baltimore, Johns Hopkins University Centre for Social Organisation of Schools.

MOOS, R.H. (1978) 'A typology of junior high and high school classrooms', *American Educational Research Journal*, 15, pp. 53–66.

PURKEY, S.C. and SMITH, M.S. (1982) 'Too soon to cheer? Synthesis of research on effective schools', *Educational Leadership*, 40, 3, pp. 64–9.

REYNOLDS, D. (1982) 'School effectiveness research — a review of the literature', *School Organization and Management Abstracts*, 1, pp. 5–14.

SAGOR, R. (1981) '"A Day in the Life" — a technique for assessing school

climate and effectiveness', *Educational Leadership*, 39, pp. 190–3.
SCHEERER, H. (1981) 'Choice schemes and the Quality of School Life in West German comprehensive schools', in Epstein, J.L., *op. cit.*
SCHONFELD, W.R. (1971) *Youth and Authority in France: A Study of Secondary Schools*, Beverley Hills, Calif., Sage.
THOMAS, R.A. (1976) 'The organizational climate of schools', *International Review of Education*, 22, pp. 441–63.
WEICK, K.E. (1976) 'Educational organizations as loosely coupled systems', *Administrative Science Quarterly*, 21, pp. 1–19.

4 Conceptualizing Curriculum Differences for Studies of Secondary School Effectiveness

Brian Wilcox

Curriculum As a Variable in School Effectiveness Studies

One striking characteristic in the current series of studies of school differences and school effects is the lack of attention which researchers have given to 'curriculum' as a variable of potential interest. This is very surprising given the fact that a large amount of senior staff time is consumed in thinking about and organizing this major aspect of a school's work. Moreover, the professional's implicit assumption of the importance of the curriculum has been massively endorsed in recent years by a plethora of advice and exhortation from the DES on the need to review and recast it.

The neglect of curriculum in this area of study may reflect the difficulty which researchers have in pinning down what is a very elusive, slippery, and complex conception. We can begin to come to grips with it perhaps if we distinguish three aspects. First, there is the way in which the curriculum is organized, that is, the pattern of subjects taught, the methods of grouping pupils and teachers together to pursue specific learning activities under such headings as history, integrated science, pastoral care. Secondly, there are the descriptions which detail what actually occurs in the groupings referred to above. This is what is often referred to as the *content* of the curriculum, a term which may be taken to mean more than just factual knowledge, and to include an account of the skills, attitudes and values which are fostered. Finally, there is the question of how the content of the curriculum is actually developed with pupils. This, of course, includes the teaching and learning methods employed, as well as the ways in which learning is supported both within and outside the classroom — something which we might call the *learning environment* of the school.

These distinctions are to some extent artificial, for the curriculum is very much a seamless robe. However, some such categorization is necessary if curriculum is to be examined as a possible influence on pupil outcomes. Furthermore, the categories provide a basis for identifying the lacunae in current research programmes. Thus in the influential study of twelve ILEA comprehensive schools by Rutter *et al.* (1979) some variables falling within the third category were examined. Some of these can be regarded as indicators of the learning environment: homework set, library use, work on walls; or of teaching/learning method: teacher praise, teacher interventions, teacher interaction style. But none of these process variables falls within the first two categories of curriculum organization and curriculum content.

The three categories can be regarded as providing descriptions at three levels of generality. The first, *organization*, is the most general, and provides a description of what may be called the surface levels of the curriculum. The next two descend to deeper levels by describing, in turn, the structure of the curriculum or individual parts of it (i.e., *content*), and the nature of specific transactions — perhaps at the level of the individual lesson (i.e., the *learning environment*). Although a substantial amount of research has been carried out at the latter level in attempting to relate teacher behaviours to pupil outcomes (for example, Galton *et al.*, 1980; Galton and Simon, 1980) this has usually ignored their relationship to the more general levels of curriculum content and organization.

Researchers studying school effectiveness in which the unit of analysis is the school might find some profitable returns in examining the effects of different patterns of curriculum organization. The main purpose of this paper is to outline a methodology for conceptualizing and quantifying curriculum organization so that it might be investigated as a possible variable predictive of pupil outcomes.

The Use of a Curriculum Notation System

The methodology involves the use of a curriculum notation system which has been developed in the Sheffield LEA. It allows one to summarize economically a large amount of the curriculum detail of a secondary school in terms of a set of standardized codes and conventions. The system is a derivative of a more rudimentary one developed by Davies (1969) which is much used on the courses for senior staff of secondary schools mounted by the HMI in the COSMOS team (Committee for the Organization, Staffing and Management of Schools).

The notation system differs from that of Davies in several ways.

1 Codes for different subjects and curricular activities are developed more fully and systematically.

2 It is possible to depict a variety of teaching and organizational structures, including streaming, banding, setting, mixed ability grouping, team teaching and others, by using the system.

3 More fundamentally, the system is used as a means of outlining succinctly the total curricular structure of even the largest secondary school.

The notation system (described in detail in Wilcox and Eustace, 1980) was introduced in the Sheffield LEA in 1976. In that year all of the LEA's secondary schools were asked to submit a description of their curriculum in notational form. As a result a substantial archive now exists consisting of standardized descriptions of the curriculum and organization of the authority's three dozen or so secondary schools for each of the years from 1976 onwards. This notation system has been adopted by other LEAs, and archives of this kind are therefore likely to be found elsewhere.

Although the system was originally developed as a tool for curriculum planning at both school and LEA level, it also has considerable research potential, providing as it does a mass of curriculum data not normally accessible to researchers and which would otherwise require the use of very elaborate questionnaires to obtain.

An examination of the curriculum returns of schools expressed in notational form presents a wealth of detail within which the range of differences between schools is revealed as being greater than is often thought. In order to discern these differences (and similarities) clearly, and also to render curriculum detail manageable as research variables, it is necessary to aggregate the data within some broader curriculum concepts. A promising one seems to be *curriculum balance*.

Analysis in Terms of Curriculum Balance

The notion of curriculum balance is a recurring one in the history of education. It can be traced back at least as far as the idea of the seven liberal arts in medieval universities. The science versus arts debate which has been carried on intermittently from the mid-nineteenth century to the present represents another manifestation of the same theme. More recently, curriculum balance has been the special concern of philosophers of education who have attempted to understand the nature of the curriculum in terms of forms of knowledge or characteristic ways of thinking (Hirst, 1975; Phenix, 1964). The ideas of the former are also reflected in the attempt of HMI to look at the curriculum in terms of 'areas of experience' (DES, 1977). Other frameworks are possible and Hurman (1978) describes a useful one based on subject groupings. The advantage of the last approach over the others is that it relates more naturally to the familiar titles of the school timetable.

In the analysis which follows, balance has been expressed in terms of the following broad subject groupings:

English studies (including literature, library, etc.)
Mathematical studies (including computer studies, etc.)
Religious education
Traditional humanities (history, geography, etc.)
Integrated humanities (social studies, etc.)
Lifeskills (including careers education, health education, parent
 craft, community studies, form periods, assembly)
Languages
Sciences
Creative/practical subjects
Aesthetic subjects (art, drama, music)
Vocational subjects (e.g., typewriting, motor vehicle mainte-
 nance)
Physical and leisure activities.

Given the diversity of the secondary curriculum — well over 100 subject titles are necessary to describe the secondary school programmes in Sheffield — some form of categorization is essential if the notion of balance is to be expressed in any meaningful manner. The set of categories given above is, of course, just one amongst many which could be suggested. The principal justification for the particular groupings used here is that they identify curriculum activities that are reasonably distinct one from another. Obviously some overlap inevitably exists. Thus although religious education may occur within an integrated humanities course, where it does so, experience suggests that its treatment and content is often different from that which usually characterizes the separately timetabled subject. Although art, drama and music are often grouped together under titles such as 'practical' or 'creative', it was felt that this concealed their distinctive contributions and placed them alongside some inappropriate curricular bedfellows. They were therefore grouped under the heading 'aesthetic subjects'. The group termed 'lifeskills' arises from the attempt to provide a label for those activities which have as their *major* aim the preparation of the pupil for life beyond or outside of school. This group also includes form periods and assemblies where these take place *within* the official timetable. Where these activities take place outside the timetable (e.g., as a ten-minute registration period) they are not included. This may, at first glance, seem somewhat arbitrary. However it does generally follow that when a school decides to consume some of its forty or so timetabled periods in this way then some kind of distinctive contribution occurs. Thus a timetabled form period often provides the form teacher with the opportunity of following a structured programme of guidance or general studies.

Another advantage of the categories used is that their number (twelve) is neither so great as to make the subsequent analysis too detailed nor so small as to make it too gross.

Curriculum balance may be expressed in at least two ways: in terms of what the pupil receives, or of how teaching resources are allocated to particular curriculum areas. One of the problems with the former approach is that different groups of pupils experience different curricula, particularly as a result of the complex pattern of option choices which operates in most schools in the fourth and fifth year. The alternative approach basically poses the question: where does the school place its curricular emphasis in deploying the activities of its teachers? This can be expressed easily by calculating the number of teacher periods per week for each subject, grouping under the appropriate curriculum category and then aggregating the results. Teacher periods for each category can then be divided by the total number of teacher periods per week and the results converted into percentages. This calculation has been carried out on each year group (S1–S5) of all secondary schools in Sheffield using the 1980/81 curriculum returns. The detailed calculations obtained were sent to each school to check whether:

(a) individual subjects were placed, in the school's view, under the right category;

(b) the curriculum return had been interpreted appropriately and the calculations carried out correctly.

The information was then returned with any modifications or corrections by the school.

Some modification was also necessary for most schools concerning the inclusion of remedial provision. Where remedial provision was separately coded on the curriculum return as Rm it was included under English studies unless clearly related to mathematical studies or some other subject. In the case of those schools which had a remedial band, the curriculum offered by that band was automatically included under the appropriate curriculum headings. Where remedial 'withdrawal' operated the schools were asked to indicate the number of teacher periods which this involved. These were allocated as appropriate to English or mathematical studies.[1] The outcome of this procedure was that an analysis of teacher periods by curriculum group was tacitly agreed with each school.

Some Results

Table 1 summarizes the results of this analysis of the LEA's thirty-nine secondary schools by giving the average percentage of teacher periods allocated to each curriculum area by year group from S1 (i.e., 11+ years) to S5 (i.e., 15+ years). It will be noted that the figures in the extreme right-hand column are obtained by adding together those falling under the two categories, integrated humanities and lifeskills. This is done because it was felt that the separation of these two categories was somewhat artificial, particularly in years S4 and S5. For example, some integrated humanities courses include a careers education and often a health education component. Thus that area of the curriculum specially concerned with preparing pupils for life beyond school and adult life generally is best represented by combining these two categories. In the absence of a commonly accepted term, the title 'general preparation for life' has been used for the combined categories.

It is thus possible to obtain a series of standardized curriculum profiles which permit comparisons to be made between schools. As examples of the kind of summary possible, the results for the S1 and S5 year groups are displayed in Figures 1 and 2. These figures present visually the variation of curriculum balance across all the secondary schools in Sheffield. Each rectangular block shows the percentage of teacher periods allocated to each curriculum area for all Sheffield schools. The left-hand side of the rectangle locates the school (or schools) which has the lowest proportion of teacher periods allocated

Table 1. *Average Percentage of Teacher Periods per Curriculum Area per Year Group*

(N = 39 schools)

	(1)	(2)	(3)	(4)	(5)	(6)	(7)	(8)	(9)	(10)	(11)	(12)	(6) and (8)
	English studies	Mathematical studies	Languages	Science	Humanities	Integrated humanities	RE	Lifeskills	Aesthetic subjects	PE	Practical crafts	Vocational subjects	General preparation for life
S1	15.7	14.4	9.1	11.0	10.9	1.9	3.6	2.5	8.8	10.0	12.0	0.0	4.4
S2	14.7	13.6	10.4	11.1	11.1	1.3	3.7	1.8	8.7	9.1	14.5	0.1	3.1
S3	13.1	12.7	10.4	13.1	10.4	1.5	3.1	2.3	8.1	8.4	16.9	0.1	3.8
S4	12.4	12.2	5.4	15.0	12.1	4.4	2.3	4.9	5.3	6.9	14.7	4.3	9.3
S5	12.9	12.3	5.1	14.9	12.1	4.7	2.3	4.8	5.0	6.9	14.7	4.5	9.5

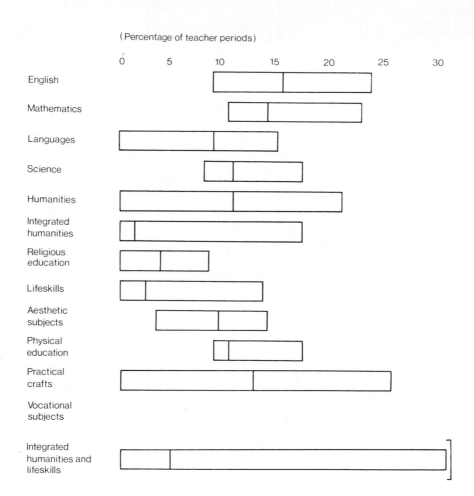

Figure 1 *Percentage of Teacher Periods Allocated to Curriculum Areas in the S1 Year*

Key:
Left-hand side of rectangle = minimum allocation.
Right-hand side of rectangle = maximum allocation.
Middle line = average allocation.

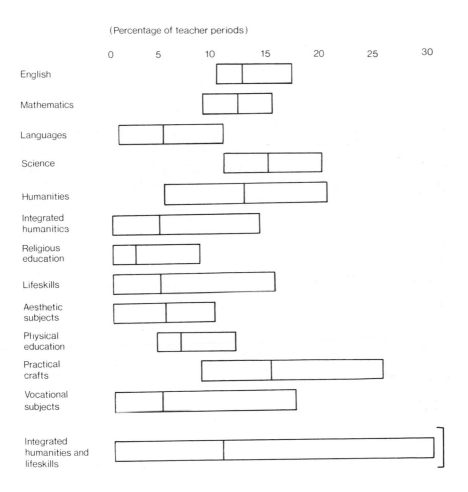

Figure 2 *Percentage of Teacher Periods Allocated to Curriculum Areas in the S5 Year*

Key:
Left-hand side of rectangle = minimum allocation.
Right-hand side of rectangle = maximum allocation.
Middle line = average allocation.

to a particular curriculum area. The right-hand side of the rectangle identifies the school (or schools) having the highest proportion of teacher periods. The vertical line between the two is the average value for all schools for that curriculum area.

Inspection of these figures reveals many interesting points. For example, the curriculum area for which the variation between schools is greatest is that represented by the combined categories referred to above and provisionally called 'general preparation for life'. However, the purpose of presenting these results is not to provide a detailed analysis and interpretation of them, interesting and important though that might be, but to illustrate something of the variation which exists across schools.

It is interesting to note that marked variation in curriculum profiles can exist for schools which are outwardly similar. This is illustrated in Table 2 for two comprehensive schools (A and B) both having an intake at S2 (12+ years), roughly similar year group sizes, small sixth forms, and drawing on comparably disadvantaged catchment areas (both were SPS (social priority supplement) schools.) Amongst the differences apparent are the greater emphasis given to aesthetic subjects by school A and to practical crafts by school B. Of course, the figures in Table 2 are averages across the year groups and do not distinguish between pupils of different abilities who may receive different curriculum programmes. However, the curriculum profiles of such pupils can be determined if required, particularly where pupils are organized on the basis of discrete streams or bands.

Some Indication of the Form Which Studies Involving the Curriculum Variable Might Take

School differences, then, are apparent in the patterns of curriculum organization. The important question, however, is whether such patterns have a differential effect on pupil outcomes such as academic success. Is there a relationship between the type of curriculum organization of a school and the success or otherwise of its pupils in fifth year public examinations (to take one of the currently favoured pupil outcomes)? It would seem that studies have yet to be done which would provide answers to this question. It is possible, however, to discern the form which such studies might take assuming they had access to curriculum notation data from a number of schools.

If the emphasis is on pupils' examination achievements in S5, it is

Table 2. *Average Percentage of Teacher Periods per Curriculum Area per Year Group for Two Comparable Schools (A and B)*

Year group	School	Number of Pupils in year group	(1) English studies	(2) Mathematical studies	(3) Languages	(4) Science	(5) Humanities	(7) Integrated humanities	RE	(8) Lifeskills	(9) Aesthetic subjects	(10) PE	(11) Practical crafts	(12) Vocationals subjects	(6) and (8) General preparation for life
S2	A	253	15.4	16.9	8.6	9.4	9.4	0.0	4.7	0.0	14.1	8.6	12.9	0.0	0.0
	B	228	16.8	13.1	10.4	11.9	0.0	13.8	0.0	0.0	5.9	13.3	14.8	0.0	13.8
S3	A	252	12.9	12.9	11.1	12.9	9.2	0.0	4.6	0.0	13.8	9.7	12.9	0.0	0.0
	B	264	14.9	14.5	8.1	12.5	12.5	1.0	2.1	0.0	7.9	5.8	20.7	0.0	1.0
S4	A	271	11.8	14.7	3.0	12.8	6.9	3.9	2.0	6.3	9.8	9.4	14.7	4.7	10.2
	B	218	15.5	13.8	2.9	14.0	9.7	3.9	1.0	1.9	6.8	10.7	19.9	0.0	5.8
S5	A	285	12.5	14.5	1.0	15.4	8.0	0.8	3.9	6.4	7.2	9.8	15.0	5.9	7.2
	B	231	15.0	14.6	2.7	15.9	9.1	3.6	0.9	2.3	6.4	4.6	25.0	0.0	5.9

perhaps a reasonable hypothesis to assume that these are, in part, the outcome of the cumulative pattern of curriculum organization throughout the secondary school from the first year onwards. It would, therefore, be necessary to aggregate the organizational pattern of S5 with that of S4 in the previous year and that of S3 in the year before that, and so on. If the pattern of curriculum organization in schools were stable from one year to another then one could, of course, aggregate across year groups for any one school year. However, this is unlikely to be the case — changes may occur from one school year to the next for a whole variety of reasons. These changes may be substantial, corresponding perhaps to major curriculum developments. Ideally, then, one wants to look at the curriculum of schools in a longitudinal sense. However, although longitudinal studies of individuals, particularly children, are an established method of educational research, longitudinal studies of *schools* appear to be rare. A recent exception is Ronald King's study of a sample of secondary schools. King originally surveyed the organization of pupil learning and behaviour in seventy-two secondary schools in 1968/69. Ten years later he was able to re-survey forty-five of his original sample, thus enabling a comparison to be made between the two points in time. As a result he was able to consider the question: '*How* have schools been changed over the years?' (King, 1981). King's study, although it examined a variety of organizational features (e.g., streaming, setting, school councils, assemblies, and systems of pastoral care) did not consider changes in the pattern of curriculum organization.

The existence of a curriculum archive built up from notational returns obtained annually provides much of the data needed for a longitudinal study of curriculum organization of schools, almost as a matter of routine. It has the added advantage of generating a description not only at two points in time, as in King's study, but also at intervening ones. Thus the development of schools, either individually or collectively, can be traced year by year in some detail, and thus the aggregated pattern of curriculum organization reliably determined.

Studies of school effectiveness which have used examination results as outcome measures have not generally differentiated between performance in different subjects. Examination results have been aggregated to give single measures such as the percentage of pupils gaining one or more O-level or O-level equivalents (for example, Rutter *et al.*, 1979; Gray *et al.*, 1983). Whilst it would be interesting to see whether such global measures were associated with different patterns of curriculum organization, it might be more revealing to explore the relationships between examination performance in specific subject or curriculum areas and the pattern of organization for the curriculum as a whole or of particular parts of it. In this way answers might be given to such questions as: Do schools which give the greatest emphasis to curriculum components such as English, mathematics, science, traditional humanities achieve the best examination results? Does an integrated approach to science or the humanities in the lower school have any effect on the examination results achieved in these areas later on? Different patterns of curriculum organization might also be expected to influence other aspects of pupil behaviour. Do schools, for example, which invest heavily in what has been referred to earlier as the 'preparation for life' area of the curriculum produce discernible effects on the personal and social competence of their pupils?

Conclusion

Simpkins (1983), in a review of the management implications of curriculum information systems, distinguishes between two processes: *filtration* and *transformation*.

> Curriculum notation involves filtration, expressing in a systematic language the way in which the school curriculum is organised, children are grouped and staff deployed. Curriculum analysis, on the other hand, comprises all the ways in which the essentially descriptive information embodied in a notation is manipulated and transformed to produce summary information — usually indicators of various kinds — which points up key dimensions of actual or proposed curricular patterns ... Curriculum notations and curriculum analysis essentially describe the pattern of *inputs* to the curriculum in terms of pupil and teacher time and, to some extent, the curriculum *process* in so far as it can be captured by patterns of pupil grouping and organization.

However, although the management applications of curriculum notation systems are increasingly recognized, the value of such systems to researchers has been largely ignored. The main argument presented here is that the use of a notation system enables researchers to quantify 'curriculum' as a variable in studies of school effectiveness. As a first stage it has been suggested that effects might be sought of different patterns of curriculum organization on pupil outcomes. *One* way of doing this which looks promising is in terms of curriculum balance. However, one of the great advantages of summarizing curriculum data in notational form is that they can be reworked in a multitude of ways to create a whole range of possible curriculum indicators.

Whilst it may be feasible to look for statistically significant relationships between school outcomes and various curriculum measures in a large sample of schools, an alternative approach involving detailed study of a small number of schools should also be considered. One way of pursuing the latter might be to identify a group of schools of comparable size, intake characteristics, etc., and examine the extent to which they vary on a range of pupil outcomes. Such a study, having access to an archive of curriculum notation and other data, would be able to plot the precise changes in the curriculum organization of the schools over time. Such data could also be supplemented with those derived from school documents (such as syllabuses, schemes of work), teacher interviews and perhaps classroom observation so as to give a comprehensive account of the curriculum at the organizational, content and learning environment levels outlined earlier.

Stenhouse (1978) has presented a persuasive case for carrying out the fieldwork aspect of the study of schools in such a way as to produce case records for lodgement in a Contemporary Educational Records Archive. Stenhouse conceives the case record as the 'theoretically parsimonious condensation of . . . data produced by selective editing' by the fieldworker. It would represent an 'edited primary source' which would form the basis from which case studies and analytic surveys might be written. It is envisaged that the case record would be derived from the much larger body of data which could be collected from schools, for example, syllabuses, schemes of work, curriculum details, supplemented by that obtained directly by the fieldworker through interviews with teachers, pupils, etc.

An archive of curriculum notation data such as exists in Sheffield, although much less ambitious in scope than Stenhouse's conception, would seem to have something in common with it. Thus the curriculum returns on which the archive is built could be said to be 'parsimonious condensations' of the total curricula of schools. In Stenhouse's terms they form at least part of a potential case record. Stenhouse also argues that an educational archive developed along the lines he suggests should be accessible to external researchers. Researchers would be able to consult the case record not only to verify studies derived from them but also to provide data for their own investigations. It would be necessary to derive appropriate protocols for dealing with such access but this should not represent an insurmountable problem. For example, Gray (1981) has noted the growth of LEA data bases on school examination results and has been able to gain access to them as an external researcher.

If the embryonic curriculum archives which probably exist in several local authorities continue to develop, then we may expect that members of the research community will seek to use them. This could well initiate a new and potentially fruitful thrust to school effectiveness studies in particular and curriculum research in general.

Note

1   In the cases where the allocation to these two subjects was not given by the school the number of teacher periods of withdrawal provision was split in the ratio 6:4 between the two.

References

DAVIES, T.I. (1969) *School Organisation*, Oxford, Pergamon.
Department of Education and Science (1977) *Curriculum 11–16*, London, HMSO.
GALTON, M. and SIMON, B. (Eds) (1980) *Progress and Performance in the Primary Classroom*, London, Routledge and Kegan Paul.
GALTON M. SIMON B. and CROLL, P. (1980) *Inside the Primary Classroom*, London, Routledge and Kegan Paul.
GRAY J. (1981) 'A competitive edge: examination results and the probable limits of secondary school effectiveness', *Educational Review*, 33, 1, pp. 25–35.
GRAY, J., McPHERSON, A.F. and RAFFE, D. (1983) *Reconstructions of Secondary Education: Theory, Myth and Practice since the War*, London, Routledge and Kegan Paul.
HIRST, P.H. (1975) *Knowledge and the Curriculum*, London; Routledge and Kegan Paul.
HURMAN, A. (1978) *A Charter for Choice: A Study of Option Schemes*, Windsor, NFER.
KING, R.A. (1981) 'Secondary schools: some changes of a decade', *Educational Research*, 23, 3 pp. 173–6.
PHENIX, P.H. (1964) *Realms of Meaning*, New York, McGraw-Hill.
RUTTER, M., MAUGHAN, B., MORTIMORE, P. and OUSTON, J. (1979) *Fifteen Thousand Hours: Secondary Schools and Their Effects on Children*, London, Open Books.
SIMPKINS, T. (1983) 'Some management implications of the development of

curriculum information systems', *Journal of Curriculum Studies*, 15, 1, pp. 47–59.

STENHOUSE, L., (1978) 'Case study and case records: Towards a contemporary history of education', *British Educational Research Journal*, 14, 2, pp. 21–39.

WILCOX, B. and EUSTACE, P.J. (1980) *Tooling up for Curriculum Review*, Slough, NFER.

5   *Pastoral Care and School Effectiveness*

David Galloway

Pastoral care emerged as a growth area in secondary education with the development of comprehensive schools. This does not imply that grammar and secondary modern schools failed to provide pastoral care, merely that they seldom gave it a name, or paid selected teachers extra money to take special responsibility for it. Throughout the 1960s and 1970s pastoral care, like Topsy, 'just growed'. The overwhelming majority of comprehensive schools established posts at middle or senior management level with specific responsibility for pupil's welfare, and a new breed of specialist was born.

The growth was haphazard and, for so widespread a movement, remarkably undocumented in its early stages. Schools varied in their definitions of pastoral duties, in the way they organized these duties, and even in the priority they attached to them. Developments which had seemed inevitable in the 1960s and early 1970s lost momentum and gradually fizzled out towards the end of the 1970s. Perhaps the most notable was the appointment of full-time counsellors in secondary schools. The decline both in training courses for school counsellors and in the number of full-time counsellors employed in schools was partly attributable to economic pressures but perhaps also to the counselling profession's inability to resolve dilemmas inherent in the counsellor's role in school. Many of these dilemmas apply also to pastoral care, and can be expected to attract increasingly critical attention in the next few years.

Gradually, though, a degree of consensus has emerged on the aims and function of pastoral care. Hamblin (1977) argued that it should focus explicitly on progress and adjustment at school, pointing out that teachers cannot hope to do much about their pupils' home backgrounds. He also believed that the first priority of senior staff was to lead a pastoral team, since all teachers should be involved in pastoral care. Button (1981) carried this argument a stage further by providing suggestions for form tutors to use in active tutorial work. Others pointed out that teachers who spend too much energy trying to resolve or reduce problems in their pupils' family lives may become frustrated or exhausted (Spooner, 1979; Galloway, 1981) and suffer from role conflict (Dunham, 1977).

In spite of this broad and somewhat ill-defined consensus, there have been few systematic descriptions of pastoral care, and even fewer systematic attempts to evaluate its effectiveness. The detailed case study of 'Rivendell', a large comprehensive school in England, provides a welcome addition to the literature (Best *et al.*, 1983) but underlines the need for information based on a larger number of schools, utilizing a range of methodologies. Criticisms have focused on the concept and process in fairly general terms (for example, Best *et al.*, 1978; 1980) or on particular practices, such as a tendency for middle management staff to investigate cases of truancy (for example, Reynolds and Murgatroyd, 1977). The first part of this chapter discusses the concept and practice of pastoral care with specific reference to recent research on school effectiveness. The second part discusses issues in the evaluation of pastoral care, and suggests possible avenues for future school effectiveness research.

Aims and Function

Hamblin (1978) has defined pastoral care as:

> that element of the teaching process which centres around the personality of the pupil and the forces in his environment which either facilitate or impede the development of intellectual and social skills, and foster or retard emotional stability ... [it] is also concerned with the modification of the learning environment, adapting it to meet the needs of individual pupils, so that every pupil has the maximum chance of success whatever his background or general ability.

A clear implication of this definition is that pastoral care is inherent in the school's educational goals. Logically, though, it is possible for a headteacher to base a school's general organization and day-to-day management on a philosophy which makes no explicit reference to pastoral care. Equally, such a school could be a satisfying, stimulating place both for its pupils and for its teachers. Conversely, schools described by senior staff as 'guidance orientated' or 'pastoral care orientated' sometimes provide a profoundly unsatisfying environment for teachers and pupils alike.

The point, of course, is that effective teaching requires pastoral skills. Yet although pastoral skills are necessary for effective teaching they are certainly not sufficient — if indeed it makes sense to talk about pastoral skills as separate and distinct from the teaching process. Uncompleted homework provides a good illustration. Possible explanations are that the pupil: (i) simply cannot understand the work; (ii) so much dislikes either the teacher or the subject that he is refusing to cooperate; (iii) lives in a crowded home with inadequate facilities for completing homework; (iv) is developing a generalized antipathy towards school, perhaps associated with membership of an anti-authority peer group; (v) is showing symptoms of personal or family stress.

Establishing the reasons will require sympathetic and possibly prolonged investigation. Some teachers will see such investigation as an essential part of their job of enabling each pupil to reach a high standard, with a consequent sense of achievement. Others will see it specifically in 'pastoral' terms. From whatever perspective it is viewed, this example illustrates the nonsense of a structural distinction between academic, pastoral and disciplinary goals. An organizational structure based on a coherent philosophy provides a starting point for effective teaching. Unfortunately this starting point is frequently lacking. Galloway *et al.* (1982a) and Galloway and Barrett (1982), for example, described schools in which subject teachers were required to refer 'pastoral' problems to a year tutor or counsellor and 'discipline' problems to the head of department. As these teachers often saw a class only once or twice a week, and received no guidance in distinguishing the two supposedly separate problems, confusion and inconsistency became inevitable.

While the explicit aims of pastoral care can be stated reasonably concisely, its actual function within a school is far more problematic. Ostensibly its function is to promote the aims of the school, generally described in pretty general terms such as educational, social and cultural development, or helping each child to reach his or her full potential. Somewhat less obvious functions are: (i) to provide an alternative career ladder to the traditional one through subject departments; (ii) to provide a 'liberal' form of social control; (iii) to respond to teachers' short-term needs by enabling them to refer disturbing pupils to a middle management specialist. The functions of pastoral care will vary from school to school, depending on the school's unstated aims for its staff and pupils, or the 'hidden curriculum', and on the degree of consistency between stated and unstated aims.

Models of Pastoral Care

An implication of this argument is that the quality of pastoral care may be assessed by reference to attitudes throughout the school and to educational and behavioural standards. It may not matter very much whether we look first at the pupils' attitudes and behaviour or at the teachers'. Headteachers could legitimately argue that their first priority should be the pastoral care of their staff. Bored or dissatisfied teachers who feel that their efforts are undervalued cannot sensibly be expected to produce alert, interested pupils, confident that their teachers will recognize and value their efforts.

It is instructive to consider some of the principal sources of stress and of satisfaction reported by teachers. Children's behaviour and progress have been reported as major sources of stress from day-to-day events in the classroom both in primary schools (Pratt, 1978; Galloway *et al.*, 1982b) and in secondary schools (Kyriacou and Sutcliffe, 1978; Dunham, 1977). Rudd and Wiseman (1962) found poor relationships with colleagues an important source of dissatisfaction, while Coates and Thoresen (1976) found tension in relationships with senior colleagues an important source of anxiety. Yet although children's behaviour and progress are potential sources of stress, a study of primary teachers in New Zealand found that they were also amongst the most important sources of satisfaction (Galloway *et al.*, 1982c).

These results need to be viewed alongside another set of research findings. There is relatively little overlap between children whose parents report behaviour problems and children whose teachers report problems (Rutter *et al.*, 1970). Moreover, within any one school children's behaviour can vary from class to class and from teacher to teacher. In other words, as predicted by social learning theory, behaviour is to a large extent situation specific. Hence, the levels both of stress and of job-satisfaction experienced by a school's teachers would appear to be determined by policies and practices for which they — or perhaps their colleagues — are responsible.

It is worth looking at how most schools organize pastoral care in the light of this suggestion. At least in Sheffield, by far the most common basis for pastoral care in the 1970s was a year tutor system. Depending on the size of the school the year tutor often had one or two assistants. A minority of schools operated a house system, while an even smaller minority centralized pastoral care on members of the senior management team. A common feature in virtually all schools was that the form tutor was theoretically the basic unit of pastoral care. The formal organization, though, tells us nothing about what happened in practice. From ten schools studied in Sheffield and four in New Zealand, Galloway (1983) identified four with exceptionally low levels of disruptive behaviour. A characteristic of at least three of these schools was the active part played by the form tutor in the pastoral care network. In other schools, which in theory attached similar importance to the form tutor's pastoral role, his position was largely administrative.

Galloway suggested five ways in which school policy and organization could defeat its own stated goal that the form tutor should play an important part in the pastoral team: (i) class tutors changed each year; (ii) they seldom taught their classes; (iii) they saw their tutor groups for only five or ten minutes once or twice daily; (iv) the year tutor's job was defined in terms of investigating and dealing with problems, rather than as leader of a pastoral team; (v) they felt that year tutors were paid to do pastoral care, and saw no reason for accepting the responsibility themselves.

The first four points illustrate the importance of analyzing the formal organization of pastoral care. In several schools the head regarded form tutors as having pastoral responsibilities, albeit usually ill-defined ones, but form tutors received no guidance in carrying them out. This was not altogether surprising, since they received little or no opportunity to undertake a pastoral role.

Analyzing the formal organization is not, however, enough. A formal structure which enables form tutors to play an active part in the pastoral network cannot ensure that they do so. Form tutors may still feel that year tutors are paid to 'do' pastoral care, and define this as dealing with problem pupils. Changing such a climate requires the opportunity for year tutors to plan tutorial work with their teams of tutors. It also requires that the head and senior staff are seen to value pastoral goals as highly as they value academic goals. Placing a high value on pastoral goals raises questions about the nature of support which teachers offer their pupils — and each other.

In the Sheffield and the New Zealand studies schools with varying rates of disruptive behaviour also differed in their organization and use of support networks. In schools which were relatively free from disruptive behaviour, teachers were generally expected to deal with disruptive behaviour themselves. Yet they were also expected to seek advice and help from colleagues. The first person to contact would usually be the form tutor, but more senior colleagues were available if needed. The immediate effect may sometimes have been to increase the teacher's feelings of stress: the problem could not be passed to someone else. In the long term, the teacher's sense of self esteem would be enhanced by having dealt with the problem himself. At other schools subject teachers were expected, almost as a matter of routine, to refer disruptive pupils to middle management. The year tutor or head of department would then investigate and deal with the pupil. In the short term this was helpful: there was someone to whom the problem could be passed. In the long term it reduced the teacher's professional confidence through the implicit assumption that the problem could only be handled by someone more experienced.

There is a parallel here in the ways schools use external agencies. Gath *et al.* (1972; 1977) have noted differences between schools in the rate of referral to child guidance clinics. Galloway *et al.* (1982a) have noted differences in their suspension rates which, like Gath's child guidance referral rates, could not be attributed to catchment area variables. Although less well documented, there are clearly differences in the motive behind the decision to refer. In some schools the LEA psychological service is seen as the Special Schools Removals Service. The message behind referral is: please remove this child; he can't/won't, learn/conform. The message behind referral from other schools is: please suggest ways in which *we* can teach/manage this pupil more effectively.

Thus, if the teacher sees the child as a *learning* or as a *behaviour* problem responsibility rests not with the teacher, but with the child, the family, or some other professional person. The teacher's problem, though, remains, and the failure of senior staff or external agencies either to solve it for him or to involve him in the solution leads to increasing frustration and resentment. On the other hand, when a teacher can see a child as a *teaching* problem he retains a personal commitment to reducing if not solving it. This perspective, though, is only feasible in schools where the solution is seen as a cooperative effort between senior and less experienced teachers, perhaps with specialist advice from outside agencies. Moreover, failure needs to be seen as a constructive learning experience rather than a sign of incompetence.

Hargreaves (1978) has argued that teaching is a lonely activity, and that teachers are notoriously bad at supporting each other. Teachers in comprehensive schools spend a lot of time discussing pastoral care for children. Perhaps their pastoral efforts might, in some schools, be more effective if they could reexamine the sort of support they provide each other, and consider whether this is consistent with the sort of support they wish to offer their pupils.

Evaluation

We have argued that effective teaching requires pastoral skills. Moreover, since pastoral care is primarily concerned with pupils' progress and adjustment at school, it makes little sense to talk about pastoral goals as being separate and distinct from educational and disciplinary goals. These conceptual points raise questions both about the methodology and the empirical criteria appropriate for evaluating pastoral care.

The problems lie: (i) in deciding what should count as evidence of effective pastoral care, and (ii) in establishing that we are in fact evaluating pastoral care, rather than some other school variable or some catchment area variable. The first is a problem both for quantitative and for qualitative methods. Demonstrating, for example, that a school places a high priority in the time-table on an elaborate, admirably planned pastoral curriculum cannot sensibly be taken as evidence of effective pastoral care if relationships throughout the school are dreadful. The second problem is more frequently one for quantitative methodologies. The point is that virtually any outcome measure can be contaminated by other variables not directly related to the pastoral variable under investigation.

A separate difficulty is that the relationship between variables is both complex and inconsistent. Rutter *et al.* (1979) found that schools which did well on one of their outcome measures tended to do well on the remainder, once they had controlled for intake. There are, nevertheless, two problems here. The first is that the outcome measures did not have a uniform effect. School attendance for example, appeared to be more strongly influenced by pupil intake than behaviour within the school. The second is that the sample of schools was relatively small, and other studies have reported conflicting results. One of the four schools with exceptionally low rates of disruptive behaviour described by Galloway (1983), for example, also had exceptionally poor exam results. The other three were able to derive legitimate satisfaction from their exam results.

The problem of selecting outcome variables cannot, however, be avoided. Teachers should presumably have some idea what they are trying to achieve through the pastoral care network, otherwise there would be no point in devoting time to it in the first place. Yet on its own quantitative evidence on outcome variables does not take us much further forward. Progress is nevertheless possible using a range of methodologies.

Discussion of research on two possible outcome variables, attendance and behaviour within the school, will illustrate this argument. These variables are selected because of their immediate and direct relevance to almost all teachers with posts of responsibility for pastoral care.

Attendance Attendance is heavily influenced by socio-economic variables in the catchment area, especially in urban areas (Galloway, 1982). This tends to obscure the school's contribution. On the other hand, attendance registers do enable teachers to identify trends over time, and hence to monitor the effectiveness of particular projects or new policies. Jones (1980) reported substantially improved attendance following the introduction of a wide-ranging pastoral policy in her London comprehensive school. Showing that attendance had improved was a numerical exercise. It would have been little use, though, without a description of the changes that were introduced and an analysis of the process of their introduction with reference to the school's overall aims and philosophy. Thus, at a fairly simple level, a range of methodologies was used to complement each other.

Behaviour at School Demonstrating school influences on pupils' behaviour is perhaps more complicated than on attendance, since relatively accessible numerical data are lacking. Nevertheless, some evidence has emerged. Galloway *et al.* (1982) showed very large differences in suspension rates between Sheffield comprehensive schools. Later they reported no relationship between suspension rates from thirty-three Sheffield comprehensives and twenty-two catchment area variables (Galloway *et al.*, 1984). The school organization variables included the organization of pastoral care. The low correlation with suspension rates was not interpreted to imply that pastoral care was unrelated to pupils' behaviour, but rather that its formal organization was relatively unimportant. The lack of significant correlations between suspension rates and either catchment area or school variables was interpreted as evidence that suspension rates were largely idiosyncratic to each school.

It does not, of course, follow that suspension rates bear a linear relationship to behaviour in the school. The study did not aim to show that schools with the highest suspension rates also had the worst behaved pupils. Informal observation in secondary schools both in Sheffield and in New Zealand did, however, strengthen the argument that both the amount and the severity of disruptive behaviour *within* the schools was largely independent of pupil intake variables such as social class. In support of this view Rutter *et al.* (1979) also found a low correlation between behaviour within London schools and all of their pupil intake variables.

Taking results from the London, South Wales and Sheffield studies together, it is clear that school influences on attendance and on academic performance can only be demonstrated by controlling for pupil intake variables. This is not nearly so obvious with respect to behaviour within the school. If this argument is valid, it follows that the level of *disruptive* behaviour within the school (which is *not* the same thing as general pupil behaviour), may have relatively little relationship either with attendance, or with academic standards, or with catchment area variables.

To summarize, the evidence from research based on statistical analyses suggests: (i) schools exert an extremely important influence over their pupils' behaviour; (ii) that this influence is not necessarily closely related to their influence on other variables such as attendance or academic results; (iii) that it is not systematically related to any readily accessible catchment area variables, nor to easily recorded organizational and structural variables within the school.

If we want to go further than this, other approaches are needed. We will need, for example, to investigate the importance and meaning of disruptive behaviour from the perspectives of teachers and pupils, the role of staff and pupil cultures in establishing behavioural norms, and the planning and progress of projects which aim to change the 'tone' of the school, to tackle specific problems such as truancy or to promote specific developments such as active tutorial work. All of these require intensive investigation using a wide range of observation and interview techniques. Quantitative data, demonstrating that change has occurred, would enhance the value of illuminative data. Too many researchers have seen different methodologies as conflicting rather than as complementary.

Conclusions

The dilemma for researchers in pastoral care is encapsulated in the question: Can you have an effective school without effective pastoral care? Most secondary school teachers would probably deny the possibility. Yet many primary schools operate successfully without any of the institutionalized pastoral systems which have characterized secondary schools since comprehensive reorganization. This cannot simply be a question of size. Quite a number of primaries are as large as small secondary schools.

It seems more plausible to argue that some primary schools provide effective pastoral care even though they have not placed it on the same formal footing as secondary schools. If so, the effectiveness of pastoral care could be independent of its formal organization. That, however, is only partially true since, as we saw when discussing the role of form tutors, the formal organization can defeat its own stated objectives. Nevertheless it does suggest that teachers should give careful thought before jumping on to the latest bandwagon.

Developments such as active tutorial work and the pastoral curriculum may clearly have much to commend them in receptive schools. Yet their effect on outcome variables such as pupils' attendance, social skills, behaviour and examination results remains largely undocumented. The limited evidence available suggests that analysis of a large data base, comprising at least thirty schools, might well reveal no significant relationship between outcome variables and either the scope of pastoral care or the time spent on it. Testing this hypothesis could surely provide someone with an MEd. or PhD.

Yet even if confirmed in a large-scale study, the results would tell us little or nothing about the relationship between pastoral care and school effectiveness. The reason is that the concepts of school and teacher effectiveness imply the sort of constructive and cooperative pupil-teacher relationships which are one of the characteristics of effective pastoral care. We know that schools exert an influence, independent of their pupil intakes, on variables which specialists in pastoral care frequently regard as their areas of responsibility. Both for teachers and for researchers there are two challenges. The first is to analyze the school's formal organization of pastoral care to see whether this is in fact consistent with the school's stated aims. The second is to look behind the formal organization, to the complex network of relationships which contributes not only to success or failure in specific objectives but also to the school's general ethos.

References

Best, R.E., Jarvis, C.B. and Ribbins, P.M. (1977) 'Pastoral care: concept and process', *British Journal of Educational Studies*, 25, pp. 124–35.
Best, R., Jarvis, C. and Ribbins, P. (Eds.) (1980) *Perspectives in Pastoral Care*, London, Heinemann.

BEST, R., JARVIS, C. and RIBBINS, P. (1983) *Education and Care*, London, Heinemann.

BUTTON, L. (1981) *Group Tutoring for the Form Teacher: A Developmental Model: Lower Secondary School Years One and Two*, London, Hodder and Stoughton.

COATES, T.J. and THORESEN, C. E. (1976) 'Teacher anxiety: a review with recommendations', *Review of Educational Research*, 46, pp. 159–84.

DUNHAM, J. (1977) 'The effects of disruptive behaviour on teachers', *Educational Review*, 29, pp. 181–87.

GALLOWAY, D. (1981) *Teaching and Counselling: Pastoral Care in Primary and Secondary Schools*, London, Longman.

GALLOWAY, D. (1982) 'Persistent unauthorized absence', *Educational Research*, 24, pp. 188–96.

GALLOWAY, D. (1983) 'Disruptive pupils and effective pastoral care', *School Organization*, 3, pp. 245–54.

GALLOWAY, D., BALL, C., BLOMFIELD, D. and SEYD, R. (1982a) *Schools and Disruptive Pupils*, London, Longman.

GALLOWAY, D. M., PANCKHURST, F., BOSWELL, K., BOSWELL, C. and GREEN, K. (1982b) 'Sources of stress for class teachers', *National Education (NZ)*, 64, pp. 164–69.

GALLOWAY, D. M., BOSWELL, K., PANCKHURST, F., BOSWELL, C. and GREEN, K. (1982c) 'Satisfaction with teaching', *National Education (NZ)*, 64, pp. 206–13.

GALLOWAY, D. and BARRETT, C. (1983) 'Disruptive pupils: a result of teacher stress as well as a cause?' *New Zealand Post Primary Teachers Association Journal*, Term 2, pp. 40–4.

GALLOWAY, D., WILCOX, B. and MARTIN, R. (1984) 'Persistent absence from school and exclusion from school: the predictive power of school and community variables', *British Educational Research Journal*, (accepted for publication).

GATH, D., COOPER, B. and GATTONI, F.E.G. (1972) 'Child guidance and delinquency in a London borough: preliminary communication', *Psychological Medicine*, 2, pp. 185–91.

GATH, D., COOPER, B., GATTONI, F. and ROCKETT, D. (1977) *Child Guidance and Delinquency in a London Borough*, Oxford, Oxford University Press.

HAMBLIN, D.H. (1977) 'Caring and control: the treatment of absenteeism', in CARROLL, H.C.M. (Ed.) *Absenteeism in South Wales: Studies of Pupils, their Homes and their Secondary Schools*, Swansea, University College of Swansea, Faculty of Education.

HAMBLIN, D.H. (1978) *The Teacher and Pastoral Care*, Oxford, Blackwell.

HARGREAVES, D. (1978) 'What teaching does to teachers', *New Society*, 43, 805, pp. 540–42.

JONES, A. (1980) 'The school's view of persistent non-attendance', in HERSOV, L. and BERG, I. (Eds.) *Out of School: Modern Perspectives in Truancy and School Referral*, Chichester, Wiley.

KYRIACOU, C. and SUTCLIFFE, J. (1978) 'Teacher stress: prevalence, sources and symptoms', *British Journal of Educational Psychology*, 48, pp. 159–67.

PRATT, J. (1978) 'Perceived stress among teachers: the effects of age and background of children taught', *Educational Review*, 30, pp. 3–14.

REYNOLDS, D. (1976) 'When pupils and teachers refuse a truce: the secondary school and the creation of delinquency', in MUNGHAM, G. and PEARSON, G. (Eds.) *Working Class Youth Culture*, London, Routledge and Kegan Paul.

REYNOLDS, D. and MURGATROYD, S. (1977) 'The sociology of schooling and the absent pupil: the school as a factor in the generation of truancy', in CARROLL, H.C.M. (Ed.) *Absenteeism in South Wales: Studies of Pupils, their Homes and their Secondary Schools*, Swansea, University College of Swansea, Faculty of Education.

RUDD, W.G.A. and WISEMAN, S. (1962) Sources of dissatisfaction among a group of teachers', *British Journal of Educational Psychology*, 32, pp. 275–91.

RUTTER, M., TIZARD, J. and WHITMORE, K. (Eds.) (1970) *Education, Health and Behaviour*, London, Longman.

RUTTER, M., MAUGHAN, B., MORTIMORE, P. and OUSTON, J. (1979) *Fifteen Thousand Hours: Secondary Schools and their Effects on Pupils*, London, Open Books.

SPOONER, R. (1979) 'Pastoral care and the myth of never ending toil', *Education*, 2nd March, pp. 251–52.

TYERMAN, M.J. (1958) 'A research into truancy', *British Journal of Educational Psychology*, 28, pp. 217–25.

6 Examination Results in Mixed and Single-Sex Secondary Schools

Jane Steedman

The relative merits of mixed and of single-sex schooling have engaged the interest of researchers and educationalists for years. Few investigations of the relation of examination performance to mixed and single-sex schooling, though, have been longitudinal, relating results at the end of school to earlier attainments. By using National Child Development Study (NCDS) data, I and my colleague Vanessa Simonite were able to take a longitudinal approach and this paper will underline its importance.

Figures from a number of sources appear to demonstrate that pupils do better in academic performance in segregated secondary schools than in co-educational schools. The investigations in 1979 and 1980 of the Assessment of Performance Unit, for example, showed that the mean reading and writing scores of pupils in single-sex schools were significantly higher than those of pupils of the same sex in mixed schools (APU, 1982; 1983). Department of Education and Science statistics, too, indicate an apparent advantage to single-sex schools, on average, in total number of O-level/CSE grade 1 'passes' (EOC, 1984).

Observations like these have probably contributed to a popular impression that, at least in academic attainments, children have more success in single-sex schools. Certainly, there are prejudices in this area. Sometimes, pressure to retain segregation comes from parents, who may associate single-sex schools with a more traditional or recognizable education. We should note that parents are more likely to have gone to single-sex schools than their offspring; the proportion of secondary schools which was single-sex dropped from 45 per cent in 1965 to 19 per cent in 1981 (EOC, 1984).

Those who favour segregation often emphasize the apparent

advantages for girls of single-sex schools. Girls' underachievement in mathematics and sciences is rightly regarded as needing attention, and some advocates of a return to single-sex schools have girls' education in mind. One expression — perhaps a rather argumentative expression — in favour of girls being segregated from boys was published in 1980, when we were starting work on sex differences in educational attainment.

> co-education is working well — for boys . . . . In many subtle ways boys are deriving benefits from an educational system deliberately established to replicate inside the school the 'normal' social environment which functions outside the school. In concrete terms, male superiority can be realised within the co-educational system . . . . The power relations of domination and subordination between the two sexes — characteristic of patriarchal society — is reproduced within co-education. (Sarah, Scott and Spender in Spender and Sarah, 1980)

The authors continues: '. . . having established that boys do better in mixed schools . . .' and go on to put the case for girls having single-sex schools.

Even though we may recognize some of those arguments, in very little of this, or of any of the material mentioned above, is there any real evidence of measurable advantages in pupils' attainments attributable to being in single-sex or in mixed schools. The official figures cited earlier could reflect the fact that pupils going to single-sex schools have, on average, tended to be at an advantage before secondary school over those entering mixed schools.

Intakes of Mixed and Single-Sex Schools

In our sample, for instance, the average attainment test scores *at 11 years old* for pupils going into mixed schools were lower than those of pupils going into single-sex schools (see Table 1). This was before they ever got to secondary schools, while they were still at primary schools (which were probably co-educational).

That average difference, at the end of primary school, between pupils going on to mixed schools and those who would be in single-sex schools, existed both for girls and for boys (see Table 2). Any apparent advantages to the pupils of single-sex schools in their

Examination Results in Mixed and Single-Sex Secondary Schools

Table 1. Schools Attended at 16 and Test Scores of the Same Pupils before Secondary School

| | | Test scores at 11 | | |
	reading	mathematics	verbal ability	non-verbal ability
Single-sex schools	19	21	26	24
Mixed schools	15	15	21	20

Table 2. Schools Attended at 16 and Test Scores at Earlier Ages of the Same Pupils

| | Test scores at 7 | | Test scores at 11 | | | | |
School at 16 and sex:	reading	arithmetic	reading	maths	non-verbal ability	verbal ability	general ability
Boys in boys' schools	25	6	19	22	24	25	49
Girls in girls' schools	26	6	19	21	24	27	51
Boys in mixed schools	22	5	15	16	20	20	41
Girls in mixed schools	24	5	15	15	21	22	43

exam averages at the end of secondary school might be products of the initial advantages with which they started secondary school.

Designing a Longitudinal Investigation

In order to look at what might be a secondary school 'effect', of whether schools were mixed or segregated, we needed to know how much was a matter of what pupils were like before secondary school. The longitudinal National Child Development Study allowed us to do this, because it is a long-term survey of all the people in Great Britain born in a particular week in 1958, which has information on the same people at 7 and at 11 years old, as well as having records of their tested attainment and examination results when they were 16. In order to find out what might be a secondary school effect, we took into account primary school attainment. We also allowed for parental 'influence': father's educational level, mother's educational level and father's occupation. We needed to do this because the proportion of pupils from middle-class homes has tended to be higher in single-sex schools than in mixed schools.

Type of School

Most importantly, we were interested to try to separate the effects of mixed and single-sex school from the effects of 'type of school', as we termed it, that is, of selectivity of schools. It is well established that selective grammar schools and independent or direct grant schools have tended to be single-sex, while the overwhelming majority of comprehensive and secondary modern schools have been co-educational. In our sample, 45 per cent of the pupils in single-sex schools were in grammar, independent or direct grant schools; only 6 per cent of the pupils in mixed schools were in those 'selective' schools. At the National Children's Bureau, we had been studying the examination results of pupils in selective and non-selective schools and knew that school differences, between grammar and secondary modern averages for instance, remained after allowance for initial attainment and home background. We therefore saw the need to disentangle effects of types of school from whether schools were co-educational or not.

In earlier work, we had taken a very limited look at results in mixed and single-sex schools, and our findings suggested further investigations would be interesting. We had compared grammar, secondary modern and comprehensive pupils' average scores on a mathematics test at 16. The only case of a difference according to whether schools were mixed or not was among *girls* in grammar schools. The averages for girls in secondary moderns or comprehensives and the averages for boys did not appear to differ according to whether their school was mixed or not (Steedman, 1980). It is very important to make any such limited application of any mixed/single-sex school differences clear. (The very well known and substantial work of Dale, on co-educational and single-sex schools, for example, is based entirely on results from grammar schools, and this is not always remembered.) We therefore wanted to pursue the mixed/single-sex distinction taking into account the 'type of school' factor. We had the information in NCDS to define 'school type' particularly carefully. We knew not only 'school type' but also how long pupils had been there, and in the case of comprehensives, how long the school had been comprehensive. So, as well as categorizing those who had been at a mixed school and those who had been at a single-sex school, we knew which of those pupils were at grammar, secondary modern, comprehensive or independent/direct grant schools.

Examination Measures

We aimed to isolate any component of examination performance associated with co-education/segregation, by relating various examination outcomes to the mixed/single-sex factor for boys and for girls, after allowing for these other factors. It was important to take a variety of 'outcome' measures. Too often conclusions (about 'under-achievement', for example) can be based on one single exam measure. Our chief measures of mixed and single-sex schools were examination results and those are what I shall report, but we also studied teachers' ratings and pupils' own ratings of performance in different subject areas, which can illuminate inferences from exam results. I have dwelt elsewhere on the need for and dangers in a variety of measures including examination results (Steadman, 1983). Different measures of examination performance do not always point to the same conclusion, and it was of interest, particularly in a study of mixed and single-sex schools, to look at a large number of subject areas. We were concerned with subjects known to show sex differences, and also with combinations of subjects, particularly what are called 'core' subjects (the sum of English, maths, French and science results). We also looked at general examination performance, such as numbers of O-level equivalents. Even within a particular subject area, we also wanted to look at different *levels* of exam performance, such as proportions with a grade A to E/CSE 1 to 3, as against proportions with a grade A to C/CSE 1, for example.

We were interested in a technical aspect of this work, too, which was to explore the use of categorical variables as measures of examinations. A program made available to us by Peter McCullagh made it possible for Vanessa Simonite to carry out both analyses of proportions (proportions passing O-level, for example) and analyses which compared groups on a sort of 'average' over all categories of examination grades, the proportional odds of reaching or exceeding any specified level of examination achievement. This does duty for a sort of mean score, without the problems of scaling which arise with examination grades and their unequal intervals.

Altogether, we carried out over thirty-five multivariate analyses; the details of variables incorporated in analyses are in the Appendix. In every analysis, pupils were grouped into four 'school + sex' groups (boys in boys' schools, girls in girls' schools, boys in mixed schools and girls in mixed schools).

What Has Emerged from the Study?

I shall present, first, the comparisons between two groups, those in mixed and those in single-sex schools. These, like all the results I am describing, are after allowing for differences at intake. I shall then go on to describe any measures which showed differences between boys and girls regardless of whether they were in mixed or single-sex schools. Then I shall look over the four groups — boys in boys' schools, girls in girls' schools, boys in mixed schools and girls in mixed schools.[1]

Mixed and Single-Sex Schools

It can be seen from Table 3 that results in mixed schools were not different from results in single-sex schools (a ratio of 1.0 indicates no difference at all).

Only on French, on science-and-French joint results, and on the proportions with five or more O-levels are there any differences at all. The ratios varied hardly at all with the particular grouping of the exam measure (or dependent variable : proportions 'passing' at O-level standard, overall proportional odds, and so on). So there were insufficient grounds there for concluding that the two categories of school differed substantially. A ratio of 1.3 is not a marked difference, as may be understood when we compare these results with some of the differences between boys and girls.

Sex Differences

Table 4 shows the similarities and differences between boys and girls. (Where the boys were higher scoring, whether noticeably or not, the figure is in the first row; where the girls were higher scoring the figure is in the second row.)

Boys were considerably likelier than girls to achieve given levels in physics and chemistry. Girls did somewhat better than boys at least at some levels of life sciences, but the average of the boys' results in their 'best' science (top science) nevertheless was somewhat higher

Table 3.

Odds ratio	Numbers of O-level equivalents	Proportions with five O-level equivalents	Maths	English	French	Physics	Chemistry	Life Science	Maths and English	Science and French	Four 'core' subjects	Top Science
Comparing mixed and single-sex schools	1.1	ss > m 1.3	1.0 to 1.2	1.0 to 1.1	ss > m 1.3 or 1.4	1.0 or 1.1	1.0 or 1.1	1.0 or 1.1	1.1 or 1.2	ss > m 1.1 to 1.5	ss > m 1.1 to 1.4	1.0 or 1.1

Key: ss = pupils of single-sex schools
m = pupils of mixed schools

Table 4.

Sex difference odds ratio	Numbers of O-level equivalents	Proportions with five O-level equivalents	Maths	English	French	Chemistry	Physics	Life Science	Maths and English	Science and French	Four 'core' subjects	Top Science
When boys ≥ girls			1.3 to 1.7			2.4 or 2.5	5.6 or 7.4		1.2	1.1	1.1	1.6 or 1.7
When girls ≥ boys	1.1	1.0		1.6	1.9 to 2.1			1.4 to 1.9	1.1	1.2 to 1.5	1.1	

Key: > 'score higher on average than'
≥ 'equal to on some measures, score higher on some measures than'

than the girls'. Girls did somewhat better than boys in French, and slightly better in English. Boys did slightly better than girls on the various measures of mathematics exams. Only one of the three measures of science-and-French showed a sex difference. Only the odds of being in the top 11 per cent on this measure, rather than other levels of performance, were better for girls. Boys' and girls' averages did not differ on the other combination of two subjects, maths-and-English. Nor did they differ according to general measures of examination performance.

So we see several similarities between boys' and girls' results, with a few striking sex differences. More notably, there was no similarly striking difference between the averages for mixed and for single-sex schools, once we had allowed for differences which existed at intake and for type of school.

The Boys and Girls in Mixed and Single-Sex Schools

What about the 'school + sex' results — that is, the pattern for boys in boys' schools, girls in girls' schools, boys in mixed schools and girls in mixed schools? In almost every analysis of exam results, the main effect of the four-level 'school + sex' variable reached a high level of statistical significance (p < .001 after 'type of school' and other factors were allowed for). But, as we saw, this had more to do with sex differences than with mixed/single-sex organization.[2] The measures of 'core' subjects and of numbers of O-level equivalents also showed an overall difference between the four groups with a probability of such a pattern happening by chance lower than one per cent. In the combinations of subjects, maths-and-English and science-and French, the 'school + sex' factor did not seem to make a consistent significant contribution. In all analyses, the main effect of 'type of school' (grammar, secondary modern, etc.) was usually statistically highly significant (p < .001).

Table 5 shows the results of comparing each pair of the four 'school + sex' groups. This complicated table has two rows for each comparison (e.g., girls in girls' schools compared to girls in mixed schools), of which one is for each direction of result (e.g., the first row is for cases where the result for girls in girls' schools is — even if only fractionally — the higher of the two, the second row for cases where it is the lower). The first two rows are comparisons among girls; the third and fourth rows are comparisons among boys. The fifth and sixth rows are comparisons among pupils of single-sex

Table 5. Sex Differences in Mixed and Single-Sex Schools

	Proportions with five O-level equivalents	Five or more O-levels	Maths	English	French	Chemistry	Physics	Life Sciences	Maths and English	Science and French	Four core subjects	Top Science
Girls in girls' schools: / Girls in mixed schools	1.3	[1.5]	1.1 to 1.4	1.1 or 1.2	1.2 or 1.3	1.0 to 1.3	1.2 or 1.4	1.1 to 1.4	1.1 to 1.3	1.3 to [1.5]	[1.1] to [1.5]	1.1 or 1.4
Girls in mixed schools: / Girls in girls' schools			1.0									
Boys in boys' schools: / Boys in mixed schools	1.0	1.0	1.0 or 1.1	1.3 or [1.5]		1.0			1.1	1.1 to 1.4	1.0 to 1.2	
Boys in mixed schools: / Boys in boys' schools			1.0 or 1.1			1.1	1.1 or 1.3	1.1 or 1.2		1.1		1.1
Girls in girls' schools: / Boys in boys' schools	1.3	1.3	[1.8]	[1.8 or 1.9]		[2.0 to 2.4]	[3.7 to 6.2]	[1.9 to 2.4]	1.1	[1.2 to 1.6]	1.1 to 1.3	
Boys in boys' schools: / Girls in girls' schools			[1.4 or 1.5 or 1.6]						1.1			1.2 to 1.4
Boys in mixed schools: / Girls in mixed schools		1.1	[1.3 or 1.7 or 1.9]			[2.5 or 2.6]	[6.5 to 7.9]		1.2 or 1.3	1.2 or [1.6]	1.2 or 1.1	[1.7 or 1.9]
Girls in mixed schools: / Boys in mixed schools	1.1		[1.5]		[1.9 to 2.1]			[1.2 or 1.7 or 1.8]	or 1.1	1.2 or 1.4	1.0 or 1.1	
Boys in mixed schools												

schools; the seventh and eighth are among pupils of mixed schools. I have outlined as worth noticing differences represented by odds ratios of 1.5 and larger.

First finding. The first two columns on the left show the general measures. The first row demonstrates that on average, girls in girls' schools had a slightly higher score on numbers of O-levels and were rather more likely than girls in mixed schools to obtain five or more O-levels. Boys in boys' schools did not differ from boys in mixed schools, on average. But, moving down to the comparisons between boys and girls, we see that it is not that girls in mixed schools are at a disadvantage relative to boys, by these measures. Rather, girls in girls' schools appear to be, by a very small margin, the odd ones out, ahead of the rest. But it is a very small margin, compared to the sex differences we have observed.

Second finding. Having seen that girls in girls' schools had marginally higher odds of five or more 'O' level equivalents than either group of boys (with girls in mixed schools scoring like boys), we explored whether this was to do with chances of a set of 'O' levels in a traditional 'core' of mainstream subjects or resulted from a tendency to accumulate examinations in a greater variety of subjects. The finding would have been less interesting if, for instance, there had merely been a propensity in girls' schools alone to put pupils in for any five subjects, rather than four 'core' subjects, in public examinations. We therefore investigated four 'core' subjects. It emerged that girls in girls' schools were overall very slightly ahead of both groups of boys in odds of a very high score on four 'core' subjects. That combination of subjects, moreover, included 'top science' grades. These results implied that the advantage over boys and over other girls for girls in girls' schools reflected differences in odds of a very high level of attainment rather than differences across the range of achievements. Girls in girls schools differed from all other pupils. The explanation may depend on performance in the subjects making up the 'core'. In one of the components, high performance in science-and-French, girls in girls' schools did better than other pupils, other girls and boys. Boys and girls did not differ significantly in mixed schools in this measure.

Third finding. Interestingly, science-and-French and French alone were the measures on which type of school interacted with 'school + sex'. The interaction showed that the superiority of girls in girls' schools over girls in mixed schools was confined to grammar and independent/direct grant schools, and was not found in secondary moderns or in comprehensives. This was an echo, in a different subject area, of the mathematics test result (Steedman, 1980). (These were the only statistically significant interactions found between type of school and 'school + sex', so there was no confirmatory evidence in mathematics or any other examinations.) So perhaps this is the restricted aplication of the small advantage to girls in girls-only schools over all boys and other girls. It may have resulted from only two sources, grammar schools and the small number of co-educational independent schools.

Fourth finding. The science-and-French results were much affected by the French component. We saw earlier that French was the one subject showing a suggestion of an overall advantage to single-sex schooling. It was the only one to show an appreciable difference for boys between mixed and single-sex schooling; boys' French was more markedly enhanced than the girls' French by segregating the sexes, or more markedly hindered by having to talk French in front of the opposite sex.

Fifth finding. There were three single subjects on which girls were at an overall advantage — English, French and life sciences. On all three subjects, the balance of findings was of some advantage to girls over the boys, both in mixed and in single-sex schools. (Only in one measure of the eight involved — odds of O-level standard in life sciences — did any difference between girls in girls' schools and girls in mixed schools approach being worthy of remark.)

Sixth finding. Similarly, there were three subjects on which boys tended to do better than girls: mathematics, physics and chemistry.

We saw earlier that sex differences in maths performance were not as striking as those in science, but *some* levels of mathematics attainment showed sex differences, even though these were not as consistent or large as some writers would seem to suggest. In any event, over the broad range of mathematical achievement, there was no advantage to girls' schools over mixed schools for girls' mathematics. There may have been a slight advantage for girls in single-sex schools over mixed schools' girls in odds of an A or B grade in mathematics O-level. The advantage, if any, from being in a girls' school to girls who were very good at maths did not, however, necessarily extend to encouraging them to do A-level, as far as could be judged from another measure, their 'highest mathematics achievement'.

In the two science subjects which showed relatively large, striking sex differences, physics and chemistry, girls scored far lower on average, as we saw, and being in a girls' school appeared to make little difference. On measures of chemistry there was no considerable advantage for girls in single-sex schools. Nor was it found that girls benefitted from single-sex schools according to most measures of physics. There was a faint suggestion of higher odds in girls' schools of a 'pass' standard at O-level/CSE in physics; a similar small advantage to *mixed* schools appeared on the same measure for boys. This was not a finding with consistent implications, but the closest and only example in all these results of the stereotyped view that 'single sex schools are good for girls and bad for boys'. Even here, any enhancement of girls' performance in physics in single-sex schools was very small, relative to the sex differences. There was no apparent advantage in single-sex schools for girls' chemistry. Differences between girls' and boys' science results were large, whether they were in mixed or in single-sex schools.

Seventh finding. On the measure of each child's best science examination result in any science, boys remained ahead of girls. Here, though, the sex difference was less marked between those in single-sex schools than in mixed schools. The only measure of 'top science' according to which girls' schools seemed to have 'better' results was the proportion passing at O-level standard. That is, there may have been a very slightly higher chance of an O-level standard pass in *some* science for girls if they were in girls' schools than if they were in mixed schools. Perhaps this resulted from the sum of small and not conclusive disadvantages in odds of O-level standard in life sciences or physics for girls in mixed schools. Were these enough to create a slightly *greater* disadvantage for girls as compared to boys in mixed than single-sex schools? There was, though, no support for this in chemistry results where sex differences were paramount, regardless of schools being mixed or single-sex.

Conclusions

These complex findings add up to suggest that very little in these examination results is explained by whether schools are mixed or single-sex once allowance has been made for differences at intake. The main subject area where some educational difference may have been made by segregation was French. The very striking differences in science performance between boys and girls existed both in single-sex and in mixed schools. Though there was a slight raising of the odds of reaching O-level standard in a science for girls in girls' schools, this was not enough to offset girls' overall disadvantage in physics and chemistry.

Nevertheless, there was a very small advantage to girls in girls' schools overall, in general examination performance, an advantage not only over other girls but also over boys. There was no disadvantage to girls in mixed schools relative to boys. This last finding appears to counter some sweeping generalizations that have been made elsewhere, and derives support from the findings of ILEA's Research and Statistics Group (ILEA, 1982). The latter showed that an apparent disadvantage to girls in mixed schools was greatly reduced when scores on exam performance scales were adjusted to take into account the ability of the intake. There was no significant difference in those ILEA results for boys or girls between pupils in mixed and single-sex schools.

The argument for single-sex schooling for girls sometimes appears to be based on an assumption that girls do worse in mixed schools than boys do; if so, in our general measures of examination results, that assumption was challenged.

There are many unresolved questions here, and I would like to mention some of them. On a technical point, I wonder, for instance, whether further exploration of sex differences in distributions of initial attainment before secondary school might be necessary, to be fully confident of the implications of adjustments made. It also seems worth considering whether it is fair to equate the groups in mixed schools, when slightly differing proportions of boys and of girls went to mixed schools.

Secondly, there is an area where a technical point meets an educational problem. Where girls in girls' schools seemed to exceed the examination performance of girls in mixed schools, this was in their chance of *high* examination attainment — the odds of being in the top 15 or 20 per cent, on four core subjects, for example. Is this a function of the emphasis the examination system or by the schools on that level of attainment and qualifications? Or are controls for higher attainments more subject to measurement error?

Thirdly, it is always possible to doubt whether findings have to do with co-education/segregation or with associated aspects of schools; the contribution of the number of hours per week spent studying a subject may be important, for example. Or, to take another example, one could investigate whether having adequate science laboratories was associated with differential exam performance. Using teachers' judgments of the adequacy of laboratories, we found very slightly lower exam results where laboratories were judged inadequate, but only for girls in girls' schools in some science subjects. Perhaps it depends on the type of school — these were unadjusted results.

Lastly, a question which is always unresolved in these studies remains: to what extent are the differences we saw between average scores at intake a *response* to examination performance (or other 'outcome' measures) rather than simply a contributory factor?

Notes

1 Results for 'co-educated' and 'segregated' groups and for boys and girls are the result of weighted averaging over the appropriate pair of groups. Tests of significance are for the 'school + sex', four-level variable. Results 'adjusted' or corrected for intake have incorporated allowance for two or three tests of pre-existing attainment, father's occupation, mother's school-leaving age and father's school-leaving age, and for type of school (see Appendix).
2 We found that the contributions, statistically speaking, of 'school + sex' and type of school were both strong and consistent, whereas there was a less consistent contribution in all exam subjects from parental variables. It did appear to be worth allowing for the level of mother's education, though, whereas, after allowing for father's occupation, his level of education contributed little to the explanation of the variance.

Appendix

Design of analyses: Analysis of exams as categorical variables, categories of grades or score (sum of exams or points for grades):
Dependent variables: Examination results by 1974 in: numbers of O-level equivalents (O-level A to C or CSE 1), maths, English, French, physics, chemistry, 'life sciences', maths-and-English, science-and-French, four 'core' subjects (maths, English, science, French), top science (best result by pupil of any in physics, chemistry, biology, botany, zoology).
Independent variables:

'school + sex'	1	boys in boys' schools
	2	girls in girls' schools
	3	boys in mixed schools
	4	girls in mixed schools
type of school	1	grammar
	2	secondary modern
	3	comprehensive
	4	rest of maintained (going comprehensive, changing school or other)
	5	independent/direct grant

'social class'	1	father's job non-manual
	2	father's job manual or no male head of household
mother's education	1	left school at 15 or older
	2	other
father's education	1	left school at 15 or older
	2	other

Various *test scores* were incorporated as continuous variables, depending on examination subjects. Analyses of mathematics and sciences results included allowance for maths at 11 and non-verbal ability at 11 and, in the case of mathematics exams, arithmetic at 7, except in the case of highest mathematics achievement ever for which allowances were maths at 11 and general ability (verbal and non-verbal). English and French examinations were analyzed with allowances for reading at 11 and verbal ability at 11. General measures, combinations of subjects and 'top science' were analyzed with allowance for three scores at 11 — mathematics, reading and general (verbal and non-verbal) ability.

References

ASSESSMENT OF PERFORMANCE UNIT (APU) (1982, 1983) *Language Performance in Schools*, Secondary Survey Reports No's 1 and 2, London, HMSO.

DALE, R.R. (1974) *Mixed or Single-Sex School?*, Volume 3, London, Routledge and Kegan Paul.

EQUAL OPPORTUNITIES COMMISSION (EOC) (1984) *Girls and Girls-Only Schools: A Review of the Evidence*, Manchester, EOC.

INNER LONDON EDUCATION AUTHORITY (ILEA) (1982) *Sex Differences and Achievement*, RS 823/82

SPENDER, D. and SARAH, E. (1980) *Learning to Lose: Sexism and Education*, The Women's Press.

STEEDMAN, J. (1980) *Progress in Secondary Schools*, London, National Children's Bureau.

STEEDMAN, J. (1983) *Examination Results in Selective and Nonselective Schools*, London, National Children's Bureau.

STEEDMAN, J. (1984) *Examination Results in Mixed and Single-Sex Schools; Findings from the National Child Development Study*, Manchester, Equal Opportunities Commission.

7 Combining Quantitative and Qualitative Approaches to Studies of School and Teacher Effectiveness

John Gray and Ben Jones

The need to combine quantitative and qualitative approaches in the study of school and teacher effectiveness may seem self-evident. Yet in Britain the two traditions have largely gone their separate ways. In this chapter we argue the case for combining the two methodologies as a practical, short-term strategy for enhancing understanding of both educational processes and outcomes.

Quantitative Studies

The dominant paradigm employed by researchers of school and teacher effectiveness in this country has been a quantitative one. At the primary school level the study of *Teaching Styles and Pupil Progress*, conducted by Bennett (1976), and the ORACLE Project, based at the University of Leicester (Galton and Simon, 1980), are probably the best-known; at secondary level the study *Fifteen Thousand Hours*, by Rutter and his co-workers (Rutter *et al.*, 1979) has commanded most attention. All three of these studies and others have collected information by questionnaire and/or observational means on the teachers or schools in their samples. They have subsequently sought to relate these data to the progress pupils have made on various measures of outcome. Their concern, then, has been to explore the correlates of 'effectiveness', where 'effectiveness' has been defined as the extent to which pupils have made greater or lesser progress than would have been predicted from knowledge of their backgrounds and/or prior attainments.

In our opinion these studies have reinforced the view (if, indeed, it needed reinforcing) that differences in outcomes remain between pupils attending different schools or taught by different teachers, even when differences in their backgrounds or prior attainments have been taken (statistically) into account. To some extent, how large or important such differences are in educational or social terms is a matter of judgment, but they appear to us in some cases to be sufficiently striking to merit more detailed investigation. Providing one is prepared to make certain assumptions, schools and teachers do seem to differ in their effectiveness.

The contribution of these and other studies (amongst which we would include our own efforts) to our understanding of *why* schools differ in their effectiveness is less impressive. Indeed, given the framework, we can put this in more precise quantitative terms. As a broad generalization, none of the factors identified in British studies to date has 'explained', even in combination, more than about a quarter of the differences in progress pupils have made. In the majority of the cases we have encountered such estimates are optimistic; figures of around 10 per cent are often nearer the mark. Even if we adopt a generous view, then, of what has been discovered to date, a sizeable three-quarters of the differences in effectiveness between schools and teachers have remained apparently 'unexplained'. Allowing for the fact that it is extremely unlikely that the social sciences will ever achieve 'perfect' explanations, all of these studies are still vulnerable to the charge that what they have 'explained' was heavily outweighed by what they *failed* to explain.

Qualitative Studies

In recent years qualitative approaches to educational research have been more widely employed than quantitative ones. There are, doubtless, many reasons for their popularity. The features of qualitative strategies that most appeal to us, however, are their apparent ability to 'capture' or 'portray' educational activities in ways that are recognizable to practitioners and to explore aspects of schools that do not lend themselves to easy quantification. Quantitative approaches, in contrast, have a tendency to disembody the situations they are explaining.

Although qualitative approaches have been popular in this country few, if any, researchers operating within this paradigm have ventured into questions of school and teacher 'effectiveness'. Indeed, we suspect that researchers within this particular tradition have been particularly sceptical of the assumptions that are part-and-parcel of the 'effectiveness' debates.

Partly as a result, so-called 'qualitative' approaches to issues of school and teacher effectiveness have become the province of practitioners. Studies conducted by members of HM Inspectorate are perhaps the most notable examples. Their small-scale study of *Ten Good Schools* (DES, 1977) and their massive survey of *Aspects of Secondary Education* (DES, 1979) both address questions of 'good practice' directly. What both have lacked, however, is a framework which might have enabled the HMI's judgments to be placed explicitly within the context of other information; and they have suffered, to some extent, from an approach which has failed to render what they have observed 'problematic'. The schools and teachers deemed 'good' by HMI have been identified on the basis of subjective preferences. They may, or may not, have been the schools and teachers whose pupils made the greatest measured progress. In other words, the distinctive contribution of a research-based approach has been largely absent.

In brief, although researchers and practitioners have shared a common set of concerns, they have approached them in markedly different ways.

Some American Experience

American researchers over the past decade have already faced some of the problems of combining quantitative and qualitative approaches. They have done so for a number of different reasons. Amongst the most important of these may have been the desire to produce models of 'good' schools to counter the view that 'schools (and teachers) don't make a difference'. In this particular respect they have been notably successful. But, not surprisingly, there has been a price. As Purkey and Smith (1982) have observed, in a comprehensive review of the most frequently cited research studies, much of the research is so methodologically weak that generalizations from it are inadvisable. It is, therefore, encouraging that many of these studies nonetheless 'ring true', but it is often difficult to decide how firmly based in empirical terms their conclusions have been.

For British researchers and practitioners there is an additional problem. Although we have become used to reading American research, the problem of cross-cultural relevance has never really been tackled in any serious way. We remain doubtful about the ease with which American assumptions about the nature and organization of schools and teachers can be translated into British contexts.

Some Modest Proposals

It is hard to disagree with the view that, in the longer term, what is required are bigger, better, more insightful studies based on British samples. This is essentially the view developed by Reynolds and Reid in the last chapter of this volume. In the shorter term, however, we believe that some more modest strategies may be more appropriate. In particular, we believe it is important to create circumstances in which the factors which (potentially) contribute to schools' or teachers' effectiveness are thrown into sharp relief.

A number of what have come to be termed 'outlier' studies have already been conducted in the USA. In essence, what such studies have attempted to do is to identify schools which appear to be 'unusually effective', once differences in intakes have been taken into account. The statistical techniques adopted in these studies are usually modelled on those employed by Klitgaard and Hall (1977) in an analysis of achievement data from some 2000 Michigan elementary schools. Schools identified as 'unusually effective' are compared with other schools of 'average' or, more frequently, 'below average' effectiveness. In this way the search for factors which appear to differentiate effective from ineffective schools is located in contexts where there is some enhanced prospect of discovering them. It is, in practice, this research strategy which has generated many of the most interesting American conclusions although, unfortunately, their often tentative nature has frequently been forgotten and they have often confined themselves to factors which could be measured easily.

Some of the methodological weaknesses of these various studies are, as Purkey and Smith (1982) remind us, self-evident. The most important, but also the most obvious, is the need to proceed cautiously towards generalization when the case studies have been conducted on very small samples. There is quite a high likelihood that, when comparing just two schools, some factors that appear to differentiate between them will have occurred purely by chance. The knowledge that this is the case must put a premium on replication.

Another major weakness of many of the studies has been their failure to control adequately for differences in the prior attainments and home backgrounds of pupils at different schools. Adequate controls for such differences are, of course, a precondition with 'naturally-occurring' samples for identifying effective and ineffective schools. It is difficult to be precise about 'how much' of the differences in results between schools or teachers such background factors should explain but our impression from British studies to date is that, when using data aggregated at the school level, the lower and upper limits lie between 50 and 80 per cent of the overall variance. These estimates are not intended to suggest that lower (or higher) figures are unacceptable but merely to indicate that, outside them, the researcher should be prepared to indicate in some detail why he or she believes adequate note has been taken of intake differences.

Finally, there has been a tendency amongst studies which have relied on the identification of outliers to compare the single 'most effective' school with the 'least effective' one. The implicit assumption here has been that any school may emulate any other and one consequence of such comparisons has been that the differential effects of schools have been dramatized. We tend to agree with Purkey and Smith, however, that such comparisons are inappropriate. The crucial and useful question, to our mind, is why a school departs from the *average* for schools of its type.

In short, there are a number of features which any quantitative framework which is to be employed should incorporate, if qualitative investigations are to be usefully pursued within it. Most prominent amongst these are the need to demonstrate that differences in social background factors or prior attainments have been taken adequately into account and that the imputed effects are consistent, either over time, across subjects or, preferably, both.

Some Evidence

In this section we propose to explore some of the consequences of employing the kind of framework we have outlined earlier in terms of three British data sets on school and teacher effectiveness. These cover, respectively: teachers of the top infant age-range (6–7); teachers of top juniors (10–11); and secondary schools' examination results (15–16). They have been chosen because, in each case, they meet our two main criteria in relation to prior attainment and consistency.

Figure 1 is drawn from a study of teacher effectiveness in the teaching of reading, conducted by one of us during the mid-seventies (Gray, 1979). Data were collected on the reading attainments of classes of top-infant children in a random sample of twenty-five schools in two local education authorities. Two terms later the same classes were tested again. The following year the research design was repeated in the same schools with the same age-group and, where possible, the same teachers. This procedure yielded pre- and post-test

Figure 1.   *Gains (adjusted) in Reading across Two Years amongst Top-Infant Teachers*

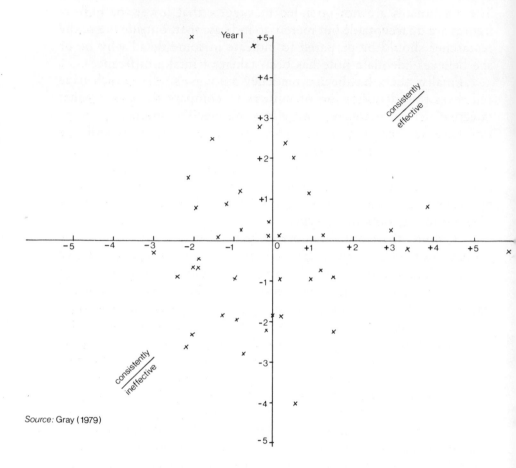

Source: Gray (1979)

data on reading performance for a large number of classes; the main study was based on the forty-one teachers in the sample for whom complete test data and other information were available for the two consecutive years.

Residual gain scores were computed for these teachers for each of the two years separately (fuller details are available in Gray, 1979) and their results for both years are displayed in Figure 1. The evidence confirms that, in both years, there were teachers who would have been identified as 'unusually effective'. For example, in Year I (described by the vertical axis) there were two teachers whose scores were considerably over two standard deviations above the mean; and in Year II (described by the horizontal axis) there was a teacher whose score was almost three standard deviations above the mean. When the evidence for Years I and II is combined, however, a different and less consistent picture emerges. Each of the three teachers just mentioned turned out to be of merely average effectiveness for the other year on which data were collected.

The diagonal line which passes from the bottom left-hand quadrant to the top right-hand quadrant describes the locations of teachers whose results were *consistent* over the two year. Some teachers fall on (or pretty close to) this line, indicating that they were consistent in both years. It is interesting to note, however, that in this particular study none of the teachers appears to have been both consistent in their effects and markedly effective (the top right-hand quadrant), although there are some tentative signs that some teachers were consistently and markedly ineffective (the bottom left-hand quadrant).

Our second example is of interest because it presents evidence of consistency across subjects. The study *Teaching Styles and Pupil Progress* (Bennett, 1976) collected pre- and post-test data for one year from a sample of top-junior teachers for reading and mathematics. Figure 2 is based on data from subsequent reanalyses of these data undertaken by Aitkin *et al.* (1981) and Gray and Satterly (1981). The vertical axis indicates the residual gain scores (based on class mean scores) for each teacher in reading; the horizontal axis describes the progress made by the same teachers' classes in mathematics. In both subjects there appear to have been teachers who were unusually 'effective' (upper-right quadrant). But neither of these two teachers appears to have been consistently effective in *both* subjects. However, since in both cases these teachers were still amongst the *more* effective teachers in their (relatively speaking) 'weaker' subject, this is probably not important. As before, there also appears to have been some evidence that some teachers were consistently (and perhaps, 'unusually') ineffective (bottom-left quadrant).

Our third example is drawn from the Contexts Project on which we are currently engaged (Gray and Jones, 1983). Figures 3a and 3b are based on data drawn from the secondary schools of one of the local authorities with which we have been working. Summary measures of fifth year examination results (the average number of O-level/CSE grade 1 passes per pupil) for each school have again been adjusted for differences in intakes (measured by the percentages of pupils at intake in each school achieving above average scores on tests of verbal reasoning). In Figure 3a the standardized residual gain scores in 1979 and 1980 have been presented for each school in the

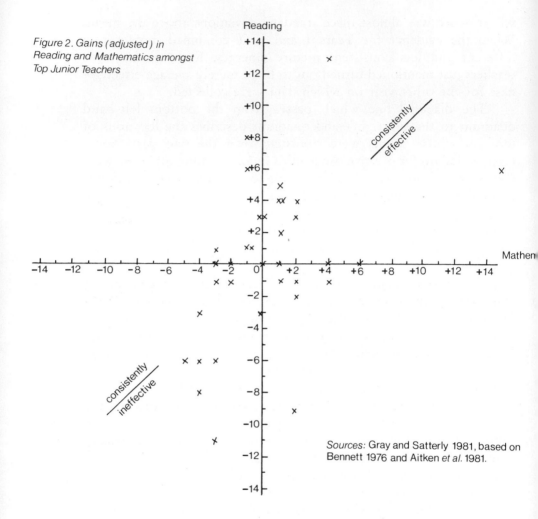

Figure 2. Gains (adjusted) in Reading and Mathematics amongst Top Junior Teachers

Sources: Gray and Satterly 1981, based on Bennett 1976 and Aitken *et al.* 1981.

authority; Figure 3b presents the same information but for the later years: 1980 and 1981. In combination the two figures enable us to look at the question of the consistency of apparent 'school effects' across several years. At the same time, however, they also underline some of the problems, and consequent compromises, that are involved.

Four schools (identified as 2, 5, 8 and 13) in the upper-right quadrant of Figure 3a appear to have combined some degree of effectiveness in both years with some degree of consistency. However, the particular location of each of the schools on the figure suggests the importance of proceeding with caution. School 13 was apparently both effective and consistent in its performance across the two years.

Figure 3a. Fifth-Year Examination Results (adjusted) in One Local Education Authority (1979/80)

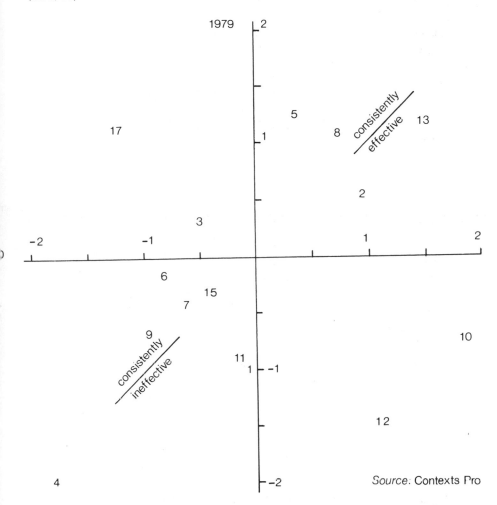

Source: Contexts Pro

However, when we turn to Figure 3b a somewhat different picture emerges. School 13 is still shown as being highly effective in 1980 but its 1981 performance (which is, of course, nearest to the present day) is merely average. School 8, in contrast, appears to have been more consistent in its performance across the three years but somewhat less effective.

It is fairly clear that the choice of which school(s) to study in greater depth needs to balance effectiveness, on the one hand, against consistency over time, on the other. If one had only had one year's data available (as has often been the case in studies of school and teacher effectiveness), it is possible that neither of the two schools

Figure 3b. Fifth-Year Examination Results (adjusted) in One Local Education Authority (1980/81)

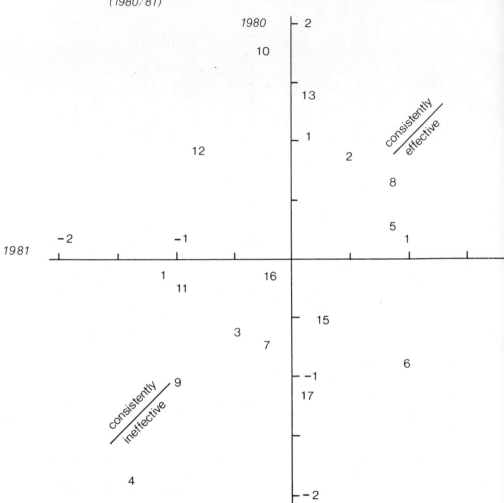

Source: Contexts Project

just discussed would have been considered worthy of detailed attention.

Up to this point the discussion has proceeded on the assumption that the changing patterns in the results of individual schools reflect substantive changes in their effectiveness from year to year. The statistical procedures we have followed are certainly standard ones which have been widely employed in studies of school and teacher effectiveness to date. A note of caution is, however, appropriate. It may be, given the relatively small number of schools and teachers available for analysis, that the statistical techniques we have employed are unduly vulnerable to fluctuations in the results of a very small number of schools or teachers with the consequence that *apparent* variability over time is increased. If this were the case, then more 'robust' statistical strategies than those currently employed in these sorts of studies might be required; we are involved in exploring some possible alternatives at the time of writing.

In sum, our analyses to date suggest that some schools and teachers may well be relatively more effective in boosting their pupils' performance and that some may well be consistent in doing so, but that identifying those that combine *both* attributes may prove more difficult.

The Next Steps?

Assuming cases of schools or teachers can be identified which satisfy our joint criteria of effectiveness and consistency, then these obviously need to be paired with other cases (matched in terms of intakes and facing similar circumstances) whose performance is merely average. In this way a framework may be established within which various comparisons of schools of differing types and effectiveness may be conducted.

The next steps are, to our mind, more difficult to define. American researchers have usually proceeded fairly rapidly towards quantitative comparisons of some kind. We are not opposed to such an approach but suspect it may be premature. Our preference is for a combination of 'detective' work and the methodology of case study (based on interviews and observation). To adopt the stance of a 'detective' may not be inappropriate, especially if one is dealing with data (such as test scores or examinations) which have been generated by administrative processes — purely clerical errors, for example, may have crept in. More importantly, when dealing with data aggregated at the level of the teacher or the school, it may be important to pursue in some depth the question of whether the bulk of the results are coming from a relatively small group of pupils or are spread more evenly. To adopt the procedures of case study allows the possibility that: (1) in the short term, the reasons why the schools and individual teachers under investigation differ in their effectiveness are actually known to those involved and, may, with some assistance, be articulated; and that (2) in the longer term such processes may actually be observed in practice. Such hopes may, of course, be overly optimistic but some investment in them is unlikely to prove costly.

To date, studies of school and teacher effectiveness have tended to converge in their conclusions. It may be that there are, in reality, just a small number of models of 'effective' practice, but we also wonder whether this assessment doesn't result from some of the assumptions in which researchers, to date, have themselves tended to invest. One important consequence of adopting the approach discussed here would be that it would be possible to generate, both fairly quickly and fairly cheaply, models of 'effective practice' for schools and teachers facing very differing circumstances. Of course, this approach only makes sense if you believe that there are several paths to 'success'. We can merely assert that, in the absence of convincing evidence to the contrary, we do.

Acknowledgements

Ben Jones is employed as a Research Fellow on the Contexts Project which is supported by a grant (HR 8602) from the Social Science Research Council, whose financial support is gratefully acknowledged. The authors would also like to thank the necessarily anonymous local authorities, schools and teachers who have generously provided data for analysis.

References

AITKIN, M., BENNETT, S. and HESKETH, J. (1981) 'Teaching styles and pupil progress: A reanalysis', *British Journal of Educational Psychology*, 51, pp. 170–86.

BENNETT, S.N. (1976) *Teaching Styles and Pupil Progress*, London, Open Books.

DES (1977) *Ten Good Schools: A Secondary School Enquiry*, London, HMSO.

DES (1979) *Aspects of Secondary Education: A Survey by HM Inspectors of Schools*, London, HMSO.

GALTON, M. and SIMON, B. (Eds) (1980) *Progress and Performance in the Primary Classroom*, London, Routledge and Kegan Paul.

GRAY, J. (1979) 'Reading progress in English infant schools: Some problems emerging from a study of teacher effectiveness', *British Educational Research Journal*, 5, 2, pp. 141–58.

GRAY, J. and JONES, B. (1983) 'Towards a framework for interpreting examination results', *SERCH*, 5, pp. 1–4.

GRAY, J. and SATTERLY, D. (1981) 'Formal or informal? A reassessment of the British evidence', *British Journal of Educational Psychology*, 51, pp. 187–96.

KLITGAARD, R. and HALL, G. (1977) 'A statistical search for unusually effective schools', in FAIRLEY, W.B. and MOSTELLER, F. (Eds) *Statistics and Public Policy*, Reading, Mass., Addison-Wesley.

PURKEY, S.C. and SMITH, M.S. (1982) 'Too soon to cheer? Synthesis of research on effective schools', *Educational Leadership*, 40, 3, pp. 64–9.

RUTTER, M., MAUGHAN, B., MORTIMORE, P. and OUSTON, J. (1979) *Fifteen Thousand Hours: Secondary Schools and their Effects on Children*, London, Open Books.

8 The ILEA Junior School Study: An Introduction

Peter Mortimore and Team[1]

The ILEA Junior School Project began in April 1980 and is due to end in June 1984. It is a longitudinal study and focuses on an age cohort of nearly 2000 pupils who entered junior classes in September 1980 and who will transfer to secondary school in September 1984. These pupils have attended fifty schools in inner London, randomly selected from the 800 primary schools within the Authority. In addition to our normal research, statistical and computing staff, we have had the benefit of working with four experienced primary school teachers seconded to the project for four years.

This chapter provides an introduction to the study and describes our means of data collection and our methods of analysis. No results are yet available although we hope, during this school year, to discuss preliminary findings with the heads and teachers of the schools participating in the research.

Why Have a Study of Junior Schools?

Differences in secondary school effectiveness in aiding the learning and development of pupils have been the subject of recent research (Rutter et al., 1979; Reynolds, 1982). There has also been considerable debate on the theoretical and methodological considerations of secondary school differences. (See, for instance, Mortimore, 1979; Tizard et al., 1979; Goldstein, 1980; Rutter et al., 1980; and Gray, 1981.)

In the United States, in contrast, most of the research into differences in school effectiveness has been carried out at the elementary school level (Weber, 1971; Brookover et al., 1976; Edmonds et al., 1978), although a study by Summers and Wolfe

(1977) and more recently the work of Goodlad and colleagues (1979) have been directed towards high schools.

During the 1980 BERA conference a speaker at the symposium on school differences argued that a comparative study of primary schools might illuminate the secondary school work as well as contributing, in its own right, to knowledge of junior schools. There have, of course, been a number of important studies of the education of children of primary school age but none has focused specifically on the question of school differences. Thus Galton and Simon (1980) have produced the most recent study of variations in primary school outcomes in terms of progress in basic skills. However, the study was primarily interested in relating pupil progress and teaching strategy rather than identifying school differences. In addition, the study did not control fully for intake characteristics known to be associated with achievement. Bennett's study of teaching style was restricted to the progress of fourth year juniors in a narrow range of educational outcomes. Michael Armstrong's study of the progress of one class of children, which revealed rich accounts of individual development under the guidance of a talented and thoughtful teacher, was of limited help in recording and understanding the variety of practice in a large LEA. Finally, the HMI primary survey (1978), whilst providing much useful information, was unable to control for intake differences between schools.

Our location as researchers within the ILEA clearly offers opportunities for the study of school differences and the question of effectiveness is of obvious and critical importance to a local education authority. Our proposal for a large-scale longitudinal study of junior schools was welcomed by the Education Officer, the Senior Staff Inspector (Primary) and members of the School's Sub-Committee of the Education Committee.

Aims of the Study

The first aim of the study is to produce a detailed description of pupils and teachers and of the curriculum and organization of schools in an inner-city area. The second aim is to study the progress over three and a half years of schooling of a cohort of 2000 pupils. We hope to be able to establish whether differences remain between schools in average pupil attainment and development, once account has been taken of the variation in the pupils' backgrounds. We have, therefore, collected detailed information about the social, ethnic, linguistic and family characteristics of the cohort.

There are, additionally, several other aims. These are to develop suitable statistical models of progress in both cognitive and non-cognitive measures; to investigate (in a sub-sample of schools) home-school relationships; to develop sensitive measures of such neglected areas of development as children's writing and speaking skills; and to explore average differences in the achievement of particular groups of pupils. Following a current educational initiative within the ILEA, special account is being taken of variation in achievement related to gender, ethnic and social class differences.

Methods of the Study

In a study of this kind it is obvious that a variety of methods will be needed. Pupil assessment (using both written and practical tasks), the completion of questionnaires, interviews and systematic observation techniques have all played their part. In addition, many statistical data have been collected from schools.

Consideration has been given to the questions of reliability and validity as well as to the comparability of the work of the field officers. Whenever possible, test scores have been adjusted for unreliability (see below, p. 128). Observation methods have included systematic training procedures and periodic reassessments of reliability. The existence of measures developed from quite different methodologies has enabled us to check on validity.

As with all fieldwork carried out in schools our research design suffers limitations. In order to overcome some of the methodological problems caused by these limitations and the variations between schools we have explored a variety of different statistical techniques (see below, p. 129). In addition, however, we have made extensive use of more qualitative data including field notes, case studies and verbatim descriptions.

Measures Used in the Study

Because the secondary studies have been criticized on the grounds of the paucity of their intake measures, we have attempted to collect as comprehensive measures as possible. Our own work (Sammons *et al.*,

1983) and the recent study by Essen and Wedge (1982) have shown that the educational effects of disadvantage may be cumulative and we have, therefore, structured our data so that this can be taken into account. Recent research by Marks *et al.* (1983) illustrates the dangers of neglecting such measures which may lead to misleading results in studies of school differences (see Gray, 1983; Gray and Jones, 1983).

Background Measures

The selection of background measures was made with reference to the results of past studies of the relationships between educational attainment and pupil characteristics (see, for example, Douglas, 1964; Davie *et al.*, 1972; Rutter and Madge, 1976). Information about pre-school experience, position in the family, parental language, child's first language and language used at home, was obtained from the primary school records. Supplementary data about the child's social and ethnic family background (including mother's and father's occupations, family size and structure, eligibility for free school meals, ethnic group and fluency in English) were also collected from schools and, in some cases, directly from parents. In addition, information about any handicaps and health problems experienced by children was collected regularly from their class teachers. Finally, information about the social and economic characteristics of pupils' home areas was obtained from the 1981 Census data.

Cognitive Development

Data have been collected about each pupil's attainments on entry to junior school. This information was necessary for the identification of differences in the 'quality' of school intakes and also in order to provide us with a baseline against which to assess an individual pupil's progress over the three and a half years of the study.

The children's reading and mathematics performance has been assessed by use of the Edinburgh Reading Test stage 1 (ERT 1) and the NFER Basic Mathematics Test A (BMT A). The children's scores on the Raven's Coloured Progressive Matrices test of visio-spatial ability have also been obtained.

We chose the ERT because this was a group test recently standardized on a suitable age-group drawn from a large population. In addition, this test is part of a series designed to cover age-bands throughout the junior school age-range. The BMT was selected following consultation with the ILEA mathematics inspectorate who considered it tested a wider range of achievement than other possible group tests. Again, this test is part of a series designed for the whole junior age-range. Raven's Coloured Progressive Matrices test was chosen in order to give a measure of general performance not dependent upon language fluency. Its advantages include ease of administration and a ready acceptability by the children.

Information about teachers' assessments of the children's performance in several areas of language and mathematics was also collected from infant school records. In addition, a practical mathematics test was administered to a random sample of pupils attending a representative sub-sample of the schools. The practical mathematics test was based upon the ILEA 'Checkpoints' procedure (devised by the mathematics inspectorate) and covered five areas of mathematics — weight, volume, sets, number and length.

Progress. The children have also been assessed in mathematics and reading at the beginning of their second and third years and, finally, at the end of the summer term of their third year in junior school. These assessments were made using the ERT and BMT appropriate for the children at each stage. Additional items of increased difficulty were included in the practical mathematics test. These later assessments are being used to establish progress over the first, second and third years of junior schooling. A final measure of outcome, the children's performance in the ILEA secondary transfer verbal reasoning test, will be obtained during the autumn term.

Writing. In addition to tests of reading, mathematics and non-verbal reasoning, we considered it important to develop a measure of creative writing. Thus, all children completed a standard story writing exercise under controlled conditions using a set topic in the first year and specially prepared taped stimuli in the second and third years. The writing has been assessed by experienced primary school teachers using measures (of technical ability and expression of language and ideas) based on scales developed by Bennett (1981). A measure of the writer's awareness of others developed by Cowie (1982) was also included.

In addition to the set tasks, we invited teachers to send us pieces of writing carried out by children on different occasions and for different purposes. We have, therefore, a considerable corpus of written work from which we hope to gain measures of the development of children's writing.

Oracy.   Many teachers place a strong emphasis upon the development of children's oral skills. In order, therefore, to take this into account, and to broaden the assessment of language development, the oral skills of a sample of children of different ability levels from each school will also be assessed during their fourth year. We will be using a number of exercises developed specially for our use by the APU Language Survey team. A discussion of the methods of assessing children's oral skills will be provided in the APU Language Survey report (forthcoming).

Non-Cognitive Development

It has been suggested that studies of school differences have tended to neglect the 'social' outputs of education (such as pupils' values or self-perception, or even attendance rates) on which, it is argued, schools may have greater effects (Reynolds, 1982). We have, therefore, included a wide range of non-cognitive measures. In this way, we hope to do justice to the diverse aims and the breadth of the curriculum of many primary schools.

Behaviour.   Information about the children's behaviour in school (as assessed by their teachers) has been collected using the 'Child at School' schedule (CAS). This instrument has been developed specially for use with the junior age-group and consists of nine items which form three sub-scales (anxious; aggressive; learning difficulties). Full details of the CAS are included in a forthcoming paper by Kysel and Varlaam (1984).

Teachers have rated all pupils individually in both autumn and summer terms of the first, second and third years. This has provided us with a detailed record of changes in teacher-assessed behaviour over time. These behavioural data have been related to attainment and progress in mathematics, reading and creative writing assessments as well as to the background of pupils. Class and school differences in the incidence of different types of behaviour problems are being explored currently.

Attitudes.   We have also developed a measure of pupils' attitudes towards different types of school activities and curricular areas, and school rules and discipline. We have called this the 'Smiley' instrument. It is a self-report measure and children have rated on a five-point scale how they felt about particular activities. The instrument is administered verbally in each classroom and the scales are represented by pictures of sad and happy faces. These attitudinal data were collected at the end of the summer term of the first, second and third years. When changes in attitudes have been analyzed we hope to be able to relate expressed attitudes to the progress of the children and to the behavioural assessments provided by their teachers. Differences between schools and classes in children's attitudes are also being investigated.

Self-concept. We would have liked to use a measure of self-concept but, despite an extensive review of the research literature, we failed to identify any suitable instrument. Many measures were too general for use in a study concerned with the child in his or her school environment. Further, most of the available self-concept instruments were developed for use in American studies and, therefore, used language inappropriate for our sample of children. As none of the published methods appeared to be suitable for our cohort we decided to develop an instrument based on the 'Child at School' schedule. We included two extra items which attempted to assess the child's perceptions of the opinions held by significant others about him or herself. The significant others we chose were the teacher and the peer group.

Because of the close relationship between the two instruments — the 'Child at School' and 'Me at School' — it is possible for us to compare the teacher's ratings with the child's self-assessment. Associations between the child's self-assessment and his or her attitudes and performance in mathematics, reading, writing and oracy are currently being explored. Again, school differences in the children's self-assessments will be examined.

Attendance. Full attendance data have been collected for each child for the three terms of each school year so that relationships between progress and attendance can be examined. Associations between attendance and background characteristics are also being investigated. School differences in this outcome will be a major focus of interest.

All these measures will be used to establish whether patterns of school differences in effectiveness are similar and whether there is a relationship between cognitive and non-cognitive measures. It will also, of course, be possible to examine differences in the various pupil measures when relationships with background factors are controlled at both the class and the school level. These analyses will indicate whether, as Reynolds (1982) suggested, there are greater differences between schools in terms of their social rather than their cognitive effects.

Teachers, Classrooms and Schools

Although the study aims to provide a description of the characteristics, development, attainments and progress of a group of pupils moving through the years of junior schooling, many data have also been collected about the classes and schools the pupils have attended. These data serve to provide not only a detailed description of differences in the learning environments experienced by our cohort, but also a guide to good primary practice.

Organization. We are developing various measures of school organization. Using interviews with headteachers we have collected information on their view of their own role and their educational philosophy as well as details of qualifications and experience. In addition, we have information on pupil grouping within the school, the methods of assigning particular teachers to classes, the allocation of staff responsibilities, methods of staff appraisal and the involvement of staff in decision-making.

Interviews with the deputy headteachers have been used to supplement data obtained from the heads and to establish the deputies' views of their roles and responsibilities, contact with children and staff and involvement in different aspects of management and decision-making. In order to obtain information on classroom organization, the teachers of our cohort have been interviewed each year to establish how the work of their classes was organized; the methods used to group pupils; extent of remedial provision; the use of textbooks and guidelines; and the type of records being kept. The teachers also provided details of their contact with other staff and with parents. Information about their responsibilities and their own philosophy of education was obtained as well as details of their involvement in decision-making within the school.

Interviews with the class teachers in the second year yielded detailed information about the curriculum experienced by the cohort. Information about the provision of remedial care (where applicable) was obtained from interviews with remedial teachers and was used to supplement data about the curriculum.

In addition, teachers in the schools (not only those interviewed) supplied information on their own backgrounds so that a full description of the teaching force working in the schools can be drawn up.

Observations.   Detailed classroom observations have been undertaken during each year of the project. Data have been collected on the classroom activity of teachers and pupils. Because of the necessity for accurate comparability over time and between classes, a systematic procedure was required. The instruments developed by the ORACLE research team for use in their studies of primary classrooms were adopted. The ORACLE instruments have the advantages of being used recently with the relevant age-group and of providing information about both the teachers' and the children's activities. The pupil and teacher records which we used are fully described by Galton *et al.* (1980). The appropriate members of our team were trained by one of the Leicester researchers.

Qualitative observations.   In addition to the systematic observations, and amended version of the SCOTS schedule (Powell and Scrimgour, 1977) was used to provide a more subjective assessment of classroom behaviour and activities. Field officers rated the classes on a number of scales (for example, 'pupil/teacher social relationship') four times during the observation day and made extensive notes about time spent in the classrooms.

Home-school liaison.   Numerous research studies have indicated that family and home circumstances can have an important influence upon children's educational achievements and behaviour at school (see, for example, Mortimore and Blackstone, 1982). Recent experimental studies have also shown that parental involvement with the child's learning at home or at school can be an effective means of promoting progress in reading (Hewison and Tizard, 1980). For these reasons it was considered important to obtain detailed information about the home and family circumstances of the children; parental involvement with the child's learning; their expectations of, and attitudes towards, education; contact with the school; and their satisfaction with their child's education. It was not practical to consider obtaining information from the parents of all 2000 pupils in our cohort. However, with the help of a grant from the Leverhulme Foundation, a sub-study was undertaken to investigate these areas and home-school links in a sub-sample of schools. A stratified random sample of eight schools was chosen and the parents of all cohort pupils in these schools contacted and interviewed.

Comparisons between background information about the pupils obtained from parents directly and that collected from the children's schools have provided a check on the reliability of our measures of pupil background for the whole cohort.

Other measures.   Information about the physical structure of the schools, the layout of buildings and classrooms and resource provision (books and equipment and other materials) has been collected and priorities in spending have been identified. In addition, field officers have used their experience of the sample schools to rate the emphasis on different aesthetic areas of the curriculum (including art and craft, music, drama and dance), science and the use of computers. Although the development of such measures is bound to be subjective, we felt it was important not to neglect these areas because of difficulties of measurement.

Methods of Analysis

As will be clear from the earlier sections of this paper, analysis of the data collected for the Junior School Project is likely to be highly complex. Early research in this country on school and teacher differences has been criticized by statisticians. (See, for example, Tizard *et al.*, 1980; Plewis *et al.*, 1981; Radical Statistics Education Group, 1983). The implications of such criticisms for analyses of school and teacher differences have been illustrated by the reanalysis of Bennett's study which resulted in substantial revisions to the original findings (Aitkin *et al.*, 1981a).

There are four general statistical problems which apply to our study. These will be described briefly before some details of the analyses we have carried out so far, and our strategies for analyzing the various data sets, are given.

General Problems

Sampling schemes.   We selected the schools from all junior schools in the ILEA to form a stratified random sample in which the proportion of schools sampled from each division remained constant. As each child, teacher and class within a particular year group was included, the sample, at both the class and the individual child level, is a clustered sample. The implication of such clustering for analysis of classes and of individual children is that, for a given dependent variable (such as, reading, for example), the values for children within a school are likely to have a different and, usually greater, degree of homogeneity than those for children overall. This violates the assumption of independence of error of the statistical techniques in commonly used programs. The SPSS package, for instance, assumes that observations arise from a simple random sample.

We have conducted some initial sub-studies of reading progress which indicate that, when regression coefficients in a multiple regression of second year reading scores on first year scores are estimated, errors usually increase. We will be cautious, therefore, in interpreting results from techniques which assume simple random sampling.

Whilst it is our intention to take into account the effects of clustering in the sample in our analyses, the practical difficulties of research using sub-samples of children and classes should not be underestimated. To date, however, studies of school differences have tended to ignore the effects of clustering and methods of taking this problem into account have not been fully developed.

Units of analysis. We are using three units of analysis: the individual child, the class, and the school. Each level is important for studies of school and teacher differences and of the progress of individuals and groups. Thus, in order to explain progress over time we need to take into account:

1 characteristics of individual pupils (such as age, sex, social class and initial attainment);

2 characteristics of the school intake (aggregated pupil characteristics which determine the sex, social and ethnic composition of the school or class as a whole);

3 other characteristics of the school (including school size, staff and pupil turnover, or staff composition).

Differences in progress are likely to be explained in terms, not only of the separate effects nor of the simple combined effects of these three sets of variables, but also by the interactions between them.

Multilevel models can be used to explain differences between schools in terms of data measured at different levels (such as the individual child, the class and the school). A summary of issues in the debate on levels (or units) of analysis, primarily concerning research conducted in the USA is given by Burstein (1980), and the importance of multilevel models has been demonstrated in the field of demography by Mason *et al.* (1981). Because of their suitability for our data it is intended to use multilevel models in our analyses of school and class differences.

Unreliability in predictor variables.   In analyzing progress in different cognitive areas we have used a conditional model. We are interested in measuring differences in a particular cognitive outcome (such as reading test scores) in year 2 for groups with similar scores in year 1. When doing this we need to control for other characteristics related to attainment, such as social class, sex and ethnic origin. It is well known that all tests (and observation instruments) have some degree of unreliability. This causes the relationship between the 'true' cognitive outcome over the two years to differ from that between the observed outcomes and may affect the results of analyses of progress. However, by incorporating estimates of the reliability for the various tests we can estimate the relationship between progress and background factors.

In our study we have retained information on the individual test items for most of the tests and this allows us to estimate test reliability using internal consistency methods. This we see as preferable to using estimates contained in test manuals collected on samples with different characteristics. Though this method appears to work well for three of our cognitive tests (the ERT, BMT and Raven's Progressive Matrices) which are constructed to measure a unidimensional trait, the notion of reliability is more complex for tests or instruments where more than one trait is operating. This appears to be the case in the practical mathematics tests and in the behaviour assessment. Thus factor analyses of the 'Child at School' schedule indicate that three dimensions of behaviour problems are operating (anxiety, learning problems and aggression) and we also expect multidimensionality to be found in the assessment of oracy and the child attitude self-completion assessment. In these cases, when considering progress, we may have to consider conducting separate analyses for each sub-scale.

Fixed versus random effects.   We selected a random sample of schools in the ILEA so that inferences could be drawn about schools, teachers and pupils in the Authority as a whole. Thus, schools and teachers are being modelled as random effects in analyses of variance models. On the other hand, some variables within the model, such as the social class of individual pupils, take the whole range of values in the sample. Since the inference is made to this range of values they have to be modelled as fixed effects.

Models incorporating both random and fixed effects are called mixed models. The multilevel models which we have described above can be translated into mixed models which allow differences between schools, classes and teachers to be explained in terms of characteristics of the school and class, while information on the individual pupils is retained. (Unfortunately, the conceptualization of school effects as random entails the use of statistical programs outside those available in SPSS; see Aitkin *et al.*, 1981b.)

We have investigated the differences in effects which result from treating schools as random effects rather than fixed effects. When we related reading attainment to the social class, ethnic group and sex of the pupil we found that the effects of social class were overemphasized in the fixed effects model in contrast to the random effects model. For this reason, mixed models are considered preferable to fixed effects models for our purposes.

Analysis Strategies

We now give some details of our strategies for dealing with the particular problems to which our data give rise.

Ways of measuring progress. For our cognitive variables we have adopted the conditional model now frequently used in educational research. This method regresses the cognitive outcome of interest on the same variable measured at an earlier stage. By controlling for each of the pupil characteristics in turn and simultaneously, the contributions of these characteristics to progress can be estimated. Problems arise, however, when the tests cannot be assumed to measure a unidimensional trait. In this case the interpretation of progress is difficult.

The sorts of questions we are seeking to answer include: are the different dimensions of particular outcomes weighted equally on measures taken at different time periods? If our answer turns out to be 'no', then the implications for the use of any general measures of progress are serious. One solution might be to identify the separate components or dimensions and to carry out separate analyses and adjustments for unreliability. This strategy may have to be applied to measures of child behaviour and attitudes to school as well as to the cognitive tests of practical maths and oracy which all appear to be multidimensional. We are reasonably satisfied, however, that tests of mathematics, reading and Raven's Coloured Progressive Matrices can be treated as unidimensional.

As yet we are also unclear as to how best to deal with outcome measures such as oracy, for which no suitable control data about previous attainment have been collected, and for which it will not, therefore, be possible to assess pupil progress directly. We could, of course, use other cognitive variables but the choice of which to use is not easy.

The longitudinal design of our study provides us with the opportunity of relating the test scores of the same pupils over three separate years. We will be interested in establishing whether, for example, tests taken in the first year still relate to third year results once the second year results have been taken into account. In addition, we are particularly interested in finding out whether the regression coefficients of the tests apply in a similar way to all groups of pupils (and to all schools).

Ways of dealing with background variables.   Different background factors have been found to have varying effects on measures of children's attainments. In addition, some background factors are 'better' predictors of attainment in tests of reading, for example, than mathematics. Because we are conscious of both conceptual and technical difficulties in controlling for background, we have carried out a series of detailed analyses in this area. The results of these analyses confirm that the effects of particular background factors vary for different cognitive outcomes. Our analyses also indicate that the contribution of a particular factor (such as a one-parent family) experienced in combination with other factors (such as poverty) may be very different from the effects of this factor when it is experienced in isolation.

The relationships between background variables and progress (as opposed to attainment) are more complex. It would appear that the determining effects of background characteristics are substantially taken into account when earlier attainment is used as the base line for measurement of progress.

Ways of analyzing observational data.   Before data about teachers, obtained either from interviews or from direct observation of class-room behaviour and strategies, can be related to other characteristics of schools or those of pupils, they must be analyzed to indicate underlying structures. We are at present examining the ORACLE and SCOTS data using factor analysis to uncover structures in the variables. We are also using cluster analysis to attempt to delineate groups of teachers and children who have similar values on the various observed indicators.

One particular issue which is relevant to our work is the question of the nature, and indeed the existence of, 'teaching styles'. Previous research on teaching methods in this country has generally collected either questionnaire data (Bennett, 1976, and the reanalysis by Aitkin *et al.*, 1981a; 1981b), or observational data (Galton *et al.*, 1980). We have adapted Galton's observation methods and, in addition, have obtained extensive interview and questionnaire data. Because of this we are able to examine the relationship between the teachers' stated methods and objectives and those observed. This issue is important but has rarely been examined in detail.

In grouping observations on teachers and pupils, an important statistical issue concerns the clustering methods used. The differences found between the teaching styles in Aitkin's reanalysis and in the Bennett data are a result of Aitkin's use of a probabilistic clustering method which assumes the conditional independence of teacher responses within a cluster. Methods of fitting mixtures of multivariate normal distributions to the observational data are being examined.

Another key question concerns which level of aggregation of data is most suitable. Theoretically it is possible to use the data at the lowest level, that of the particular utterance (observation) on each sampled occasion, or at the intermediate session level. However, useful summaries of overall teacher characteristics can be obtained by aggregating over each teacher separately for each term. This gives the proportion of utterances of different types for each teacher and enables differences between teachers to be identified. However, examination of more detailed questions, such as the relation of types of teacher management to type of audience, may require analysis at a lower level.

Ways of relating school variables to pupil outcomes. The multilevel analyses described earlier enable variation within the individual school to be taken into account. In addition, these analyses identify the extent to which the school effects can be explained by characteristics at the school level. By an extension of this approach, variation in and between classes can be incorporated.

As this discussion illustrates, these models can become very complex, particularly when account is taken of the number of time points at which attainments are assessed and observations are taken. Given the complexity and range of our data, and the variety of analyses and model building which we are attempting, much further work — including exploratory analysis of individual instruments — remains to be carried out before any interpretation of our results will be possible.

How the Findings Will Be Reported

Once the fieldwork phase of the study is completed, we are planning to hold discussions in each of the schools that have participated in the project. Thus the heads and teachers most closely involved in the study will have an opportunity to comment on the research, and on any findings which, by that stage, have emerged. We will then report to our colleagues in the ILEA administration and inspectorate before presenting summaries of our findings to the elected members. Clearly any study of this scope will produce complex findings, and detailed discussions with people involved in many different parts of the education service will be essential. We then hope to report the findings in a form that teachers, parents, advisers and fellow researchers, as well as interested general readers will find accessible. We will, in addition, publish technical papers in the appropriate scientific journals.

Conclusions

Longitudinal educational research involves commitment and work for heads and teachers of participating schools, for pupils — who are assessed more frequently than usual — and for field officers, researchers, computer programmers and statisticians.

The organization and storage of data over a three-year period is, itself, a major task. Methods of analysis enjoying current interest are also complex and frequently involve small development projects to ensure their suitability for the data. Assessment techniques are, in many fields of education, still rudimentary and have, therefore, to be adapted and piloted extensively before use.

Research can offer few guarantees. However, it is likely that the detailed descriptive information on how schools work, how teachers organize classes, and how pupils — of different aptitudes, attitudes and backgrounds — learn, will prove useful. We hope, too, that the evaluative aspects of the study will provide clearer indications of effective schooling.

Our study will not answer every question that could be asked about junior schools. Many areas of school life have, of necessity, been neglected. Furthermore, all our schools are located in the inner-city and the findings may be of less relevance for those concerned with education in suburban or rural areas.

The importance of educational research, however, must not be underestimated. The costs of society's investment in education are high. Research on current practice and, especially, on school and teacher effectiveness is important. For pupils, the years between 7 and 10 are critical in shaping their future performance in secondary schooling and in determining the opportunities available to them in later life. We hope that our study will contribute to the understanding of this phase of schooling and, more generally, to the goal of effective education.

Acknowledgements

We wish to acknowledge our debt to the heads and teachers of the schools involved in the research. We also wish to thank the various members of the ILEA Inspectorate who have provided specialist advice. In addition, we wish to thank all other colleagues in Research and Statistics who have helped in any way with the study. Finally, we wish to record our thanks to Dick Cooper and Pamela Glanville who worked a field officers for two years of the project, to Christine Mabey and Brian Clover, former members of the research team, and to Andreas Vaarlam who devized the sub-study of parental involvement.

Notes

1 The Team comprised: PETER MORTIMORE, PAMELA SAMMONS, RUSSELL ECOB, ANNE HILL, AUDREY HIND, MARY HUNT, LOUISE STOLL, JENNIFER RUNHAM and DAVID LEWIS.

References

AITKIN, M., BENNETT, N. and HESKETH, J. (1981a) 'Teaching styles and pupils' progress: A re-analysis', *British Journal of Educational Psychology*, 51, 2, pp. 170–86.

AITKIN, M., ANDERSON, D. and HINDE, J. (1981b) 'Statistical modelling of data on teaching styles', *Journal of the Royal Statistical Society* (Series A), 144, pp. 419–61.

BENNETT, N. (1976) *Teaching Styles and Pupil Progress*, London, Open Books.

BENNETT, N. *et al.* (1981) *The Quality of Pupil Learning Experiences,* Centre for Educational Research and Development, University of Lancaster.

BROOKOVER, W.B. *et al.* (1976) *Elementary School Climate and School Achievement*, East Lansing, Michigan State University, College of Urban Development.

BURSTEIN, L. (1980) 'The role of levels of analysis in the specification of educational effects', in DREEBEN, R. and THOMAS, J.A. (Eds), *The Analysis of Educational Productivity. Vol. 1: Issues in Micro-Analysis*, Cambridge, Mass, Ballinger.

COWIE, H. (1983) *An Approach to the Evaluation of Children's Writing*, London, Department of Psychology, Froebel Institute.

DAVIE, R., BUTLER, N. and GOLDSTEIN, H. (1972) *From Birth to Seven*, London, Longman.

DOUGLAS, J.W.B. (1964) *The Home and the School*, London, MacGibbon and Kee.

EDMONDS, R.C. *et al.* (1978) *Search for Effective Schools*, Cambridge, Mass., Harvard University, Center for Urban Schools.

ESSEN, J. and WEDGE, P. (1982) *Continuities in Childhood Disadvantage*, London, Heinemann.

GALTON, M. and SIMON, B. (1980) *Progress and Performance in the Primary Classroom*, London, ROUTLEDGE and KEGAN PAUL.

GALTON, M., SIMON, B. and CROLL, P. (1980) *Inside the Primary Classroom*, London, Routledge and Kegan Paul.

GOLDSTEIN, H. (1980) 'Fifteen Thousand Hours: A review of the statistical procedure', *Journal of Child Psychology and Psychiatry*, 21, 4, pp. 363–6.

GOODLAD, J.I. *et al.* (1979) *A Study of Schooling*, Indiana, Phi Delta Kappa.

GRAY, J. (1981) 'A competitive edge: Examination results and the probable limits of secondary school effectiveness', *Educational Review*, 33, 1, pp. 25–35.

GRAY, J. (1983) 'Questions of background', *The Times Educational Supplement*, 8 July 1983.

GRAY, J. and JONES, B. (1983) 'Disappearing data', *The Times Educational Supplement*, 15 July 1983.

HEWISON, J. and TIZARD, J. (1980) 'Parental involvement and reading attainment', *British Journal of Educational Psychology*, 50, pp. 209–15.

HMI SURVEY (1978) *Primary Education in England*, London, HMSO.

KYSEL, F. and VARLAAM, A. (1984) *The Child at School — A New Behaviour Schedule*, Research and Statistics, ILEA.

MARKS, J., COX, C. and POMIAN-SRZEDNICKI, M. (1983) *Standards in English Schools*, National Council for Educational Standards.

MASON, W.M., WONG, G.Y. and ENTWISTLE, B. (1983) 'The multilevel linear model: 'A better way to do contextual analysis', *Sociological Methodology*.

MORTIMORE, P. (1979) 'The study of secondary schools: A researcher's reply', in *The Rutter Research: Perspectives 1*, School of Education, University of Exeter.

MORTIMORE, J. and BLACKSTONE, T. (1982) *Disadvantage in Education*, London, Heinemann.

PLEWIS, I., GRAY, J., FOGELMAN, K., MORTIMORE, P. and BYFORD, D. (1981) *Publishing School Examination Results: A Discussion*, Bedford Way Papers 5, University of London Institute of Education.

POWELL, J.L. and SCRIMGOUR, M.N.G. (1977) *System for Classroom Observation of Teaching Strategies*, Edinburgh, Scottish Council for Research in Education.

Radical Statistic Education Group (1982) *Reading Between the Numbers: A Critical Guide to Educational Research*, London BSSRS, 9 Poland Street, London WIV 3DG.

REYNOLDS, D. (1982) 'The search for effective schools', *School Organization*, 2, 3, pp. 215–37.

RUTTER, M. and MADGE, N. (1976) *Cycles of Disadvantage*, London, Heinemann.

RUTTER, M., MAUGHAN, B., MORTIMORE, P. and OUSTON, J. (1979) *Fifteen Thousand Hours*, London, Open Books.

RUTTER, M., MAUGHAN, B., MORTIMORE, P. and OUSTON, J. (1980) 'Educational criteria of success: A reply to Acton', *Educational Research*, 22, 3, pp. 170–4.

SAMMONS, P., KYSEL, F. and MORTIMORE, P. (1983) 'Educational Priority Indices: A new perspective', *British Educational Research Journal*, 9, 1, pp. 27–40.

SUMMERS, A.A. and WOLFE, B.L. (1977) 'Do schools make a difference?', *American Economic Review*.

TIZARD, B. *et al.* (1979) 'Fifteen Thousand Hours: A discussion', *Bedford Way Papers 1*, University of London, Institute of Education.

WEBER, G. (1971) *Inner-City Children Can Be Taught to Read: Four Successful Schools*, Washington, D.C., Council for Basic Education.

9   The Theoretical Underpinnings of School Change Strategies

Jill Lewis

The institutions in which we educate our children appear to be permanently subject to change. There can be change imposed from without due to economic and political pressures, and change from within evolving from new circumstances and new insights. However, the atmosphere within which change takes place in schools is frequently an atmosphere of crisis, seemingly endless crisis. Whatever one's status within education — pupil, parent, teacher, administrator — we are all a part of one system, whether we wish to resist, ignore or implement change. If we can make this assumption, then it reduces much of the inflamation and the conflict which exists. We do not then waste time searching for villains to blame and we thus accept all the forces present in the situation and may begin to accept, approach and attack the problems which so clearly exist. Clearly cooperation is more productive than conflicts produced by crises.

When Hargreaves (1967) described the conflict between the sub-cultural groups in Lumley School, he was describing within a school a traditional view of the division within society: the Haves and the Have Nots — the 'A's and the 'B's. The egalitarian dream of the late nineteenth and early twentieth centuries has been deferred. No longer can we hope that school will enable children to overcome the conditions of their birth; nor can we assume that if opportunities are equalized that outcomes would be more nearly equal as well. In the school situation 'A's are the teaching staff with many and various hierarchical structures and also the 'successful' pupils — the pupils who achieve the institutional goals enshrined within our examination system. The 'B's are the less able, underachieving and alienated 40 per cent. Another A and B split is the one which is directly between teachers and pupils — between those who make the rules and those for whom the rules are made. Rules, of course, cover not only the means by which the pupils receive their education and which classes they attend but also personal processes, what they may wear, when and where they eat, under what conditions they may talk to each other and even when they may go to the toilet.

The concerns expressed about disruptive behaviour, concern with the management of the B group by the A group, is evidence that the more traditionally submissive B group is becoming less so. To date, there is little cohesion to such a revolution and the young people show their alienation in a sullen and withdrawn way.

The response to the threat implied in such behaviour takes a number of forms. On the one hand there is the traditional 'Ostrich' approach, the hierarchies who are continually 'in conference' — fiddling while Rome burns. There is the 'Machiavellian' approach, where those who are refusing to conform are paralleled with other negative groups in society — the feckless, the agitators — and more penal solutions are then justified. There is the 'Humpty Dumpty' approach which blandly acknowledges what is happening, even makes sympathetic noises about it, but sits kicking its heels on the fence, waiting for more frustration and anger to come along to tip it off. Finally, there is the 'Columbus' approach — those who are convinced that there is a new land out there, even though they are told by the majority that they will fall of the end of the world if they sail off to find it. This more daring approach has its hazards and, like Columbus, one may return from such explorations in chains!

None of these responses seems adequate, and I would suggest that we need to move from confusion and conflict and inadequate responses towards cooperation; and that we need to do it now. I have been working for the past five years with colleagues in the teaching profession, who are more like fifteenth century explorers than sixteenth century Italian politicians! The focus of attention has been behaviour problems and learning difficulties in our Welsh secondary schools. The processes by which we attempt to find strategies appropriate to each individual school are, I believe, a positive move towards finding that cooperation we so badly need.

Constructing a programme which would provide a reliable yet flexible basis within which to work with individual teachers and institutions necessitated investigating other programmes which were involved in this area of institutional change. In practical terms in 1978 there were two which were formative in my thinking, one in Sweden and one in New York. There was also an experiential training programme for school leaders devised at the University of Nebraska. However, the genesis of these schemes appeared to me to lie in a movement in education called Organizational Development. It is this movement, its theoretical base and its practical application which has had a major effect on the evolution of a successful cooperative venture.

Organizational Development

The focus of Organizational Development is institutional rather than individual factors. The founding father of Organizational Development was Kurt Lewin who, along with other social psychologists and educators, formed the National Training Laboratories at Bethel, Maine, USA in 1947. The concept that Lewin brought was that of action research; the action was to come from members of a group or organization and the research was in the collection by the individuals of information about their functioning. The aim was to utilize the information to collaborate in a problem-solving process which would improve their functioning professionally. In origin it was quite intensively self-analytical. Industry was the first to identify the potential this new movement offered, and extended the innovation using the methods within departments in industrial companies. Organizational Development design was advanced by working with discrete groups of both management and labour. The issue for industrial concerns was productivity, and a way forward was seen to be the structuring of a process whereby trust could be built which would underpin improved collaboration. Risks were taken in exploring interpersonal and interdepartmental conflict but control was maintained by the scientific design, the first rule of which was the collection of data — the accumulation of knowledge. It took a decade before education began to explore the possibilities which industry had pioneered and the first research project (COPED, 1965) which collected data in over eighty schools confirmed the hypothesis that a school's educational effectiveness was associated with the morale of the staff, the power structure, the problem-solving process and the degree of trust amongst colleagues. An experiment in the mid-1960s which attempted to train the whole staff of a junior high school in Organizational Development, hoping to strengthen the problem-solving capacity of the school, was highly successful. There was a measurable reduction of frustration and confusion amongst colleagues, improved communication among all parts of the school community and an increase in innovation within the classrooms (for an account of this experiment see Schmuck *et al.*, 1969).

One important element underlying the scientific design of

Organizational Development is the conscious collection, use and application of knowledge. Such knowledge may be powerful in suggesting changes in school groupings, changes in relationships between teachers, between teachers and children, between teachers and headteachers, between schools and parents. Knowledge itself can be seen as a powerful change agent if we believe that wo/man is primarily a rational being, but this view seems somewhat utopian: knowledge will give enlightenment and enlightenment will produce change? It is much more realistic to say that where knowledge about individuals' and institutions' functioning connects with personal or group self-interest then change can be effective.

Change can also be produced where knowledge is seen as not so much new information about the external world but rather new information about the internal world — expanded self-awareness, self-understanding and self-control. Many of our actions both personally and professionally are based on our individual commitment to, and internalizing of, norms of which we are unconscious. Perhaps the most dramatic illustration of this reality which we can translate into our professional world is to be found in the work of Freud. He aimed to be collaborative with his patients in an effort to *raise consciousness* and *re-educate* to bring about a change of attitudes. If we substitute change agent for therapist, and client for patient, its potential is vivid. The data base of Organizational Development need not be information about parent/teacher associations but rather about attitudes to parents; need not be about pastoral structures but about attitudes to care; need not be about teaching groups but about attitudes to labelling.

One further exploration of the use of knowledge is important, and that is that knowledge is one of the ingredients of power. Within our education system there are different bases of power which are quite legitimate and many countries have envied the autonomy of British schools — the power invested, for example, in the position of the headteacher within the school or the position of the teacher within the classroom. Knowledge which makes the individual or the institution aware of the dimensions of power is important if it is only for the increased awareness that power can be coercive. In the education system as a whole we experience the coercive power of imposed change by political decision, by economic pressure, and we also experience the anger and frustration which results. Punishment systems and rules within schools can also be coercive and lead to confrontation. Knowledge may suggest that power imposed over people is of short-lived effectiveness but power shared with colleagues, with parents and with children has a better chance of lasting commitment.

Sharing power is very important to real growth; actively seeking to empower others is potentially creative yet feared. For example, government talks of the partnership between home and school but the reality to date has been deliberately limited by the schools, and any change is being forced on schools by statute.

Empowerment means different things to different people. It is a means of taking of control. Empowering others, then, means encouraging them to take control. It is a process through which individuals gain knowledge (about themselves and their environment) and skills which result in their feeling more confident in themselves and thus more in control of their environment and more able to effect desirable changes. Ideally, fully empowered individuals are aware of their own strengths and can act effectively on their own behalf. They are also able to act cooperatively with others who have similar concerns to begin to change elements of the context in which they live and work. Although in our minds the empowerment process begins with individuals, in the long run it is directed at creating responsible social change.

The empowerment process can be thought of as one which begins with changing individuals' perceptions of themselves so they feel more control over their immediate lives. The basis for this positive change is their own recognition of the validity of the knowledge they have gained from their own life experience, the development of skills necessary for acting on their own behalf, and the acquisition of knowledge about themselves and their environment. These processes result in a person's feeling better about her/himself, having a greater sense of her/his own value, and feeling more self-confident. The combination of a stronger positive self-concept and the skills and knowledge to deal more effectively with one's environment increase a person's sense of being able to have some control over that environment and thus to act accordingly.

Over time, as a person's concept of her/himself changes, her/his perceptions of others and of the world also change. As a result of these changed perceptions and increased skills combined with joining others to take a group action, people will begin to act more powerfully, by taking more control and responsibility in all levels of their social world. (Vanderslice, 1983)

We now move from the theoretical, conceptual and experimental base of Organizational Development to practical applications in educational settings. The primary goal is to acquire the necessary knowledge on which to base an informed assessment of the present in the light of development towards future requirements. Giving a priority in terms of time to this process is not something which the teaching profession has demanded. More often the profession has been faced with imposed decisions and expected to cope with the practice in the best possible way. School populations increase and decrease, subject specialities acquire and lose status, examination systems are changed. Educational planning appears to be erratic, almost whimsical, and does not enshrine the fundamental principle that educational planning is planning an education worth having.

In order to plan effectively we need to acquire knowledge and communicate effectively with our professional colleagues. Organizational Development provides some pointers towards what is involved in the process of effective communication.

1   *Clarity of communication*   is essential to school effectiveness. It opens up channels between ourselves and our colleagues, between ourselves and the community. If we can dare to communicate with less reserve and increasing objectivity then we can:

2   *Establish clear goals*   The range of the educational needs is as diverse as the different levels and abilities of the children we teach and the institutions created to meet them. Goals can therefore be diffuse; recognition of this pluralism can lead to definitions which will not deny differences but emphasize integration and the shared ownership of a common goal. Warnock has prescribed integration; we need to feel included in, and committed to, the process of achieving this goal. This will involve a courageous and calm acceptance of:

3   *Conflict*   If we are to communicate effectively and commit ourselves to defining goals we will expose a conflict of interests between individuals, departments and institutions within the system. There are techniques for the management of conflict and for the positive use of the human energy involved. This requires a better understanding and experience of:

4   *Group process*   Most of the management of the life of schools is done through the working together of groups. Yet the

instrumental importance of the group and the time spent in group activity of varying sorts is disproportionate to the limited knowledge of group dynamics. The non-productivity of termly or yearly staff meetings is an example. The task-directed group at all levels has excellent potential. The bad experiences of the teaching profession in collaborative group effectiveness has minimized this resource and limited the interest in schools to address, and build on, its own adaptability and success in:

5 *Solving problems* Problems exist when there is a difference between what is happening in the present, and a preferred target. The degree of difference indicates the size of the problem. The present in many schools would indicate problems of truancy, sullen alienation, lack of resources. At this point I could almost leave the page blank and ask you to fill in your own. The technique involved here is, first, to stop running long enough to identify problems and to find a mutuality amongst colleagues as to which of many to deal with first. This means being open to consensus in:

6 *Making decisions* Here I would briefly mention the power of inclusive process. We have all experienced the lack of commitment to a decision which has been made by an exclusive few and which affects a whole school. Whatever our status, we avoid the more demanding process of consultation; yet the rewards are great, both in the creation of an effective learning environment and in personal satisfaction for the majority of our colleagues.

Since Organizational Development was tested initially in the world of business, it is useful to ask the question: how do schools compare with business?

	Business	*Education*
1	Clear goal — make a profit	Diffuse goals: instruction, socialization, control? Towards what end?
2	Accountability — to a Board of Directors	Accountability to the public in general — government, parents, industry — low-risk taking short-term planning.
3	Business requires collaboration	Schools attract people who have high autonomy needs. There is less requirement for collaboration.
4	Business is less secure	Schools are a refuge for those who are security orientated. There is more inbreeding from the classroom through to the school administration.

| 5 | Business looks to constantly increase its market | Schools exist in a decreasing market. |

(Derr and De Long, 1982)

However schools differ from business, neither can safely be bundled into a single image for comparison. Yet the future for both has a shared enemy at their gates — the enemy without. For both, external pressures will directly cause internal change; neither will escape economic and political forces. If we relate these external pressures directly to education they look like this:

1 Falling rolls will close schools, make staff redundant, endanger the quality of educational provision;
2 Demand for greater accountability will require new evaluations of school competence and educational outcomes. These will occupy the centre stage of public scrutiny;
3 External groups, parents, industry, politicians are already important and their desire to collaborate, if frustrated, could become a need to dictate.

The Swedish Programme: School Leader Education

Objectives

There were two main and interconnected objectives. The first was to make changes at a local level and institute developments in each of the schools represented. This aimed, with a wise sense of present educational difficulties, at obtaining a better balance between education for achievement and education for co-existence. The second objective was to develop the function of the school leader (in this programme it was the headteacher), and it was expected that more effective functioning in a leadership role would result from participation in the programme.

The Programme

The programme had three separate components:
1 *The course period.* This was a period of twenty-five days over two years, concentrated into blocks of two to four days. These

periods were called 'course summation' periods and aimed at enabling participants to acquire a deeper understanding of the working process of their own school and of their role as the leader of that school. During these meetings the group as a whole comprised no more than thirty and was broken down into smaller analytical groups of five or six. Each of these smaller groups was devised to contain a variety of school backgrounds.

2   *The home period.*   During the home period the main thrust of the work was observation and analysis of the working process of the schools represented. Consultation between programme staff and participants in formulating assignments for use during the home period took place during the course period. Links were also made with others involved in the local areas and study circles were devised involving school leaders, district administrators and local politicians. The subjects for discussion in these local groups were chosen by the circle in the locality.

3   *The society-orientated period.*   In 1976 the Swedish Government decided that school leaders should receive some practical, society-orientated experience. This was built into the scheme and comprised two, two-week periods. In the first period the participants worked in an industry typical of their local area. This aimed at helping school leaders to acquire a real knowledge of the conditions under which parents work and which the young people would meet when they left school. The second period involved working with a branch of the local child and youth welfare services. This was expected to facilitate more effective cooperation between all the agencies in the locality working with children (Swedish Leadership Programme, 1977).

The American Programme

Objectives

The goal of the American Programme was, first, to enable the participants to define their role as principals of New York City elementary schools, and to explore differing leadership styles. Secondly, it was designed to help individuals operate within that defined role in a manner best suited to their particular style of leadership. A third goal was to explore the concept of the educational leader as a humanistic change agent. There were eleven training objectives (Klopf *et al.*, 1979) which included an assessment of the individual schools, including staff competencies and the processes of staff development. There was also a specific focus on effective cooperation with parents and the wider community.

The Programme

1 To analyze each school's situation in cooperation with programme staff and participating peers.
2 Participant competencies within their defined roles were analyzed by programme staff and other programme participants.
3 To identify school problems leading to the formulation of school objectives for one year at a time.

There are some interesting differences between the programmes in Sweden and New York and that in Cardiff. All three programmes involved teachers continuing to work in their normal roles yet engaged in a structured analysis of the problems of their individual schools. In all three schemes the participants had autonomy over what was included in the analysis and the first priority was consultation with their own colleagues. The Swedish programme had the very interesting society-orientated aspect which engaged the cooperation and involvement of the wider community. The American programme placed a firmer emphasis on an analysis of individual participants. An awareness of self, attitudes, values, aims and competence was seen as the first and most important step, since a more complete understanding of self was seen as essential to better performance in the role as school leader. The process of increasing personal and professional self-awareness was seen as a developmental model for staff colleagues.

An Experiential Training Programme

The latest source of influence was an experiential training programme for educational leaders published by the Centre for Urban Education at the University of Nebraska (Barr *et al.*, 1980). The programme was aimed at senior management in American schools and drew on material already proven to be successful to develop new ideas interrelating theory and practice. Again, the focus was leadership in schools, but the definition of leadership in this context was specific:

> ... leadership is a function of group process. A leader does not exist apart from some group; therefore it is impossible to

describe an ideal leader or to isolate traits which leaders possess. One leads because particular groups have particular needs in particular environments. (Barr *et al.*, 1980)

The leadership skills presented were not to be seen as an end in themselves but related to improving the learning of students. The orientation of this programme seemed particularly useful since it was clearly aiming at what was termed the 'missing ingredient' in other programmes and which was a fundamental principle of my work with school colleagues: the principle that the day-to-day reality of accomplishing tasks effectively and efficiently would be seen in the context of the numerous other demands of the daily life of a school. The training programme had ten modules: Communication, Time Management, Constructive Stress, Small Group Decision-Making, Planning, Structuring and Conducting Large Group Meeting, Institutional Problem-Solving, Diversity: Cultural, Racial and Sexual, School/Community Involvement, Creating Observation Instruments and Self-Evaluation.

The Cardiff Programme

The experience of working for the past four years on an action/research programme aimed at making institutions change has echoed the suggestion of Georgiades and Phillimore (1982):

> Organizational change that is to be permanent is a lengthy business and results cannot be achieved hastily. Currently it is estimated that 3−5 years are needed for fundamental change in commercial or industrial organizations. There is no reason to believe that hospitals or schools would be any more amenable to change.

The School-Based Studies are conceptually the most exciting element in the Cardiff programme and potentially the most amenable to future development. Giving colleagues in school the framework within which to do an objective analysis of their individual school's problems was a primary aim of the programme. This has meant presenting the technology of the social sciences to experienced teachers, and supporting the development of the instruments for data collection and data analysis which are seen as the most suitable and acceptable to course participants and their school colleagues.

The School-Based Study is an exercise in which an attempt is made to more clearly understand the institutional framework of the school. In common with all other institutions within society, a school has structures and systems. The aims of these structures and systems should be the creation of the best environment within which the most effective education of the child takes place. I use the word 'education' here in its most universal sense.

The British education provision presents us with a variety of institutional frameworks intended to meet the needs of a variety of children at different levels of development and attainment. Using the words 'structures' and 'systems' may create the impression that we are attempting to understand something detached from the individuals within. I would emphasize that it is the individuals who create, operate and affect the structures and systems, and there is value in exploring the operational realities of the structures and systems within one school.

The people are always more important than the system. The statement, 'schools make a difference', is part of the educational research literature. Each individual school makes a difference to its professional staff and its clients. The School-Based Study provides a valuable opportunity for objective assessment.

The Guidelines for the School-Based Study

1 Decide on the school where you would like to base your study.
2 Decide on one aspect of the institution which you would like to investigate. The considerations affecting your choice should be your own professional judgment about the insights an in-depth investigation of a particular aspect will bring to your future professional expertise.
3 Discuss your choice with programme staff.
4 Approach the school to obtain permission and cooperation.
5 Discuss your choice with the headteacher and colleagues in the school — the School-Based Study should be of value to that school and be available as a working paper for discussion and possible action.
6 Development in consultation with programme staff of data collection procedures minimizes the amount of disruption to staff and school — many staff colleagues are allergic to questionnaires and you may prefer to work from records already available at the school.

7 Analyze and interpret the data in the light of any literature available — it would be useful at this point to share your interpretation with the school.

8 A useful conclusion would be the formulation of action alternatives.

9 Give a copy of the completed assignment to the school and ask them to comment.

The School-Based Study is the first stage in a complete problem solving process (see Figure 1). School-Based Studies which have been completed have covered a variety of topics:

1 Background information on pupil intake and catchment area;
2 Structural information on hierarchies, communication, pastoral organization and sanction systems;
3 Statistical information on the nature and extent of behaviour problems and learning difficulties, absenteeism, truancy and examination results;
4 Evaluation of the curriculum, of school support agencies, of school ethos and of the process of instituting change;

Figure 1 The Process of Problem-Solving

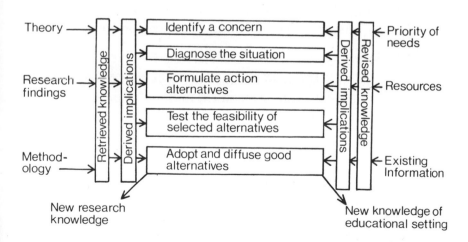

Source: Fox *et al.* (1973).

5 Studies of the stress element for staffs of both comprehensive and special schools;

6 Investigations of remedial provision, of involvement of parents as partners in the education process;

7 Exploration of transition processes between all types of schools.

All these studies have followed the model faithfully, at least as far as the third stage in the central process — 'Formulate action alternatives'. In other studies the process has included stages 4 and 5 — 'Test and select alternatives; 'Adopt and diffuse good alternatives'. The following School-Based Studies relate to children:

1 Identification and 'treatment' of the large number of pupils in the 'grey' area who have reading problems — setting up a withdrawal system;

2 Unsatisfactory transfer situation from junior to secondary and serious mistakes in grouping pupils because of limited information supplied by junior schools has been changed;

3 A weekly check on all Form 4 registers to follow up truancy. Home visits are being made to parents who cannot be reached by telephone;

4 Merit certificates are being awarded to first and second year pupils as recognition of effort and achievement;

5 A compact course for the non-academic sixth form (to supplement a diet of re-sits) has been introduced;

6 An effort has been made to provide greater stability for the lower school — less commuting of staff between sites.

The following School-Based Studies relate to staff:

1 Greater staff communication: meetings; working parties;

2 Developing the role of the form tutor — to promote greater pastoral commitment;

3 As a result of the involvement of colleagues in the School-Based Study (inclusion) there will be in-service courses for colleagues to diffuse information;

4 An improvement in the back-up facilities necessary to improve resource-based learning;

5 Closer liaison between heads of English and mathematics and special education staff;

6 Working party to develop assessment techniques beyond the exam mark/formal school report.

Organizational Development in the context of the school offers a process but not, I hope, the restrictions of a straightjacket. Individual differences in a personal and institutional sense are powerful determinants of action. However, we share common problems in working within a social unit of individuals with a specialized function.

The following list includes some ideas that have arisen from Organizational Development theory and research in relation to schools and which are worthy of discussion among colleagues:

1   The more *influence* staff members see themselves having, the more positively they regard staff meetings;
2   *Inclusion* has a positive advantage;
3   *Exclusion* breeds discontent;
4   In most schools teachers *consult* the headteacher to get help with acquiring teaching materials, clarifying attendance procedures and matters of discipline;
5   Teachers *consult* with fellow teachers on curriculum planning, classroom organization and teaching methodology;
6   Staff who feel *influential* in school decision-making more often are involved in professional innovating;
7   Staff who view their headteacher as *influential* are more likely to innovate;
8   Staff who do not feel pressured are more likely to *innovate*;
9   Most teachers want to have more decision-making *power* than they have;
10   Staff who feel *influential* with their colleagues are less alienated from the school;
11   When the headteacher and staff perceive the school's priorities in the same way they are likely to *collaborate* effectively;
12   In schools where the communication system maximizes dissemination, teachers *innovate* and share more than in schools with a hierarchical communication structure. (Watson, 1967)

I have experienced the value of a developmental model for the practitioner. It provides a passage towards a goal but not a corridor with only room for one. It involves defining, testing and refining individual and institutional aims. It has the security of observation and analysis of the here and now. It is not limited temporally but implies progression.

However, the evaluation of problems and the devising of change strategies is only part of the problem-solving process. Instituting actual change is the satisfactory completion. Again the guidelines of Georgiades and Phillimore (1982) are relevant: 'often the best supporters of innovation and change are among the ranks of people just below the top where personal commitment to the present is less and where the drive for achievement may be higher than at the top.' Certainly it seems true that autonomy in a small, closely defined area of school life is the most conducive environment for change.

Colleagues following the programme suggest that minor changes which are generally superficial are achieved, whereas more major change involving upheaval gets no further than the headteacher's office, where it is appreciated but not operationalized. They do, however, highlight important achievements which are more informal; their journal, their work and their advice is sought and feeds into many appropriate decision-making parts in the school. Their ability to contribute is recognized by colleagues, but that this specific contribution must melt into the general foray seems clear.

Hargreaves (1982) has recently asked whether teachers are to remain the relatively passive and acquiescent body of men and women on whom yet further problems are to be unloaded. The experience of working with individuals to promote school development would suggest that the answer is negative. Individual programme participants are neither acquiescent nor passive, although the passivity and acquiescence of the school staff as a corporate body seems clear. It is the cooperative model that needs building. Our basic institutions, including our schools, are caught up in endless crises. I would suggest to our profession that each crisis is in fact a missed opportunity.

References

BARR, D., ELMES, R. and WALKER, B. (1980) *Educational Leadership for In-School Administrators*, Centre for Urban Education, University of Nebraska.

BURNS, J.C., KLOPF, G.J., SCHELCLAN, E.S. and BLAHL, S.M. (1975) *Report of the Program for the Development of theElementary School Principal as an Educational Leader*, Bank Street College of Education.

COPED (1965) *The Co-operative Project for Educational Development*, US Office of Education, Project No. 1603.

DERR, B.C. and DE LONG, J.T. (1982) 'What business management can teach schools', in GRAY, H.L. (Ed.) *The Management of Educational Institutions*, Lewes, Falmer Press.

EKHOHM, M. (1977) *School Leader Education in Sweden*, Report No. 1, Linkoping, Sweden.

FOX, S., SCHMUCK, R., VAN EGMOND, E., RITVO, M. and JUNG, C. (1973) *Diagnosing the Professional Climate of Schools*, Virginia, NTL Learning Resources Corp.

GEORGIADES, N.J. and PHILLIMORE, L. (1982) *The Myth of the Hero-Innovator and Alternative Strategies for Organization Change*, (mimeo).

HARGREAVES, D.H. (1967) *Social Relations in a Secondary School*, London, Routledge and Kegan Paul.

HARGREAVES, D.H. (1982) *The Challenge for the Comprehensive School*, London, Routledge and Kegan Paul.

LEWIN, K. (1948) *Resolving Social Conflict — Selected Papers on Group Dynamics*, Harper and Row.

LEWIN, K. (1951) *Field Theory in Social Sciences: Selected Theoretical Papers*, Harper and Row.

VANDERSLICE, G. (1983) *Communication for Empowerment*, Ithaca, N.Y., Cornell University Media Services.

WATSON, G. (Ed.) (1967), *Change in School Systems*, Virginia, NTL Learning Resource Corporation.

Pathways to Institutional Development in Secondary Schools[1]

Derek Phillips, Ronald Davie and Eileen Callely

As the findings reported in this chapter come directly from the evaluation of a part-time in-service course for teachers, it is essential, first, to give a general background to the course, its aims and some of its philosophies. These are described briefly and in outline only, and form the first part of the chapter.

The Course

In 1978 a rather special and, as far as we were aware, innovative course was set up in the Department of Education, University College, Cardiff. It was supported by the three local education authorities in the area and some of its principal features were to be the following:

1   It would address behaviour problems and learning difficulties occurring in secondary schools. (At that time, not all secondary schools in the area were comprehensives.)
2   It would be equivalent to a one-year, full-time course. Participating teachers would enrol for a BEd or MEd degree, or for an Advanced Diploma. (In fact, no one yet has enrolled for the Diploma.)
3   The taught part of the course would last for two years, but for the large majority of the teachers the course would spread over three years. Candidates for first degrees would be normally required to undertake a rather general Part 1 of the BEd in their first year, then would join their higher degree colleagues for the more specialized Part 2, which was the course proper. MEd candidates would be expected to complete their dissertations in their third year.

4 The course would require the teachers to attend the university for one afternoon and evening session each week of the term. The teachers were to be released from their schools by the local authorities for the afternoon sessions.

5 It was envisaged that local authority advisers and educational psychologists would be called upon to assist in the course work. It was expected that they would become involved in lectures and seminars, but perhaps their most important task would be localized 'field' support for the participating teachers when they were preparing to carry out empirical work in the form of 'School-Based Studies' in their own schools. (We shall discuss these studies later).

6 Considerable attention would be paid to institutional change, staff development and school-based in-service training. These would be crucial and integral elements of the course.

7 It was made clear to all concerned that the main objective of the course would not be the professional development of the teachers who would attend. The intention was that, through the participating teachers, the schools involved would be helped to understand, assess and respond to those problems they judged to be chronic, most urgent, or most amenable to immediate intervention. Thus, the participating teachers were to be seen as 'links' between the course and their schools, and as 'change agents', rather than course members in the conventional mould.

8 It was appreciated that selection of teachers who would participate in the course was of critical importance. It was considered that the person chosen should be someone with formal authority and responsibility in the school, probably within its pastoral system. Because of the aims of the course, it was hoped that the person selected (initially by the headteacher, then agreed by the local authority and the course staff) would be one whose judgment was trusted not only by the head, but also the rest of the management team and by other colleagues at all levels in the school. It was envisaged that his/her role would be to have a catalytic function, and this would need to be appreciated by colleagues. The person who would participate in the course would, hopefully, be a rather special teacher.

9 With funding from the Welsh Office, the course was to be monitored and evaluated by two full-time associates of the research director, who is one of the co-authors of this

chapter. He was also, it should be pointed out, the course director.

The results of the evaluation presented here are just a small part of the complete report presented to the Welsh Office, and they cover two specific areas: the pathways into the school process which we found were available to course members, and some of the characteristics of the teachers who were able, directly or indirectly, to bring about institutional developments in their schools. The two areas are related.

The Evaluation

The task of the research team was to monitor and evaluate any change or development which occurred in the participating teachers and their schools, and which could be attributed to the course. Stated simply, the remit of the team was to find out if, and to what extent, the course was successful in achieving its objectives.

It is not intended to dwell upon the methodology adopted; however, so that the findings presented here may be seen to have validity, it is necessary to outline the research design.

Basic Assumptions

We assumed that, if the course were to reach and ultimately modify the behaviours of pupils that were of concern to the schools (truancy, disruptive and anti-social behaviour, vandalism, low motivation and high disaffection levels, poor educational standards and general underfunctioning), this would be done through the participating teacher to his/her colleagues at the school, into the school system and thence to the behaviours of the pupils. This could be seen as a 'knock-on' effect but, en route, there would be interactions amongst all the elements which, themselves, could lead to change at various levels. The original model by which we visualized these 'paths to change' is represented diagrammatically in Figure 1.

It will be appreciated that this model is not inclusive of all the interactions which may be possible, and other elements could be added to it, for example, other agencies such as the police, the social services, advisers, psychologists, and the pupils' parents. But the model illustrates our thinking early on in the research project and

Derek Phillips, Ron Davie and Eileen Callely

Figure 1. Original Model Representing Basic Assumptions of Paths to
    Change

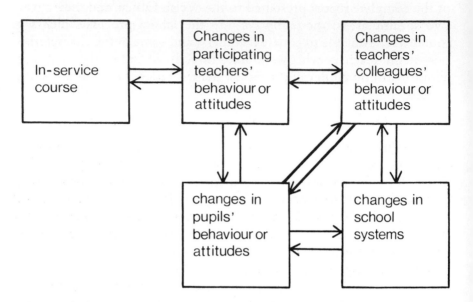

allows an indication of the threads from the course to prospective
pupil behavioural change which we intended to unravel.

A Mixed Strategy

In the unravelling, we would be required to validate each change or
development. We were to do this by a mixed strategy of the
quantification of data (where this was possible) and an ethnographic
approach of finely structured interviews in the schools. (See Phillips
and Callely, 1982, for a full explanation of this 'mixed methodology'.)
    We combined the quasi-experimental research design (Hamilton
et al., 1977) and the illuminative-evaluation model (Parlett and
Hamilton, 1972) because we felt it vital not only to identify *if* change
had occurred (or not), but also to examine, analyze and report change
processes where this was possible. To do so, we avoided the purely
descriptive account of what we believed had happened, and reported
only that which was substantiated, or shared, by many of the
teachers' colleagues in their schools, or other outside agencies, as well
as being corroborated by other factual data.'

To validate the specific findings revealed in this chapter, we used the technique of multiple-data triangulation (see Bynner, 1979; Schwartz and Kaplan, 1981). Through this, we cross-checked perceptions and statements of one person, taken from different sources, against those of others. We were interested only in those developments that could be reliably and validly attributed to the course.

The Schools and the Participating Teachers

The Schools

The original hope of the course staff was that each of the schools in the three local authorities would have been represented by one of its teachers at the end of a four-year period, with thirty teachers to each cohort. The research covers the first two cohorts. Over this period fifty-two teachers registered for the course. Nine dropped out for various reasons, leaving forty-three teachers; but because of duplications of teachers from some of the schools, we were able to investigate fully thirty-eight schools.

The teachers were not deliberately selected from schools with the most difficulties, or where there had already been demonstrated a considered response to their problems, or from schools which had particularly disadvantaged catchment areas, or upon any other specific criterion, although the aim of the course director was for a reasonably balanced intake. Using data easily available from the Welsh Office, we examined some of the characteristics of the schools in the first cohort and found that they did not differ statistically from the rest of the schools in the three authorities. The variables used for this comparison were: Burnham group (that is, the size of the school in pupil number); the number of pupils taking free meals; the number of pupils providing their own meals; attendance figures, and pupil-teacher ratio.

The Teachers

We have mentioned above that some schools sent more than one teacher to the course, so, although our sample consisted of thirty-eight schools, these were represented by forty-three teachers.

It was the original aim that teachers in relatively senior positions should attend the course because of the 'link' and 'change agent' roles which were envisaged for them. The sample of teachers we investigated reflects this. Table 1 shows the number of teachers in the various hierarchy positions in the schools they represented.

Table 1.   Position in School of Course Members

Position	Number	(Percentage)
Headteachers	5	(12)
Deputy heads (including one academic registrar)	15	(35)
Heads of school (i.e., upper, middle or lower)	13	(30)
Year tutors	7	(16)
Head of house	1	(2)
Careers teacher	1	(2)
Teacher in charge of special class/unit	1	(2)
	43	

Also reflected in this pattern of seniority were the ages of the teachers. Thirty of them (70 per cent) were over 40 years of age. In the group, there were thirty-four men (79 per cent) and nine women (21 per cent).

The teachers were required to write, each year, self-report essays on personal, colleague, institutional and pupil change. Every week they submitted Course Journals, occasionally writing on the various developments taking place. They also presented their School-Based Study as an academic piece of work; this was done in their first year on the course, and usually took the form of a small-scale empirical study carried out by them in their own schools. From all these sources, and from our periodic visits to the schools, we amassed a considerable amount of information which formed the base for the multiple-data triangulation check by which we were to validate each of the supposed developments and trace the strands of the interactive model shown in Figure 1. We did so through our structured interviews with members of the school staff well placed to confirm or refute any changes or developments reported by course members or their colleagues.

The Results Related to Pathways of Development

A Developing Model

Even while we were gathering the data we were becoming increasingly aware that the quite elaborate model we had basically assumed would operate was insufficiently complex to describe the 'Paths to Change' which had been formed. For example, we found that the original model had not stressed the importance of the considerable influence of course member upon course member. This was clearly shown by the number of times we uncovered new developments in the pastoral system, the curriculum, etc., which had been cross-fertilized from one school to another via course members. We also found that the research itself was having an effect upon both the course members and their colleagues in the schools. The latter was the result of our visits to the schools and our conversations with members of staff. In this way we were, if doing nothing else, heightening their awareness of what the course signified and what their colleague, the course member, was trying to do.

The 'investigator effect' has thrown many an experimentally-based methodology into disarray (if not the dust-bin!). But we were aware, from the start, that it was likely our research would affect some aspects of the course outcome. We had attempted to insulate the research as much as possible and to optimize objectivity in the research associates by deciding not to be drawn in to giving advice to the teachers or acting as 'consultants' to the schools. However, this attempt proved increasingly difficult and even counterproductive, as far as our own relationships with the course members and their schools were concerned.

The course members were persistent in their approaches to us to find out exactly who we were and why we sat, scribbling at the back of the lecture room, or listened-in to their seminar conversations, or asked if we may look at the current Course Journal (one member of the course christened us the KGB!). In addition, we found that their colleagues in the schools had a need to talk to us about the course, so we felt, if we were inevitably to 'contaminate' by our very presence and the nature of our procedures, then we had better know exactly what contamination we were spreading. We decided to systematically record those circumstances where we believed, or knew, that we had acted as change agents ourselves. As Powdermarker (1967) remarks, 'Conscious involvements are not a handicap for the social scientist. Unconscious ones are always dangerous.' In addition, we recognized that some course members had used outside agents in attempting some form of development in the school. Most importantly, however, we found that there were different avenues of approach, different 'pathways' to change, which were being followed by different course members, not only to those outside agents whose aid had been enlisted, as might be expected, but also *within* the school system itself.

Pathways to Development

While we identified the 'pathways', we also found that they did not always lead to new developments in the schools. Occasionally, 'blocks' would occur, it seemed, along the strands and the potential changes would go no further. To use a neurological terminology, there seemed to be 'synapses' along each thread. Given the appropriate 'excitators', the pathways would be open and the developments flowed forward. Without these, or with the blocking presence of 'inhibitors', the potential died. Some of the facilitators and blocks to change found by us are discussed below. One of the first things we wished to do, however, was visually to represent the developing model. Figure 2 shows a diagramatic representation of these pathways to potential change. The cusps along each line signify potential synapses that have to be bridged, perhaps by motivating factors that may overcome antipathy to change rather than harnessing forces to operate against active 'blockers', before the development is complete. It must be stressed here that Figure 2 is not a theoretical model but is, rather, a schematic representation of what we found, from our observation and interviews, had actually happened in the schools.

There are two significant features to consider in Figure 2. First, there is the bilaterality which follows the arrows from 'Course'. The pathways used seemed to depend upon the position in the school of the teacher participating in the course. It was clear that the group of teachers on the left of the diagram (headteachers and heads of schools, or heads of sections as they are sometimes called) had used direct pathways not only to other course members on the right and to colleagues in their schools and the pupils, but also to 'School Process'. That is, they had direct access to potential institutional developments. In contrast, the pathways used by 'Course Members — Others' (these were deputy heads, year tutors, careers and special unit teachers) had no direct approach to 'School Process' but reached it through 'Colleagues' and — more often — the 'Headteacher'.

The second feature of the model is that all the contacts between teachers and educational psychologists we were able to confirm were to and from headteachers or heads of school. On the other hand, contacts with education welfare officers and police were via deputies and 'others'.

Figure 2. Model of Pathways of Communication Which Influence Development in
         Secondary Schools

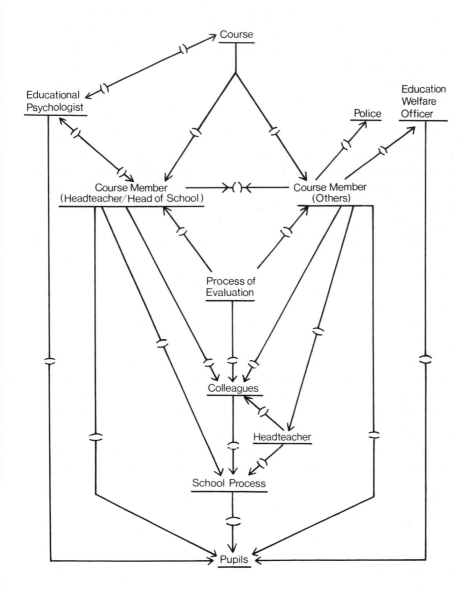

The Status of the Teachers

The taught part of the course was intended to input identically to each member, whether graduate or non-graduate. We found that there was a statistically significant change of attitude to pupils with behaviour problems amongst non-graduates, but that this was not so with the graduates. So, it seems unlikely that the course was the cause of the bilaterality shown in the model, for the majority of the deputy heads (twelve out of fifteen) were already graduates, and so were many of the other teachers who used the pathways on the right of the diagram in Figure 2. It did appear, then, that the pathways the teachers followed depended upon the position in the school of the participating teacher. Perhaps it was not the *level* of status in the hierarchy of the school which dictated which pathway to institutional change would be used, but the *quality* of status of the teacher, represented by his/her power as the head of an autonomous unit.

We quantified the type and number of institutional developments directly or indirectly initiated by the teachers in our sample and found that twenty-six of the forty-three reported verifiable changes. (In passing, it may be of interest to note that we found a total of ninety-six institutional developments in the represented schools that could be validly attributed to the effects of the course.)

Certainly, change could be achieved through either route. This was exemplified when we considered the positions of the twenty-six teachers in the schools where developments had taken place, compared with those of the seventeen teachers where no developments were verifiable. Table 2 shows our analysis of this characteristic.

Table 2. *Teacher's Position in School and Institutional Development in School*

| | Position in school | | | | |
	Head	Deputy	Head of school	Other	Total
Institutional development	5 (100)	8 (53)	8 (62)	5 (50)	26 (60)
No institutional development	0 (0)	7 (47)	5 (38)	5 (50)	17 (40)
	5 (100)	15 (100)	13 (100)	10 (100)	43 (100)

Note: Percentages are shown in brackets.

We also looked at the number of developments *directly* or *indirectly* attributable to the teachers whose hierarchy positions are shown in Table 2. Table 3 shows this analysis, with average number of developments for each position.

Table 3. Teacher's Position in School and Number of Institutional Developments (with averages)

	Head (n=5)	Deputy (n=8)	Head of school (n=8)	Other (n=5)
Total number of institutional developments	28	30	30	8
Average (rounded)	6	4	4	2

At this level of analysis, both Tables 2 and 3 seem to indicate a trend related to the seniority, or position, of the teacher. But another variable we examined was the number of those teachers who were *directly* responsible for initiating the developments in their schools, linking them with their positions in the schools.

As far as those course members who were heads were concerned, quite naturally it was relatively easy to trace the movement back to their hand on the tiller. But in none of the cases of institutional change reported to us, and which we were able to validate, was there a single instance of the developments being 'actioned' by a deputy headteacher. On the other hand, of the thirty developments which occurred in the eight schools represented by heads of schools, nineteen came directly from these teachers. (Sometimes the changes were made not only without prior consultation with the head but also without his knowledge after the event.)

In every case we were able to validate these changes as having come from the course in some way. But by no means was it always the participating teacher who took the final decisions which led to the developments we verified. Whereas this may be readily accepted in the cases of the year tutors, and the other, relatively junior, teachers, it is perplexing that none of the deputies took the final decision.

It must be stressed that as many developments happened in schools represented by deputies as occurred in schools where heads of schools were the representatives. (This is clearly shown in both Tables 2 and 3.) We could say, then, that the deputies were at least as effective in producing change, by indirect routes, as heads of schools were by both routes. But deputy heads 'outrank' heads of schools, so far as status is concerned. The interesting fact was that the heads of school were able to equal (and exceed so far as percentage is concerned) the superior-positioned deputy heads in initiating institutional developments. It seems to us that either the nature of the responsibilities of a deputy, or the limited extent of his/her autonomy (the 'quality' of the power), or perhaps his/her traditional way of functioning, is different from that of a head of school.

We believe that what the pathways in Figure 2 suggest is that direct access to the school process is either not available to the deputies, or is not the route they normally take. It may be politic for them not to take the direct route to the heart of the system. It follows that it may be a truism to state that part of our model represents the job of a deputy: to deputize. So, it may be expected that all action affecting the school which emanates from a deputy head would be politically filtered through the headteacher and would then seem to come from that position. If that is so, then our findings support it.

A question might be asked, however, about the prudence of a management system that did not allow, encourage or actively develop in teachers with the status of a deputy head, who might well be required to act in place of the head with little forewarning and for extended periods, some greater autonomy of action than was evidenced by our evaluation of initiatives directly taken by them. It would seem to be sensible, if only in terms of their training as future heads, to allow them greater flexibility of role, greater possibilities of direct action, and a wider remit in regard to the school processes than seemed to be revealed by our findings. Of course, our sample is small. Of the fifteen deputies, we found verifiable developments in schools represented by only eight of them. But our results do seem to highlight the need for an examination of the role of the deputy head, either generally or in particular schools.

As far as the second form of bilaterality is concerned — contacts with 'outside agents' — we are unable to explain definitely why heads and heads of schools interact with educational psychologists (and deputies and 'others' on this course did not) and why the 'Others' interacted with education welfare officers and the police. We suspect that these may be traditional routes of contact, perhaps emanating from the quality of the autonomy residing in the various positions. On the other hand, both sorts of contact occurred so infrequently that it could have been idiosyncratic to these course members.

Other Teacher Characteristics

We looked at a number of other variables besides the teacher's position in the school, in association with institutional development:

The sex of the teacher;

Age (younger or older than 41 years);

Motivation for attending the course (was it self-interest before school, or was it actually to help the school develop new strategies and responses to attempt to solve its problems?).

With none of these variables was it found that there was a statistically significantly likelihood of change being associated with one group or the other.

The School-Based Study

We examined the part played in institutional development by the School-Based Study. The intention of the course staff was that this project, carried out by the teacher in his/her own school, might more clearly define the problems concerning the school and would lead to responses designed to alleviate the problems.

It was planned that schools would, in the process of carrying out the School-Based Study,

1   specifically detail the problems,
2   gather empirical evidence of the problems,
3   analyze the evidence.

It was clearly expressed that course members should enlist the support of their colleagues in the schools, explaining the purpose of the Study and should approach the investigation in a spirit of cooperation and commitment to development. (For further details on the philosophy of the School-Based Study as it was developed then applied to this course see Davie, 1980; Lewis, 1982.)

Although they were encouraged to do so, it was reported to us (and validated) that only eight of the forty-three teachers did consult their colleagues before starting the Study. Twenty-six of them did so after completing the Study. We examined the apparent effects of these 'before' and 'after' consultations upon subsequent institutional developments. Tables 4 and 5, respectively, show our findings for each condition.

Derek Phillips, Ron Davie and Eileen Callely

Table 4. Prior Consultation with Colleagues on School-Based Study and Institutional Development

| | Prior consultation | | | |
	Colleagues consulted	Colleagues not consulted	Not known or no data	Total
Institutional development	7 (88)	18 (58)	1 (25)	26 (60)
No institutional development	1 (12)	13 (42)	3 (75)	17 (40)
	8 (100)	31 (100)	4 (100)	43 (100)

Note: Percentages are shown in brackets.

Table 5. Post-School-Based Study Consultation with Colleagues and Institutional Development

| | Post-consultation | | | |
	Colleagues consulted	Colleagues not consulted	Not known or no data	Total
Institutional development	20 (77)	5 (42)	1 (20)	26 (60)
No institutional development	6 (23)	7 (58)	4 (80)	17 (40)
	26 (100)	12 (100)	5 (100)	43 (100)

Note: Percentages are shown in brackets.

There seem to be similar trends revealed by the figures in both Tables 4 and 5: that is, if colleagues are consulted, either before or after completion of the Study, there is a greater likelihood of institutional development than if they are not consulted at all. However, the fact that only eight teachers consulted their colleagues *before* their investigation demands a cautious interpretation, and the distribution is not statistically significant.

On the other hand, Table 5 does show a strong association between consultation with colleagues over the *results* of the School-Based Study and subsequent institutional development. Here, the distribution produced a significant difference between the groups (χ^2 = 4.5; 1 df; $p < 0.05$). But perhaps it was not the post-hoc consultation itself that increased the likelihood of change, but the manner in which consultation was carried out, and with whom.

It was clear to us from our many visits to the schools that the majority of the course members had not entirely adopted the cooperative strategy for the School-Based Study which had been envisaged by the course staff. The contacts we found (when we did find them) between the course members and their colleagues usually consisted of requests for information: the completion of question-naires, interviews, or the supply of numbers related to some aspect of the problems being investigated (attendance, disruptive episodes, etc). Rarely was there evidence of a cohesive attack made upon the problem via the School-Based Study that had been advocated by the course staff.

Beyond this 'surface contact', generally, the teachers in the echelons of the school system below the senior management team had little idea of why the data they were collecting for their course-attending colleague were needed. In one school, a teacher strongly objected to 'getting his degree for him' by collecting the data at all. Indeed, in some cases, even the head did not fully appreciate which aspect of the school's problems the course member was investigating.

After the event, however, when the participating teacher's research had been completed and the report written up (and many of them showed a high standard of research expertise and produced valuable insights into the problems) the whole study, or specific parts of it, with the agreement of the head, was duplicated and distributed to members of staff for their comments. Occasionally, we found evidence of a more formal display of the results, when the course member would address staff meetings and explain the implications of the findings of the research. Through these means the outcome of the Study reached groups of teachers more junior than the ones we found were briefed on the purpose of the Study, and in a much more coherent form. It would seem from our evidence that this strategy was more successful than was the type of prior consultation we had noticed.

Change in Colleagues' Behaviour

It is highly likely that the School-Based Study brought about changes in the professional behaviour of the colleagues of the course mem-bers. Certainly we found that this occurred in many cases when the Study's results were revealed to the staff. This appeared to be another facilitator operating along the pathways to change (Figure 2). It will be remembered that change in colleagues' professional behaviour was

Derek Phillips, Ron Davie and Eileen Callely

one of our theoretical 'stepping-stones' to institutional development described earlier and shown in Figure 1. What we now found was that, while it was not entirely a 'sine qua non', for there were other routes available to both types of course member by which they could reach the school process and institutional development, it did ease the way when it was present.

Continuing with the triangulation technique, we looked at the association between change of colleagues' behaviour and institutional developments. Our findings are shown in Table 6.

Table 6. *Colleagues' Change in Professional Behaviour and Institutional Development*

| | Colleagues' change | | |
	Yes	No	Total
Institutional development	24 (77)	2 (17)	26 (60)
No institutional development	7 (23)	10 (83)	17 (40)
	31 (100)	12 (100)	43 (100)

Note: Percentages are shown in brackets.

The differences between the groups shown in Table 6 are statistically highly significant ($\chi^2 = 13.38$; 1 df; $p < 0.001$). There are two inconsistent groups in this table, however: first, where 'colleague change' had been noted and validated, yet no institutional developments had been verified; second, where there was no 'colleague change' yet developments had been verified. These apparent paradoxes to the general trend could serve to indicate that we, as researchers, were attempting to identify institutional changes too early (we had to start the final evaluation relatively early in the programme to complete the research in the time available), or that we were unable to confirm — to meet the stringent criteria we were working with — that something had occurred which could be *clearly attributed* to the course. Neither of these possibilities detracts from the high level of confidence given to the association between 'colleague change' and institutional development.

Conclusions

Importance of the Head's Support

Although deputy heads and 'other' teachers (on the right side of the model in Figure 2) were found not to be able to reach the school process directly, at least not to 'action' institutional developments, approximately 50 per cent of that group did so through the head-teachers. This does not imply that the heads so involved, as had been the case with other colleagues, changed their attitudes for development to take place. In some cases this was so, but in many other instances the heads already had a clear idea of the benefits they wished to bring to the school via the attendance on the course of a particular teacher. Some of the heads set out to use the course in that way: using the course members as facilitators for change. This strategy was not always successful, due — in part — to the pathways of communication which some of the teachers were often forced to take, or were used to taking, to the school process. Where these were through colleagues and changes of professional behaviour resulted, then the potential 'synaptic gap' was bridged and changes occurred.

Some other heads used the course to enable selected teachers to gain an initial, or higher, degree. A number of these heads were antipathetic to institutional change, During our visits to these schools, it was clear that, although the course members understood their roles as 'links' between the course and the school, and as 'change agents' (they were stressed often enough on the course!), the heads did not seem to. A cry frequently picked up by us at these schools was that the participating teacher was not being 'given a platform' from which to reach colleagues on the staff.

The head's apparent lack of commitment to the agreed aims of the course was a dead hand laid upon potential change and the head him/herself became the block to development. This may have been due to a disinclination on the part of the head to initiate developments or to encourage their propagation. However, there were occasions even in those schools when, given the right 'quality' of power and the appropriate autonomy, change, initiated by heads of lower and middle schools particularly, did take place.

Nevertheless, our evaluation of the course in respect of institutional developments showed, quite clearly, the importance of the head's commitment to change in the system. Whilst there certainly were instances of change having taken place without the knowledge of the head (always via the heads of schools), in the large majority of cases the head knew exactly what was happening and ultimately facilitated the development by personal decision, or 'nodded it through'. Some heads maintained a 'watching brief' on the developments, allowing the heads of school to take the initiative within their autonomous areas of control.

Interestingly, there were some heads who felt (and expressed this to us) that there was a possibility of a 'back-lash' effect from staff if they took an active position themselves in regard to institutional developments. It was felt, by these, that an edict seen to come from the head may have been met by a passive (in some cases active) resistance from some sections of the staff. Such heads, we found, preferred to infiltrate the system with ideas of development proposed by the course member, themselves giving tacit agreement, but not outright support, until the avenue to the 'colleagues' had been firmly established. This more subtle approach casts these heads in the role of 'undercover change agents', perhaps.

Whilst both the open support and the more covert approaches were seen to work, we were not able to measure differences in effect of either. What was clear, however, was that twenty-four of the twenty-six schools which introduced developments also showed changes in the attitudes and professional behaviour of the colleagues of the participating teachers.

Change and the School-Based Study

The importance of the School-Based Studies was also evident from our evaluation. In 77 per cent of the cases where change took place (twenty schools) colleagues had been consulted after the Study had been carried out. Our findings indicate that it was likely the School-Based Study was one of the most important factors to colleague change. Our suggestion is that such a Study, based upon the school's problems, could be grafted on to other, perhaps more conventional, in-service training courses.

Deputy Heads: The Right System?

Perhaps one of the most important findings to come from our monitoring of course effects upon the participating teachers and institutional developments in their schools was the relative inability of the deputy heads to go straight to the heart of the school system and directly 'action' institutional change themselves. On the other hand, we found that approximately half of the heads of schools (lower, middle and upper) were able to do this, because — we suggest — they have greater flexibility of action and greater autonomy in their areas of responsibility. Of the total of fifteen deputies on the course in the first two cohorts, none was also head of school. Conversely, of the thirteen heads of school none was also a deputy head. The possibility is suggested that, had there been a system of dual responsibility where the heads of school were also deputy heads, then there may have been more changes in the school we monitored.

Other models for the role of the deputy head, already proposed elsewhere, could also facilitate change in the secondary school. In their discussion of alternatives Matthew and Tong (1982) mention the possibility of a number of models, two of which are echoed by our comments upon what we see as the limited effectiveness of the deputy head to directly institute change in secondary schools. They have suggested, first, that the head becomes more a consultant than at present, where the deputies take more immediate decisions; second, a more extended partnership than is currently normal, reaching beyond the senior management team, in line with the Countesthorpe system (see Watts, 1976), where the deputies will necessarily '. . . undertake a major part of the informal and formal processes of consultation and transmission of ideas and policies.'

Of course, there is a danger inherent in partnership models that the deputies will lose all defined responsibilities. But, so far as institutional development is concerned, we feel that the responsibility in many schools at present is of such a character that few deputies may be in a position to reach, directly, the school process, negating their seniority in the system and limiting the possibility that they may bring about directly actioned change.

We hope it is clear that we are not advocating the removal of the position of deputy head; it would not be possible, or advisable, to do so. In any case, we are not in a position to recommend such a radical move based upon our limited sample. What we are suggesting is that the pathways model to institutional development points to an urgent need to look critically at the role of the deputy head in the comprehensive school. What our findings further suggest is that the current activities of deputies may be hamstrung by lack of autonomous power.

Without more wide-ranging and substantial research to investigate the functional aspects of the post of deputy head in relation to the school's institutional developments, it is, perhaps, expedient to go

only a little further in our comments. What has been highlighted by
our evaluation of the course in Cardiff is that, in the post of head of
school, there resides a considerable executive responsibility. There is
a potential danger to secondary schools that, when such teachers of
high ability and long experience seek, and are promoted to, the
position of deputy head, they may be surrendering the direct
management role for an insubstantial and superficial quality of power
projected by an illusion of the status of the job of the deputy head
rather than the real weight it carries, currently, in the secondary
school's organizational system.

Notes

1 The research project described here was funded by the Welsh Office. The
  views expressed here are those of the authors and not necessarily of the
  Welsh Office.
2 This 'mixed methodology' has been commended by others in this field of
  research: see Henderson (1978); Bolam (1979).

References

BOLAM, R. (1979) *Evaluating In-Service Education and Training: A Nation-
    al Perspective*, University of Bristol.
BYNNER, J. (1979) *Research Methods in Education and the Social Sciences*,
    Open University Course D 304, Block 4, Part 1, Milton Keynes, Open
    University Press.
DAVIE, R. (1980) 'Behaviour problems in schools and school-based in-
    service training, in UPTON, G. and GOBELL, A. *Behaviour Problems in
    the Comprehensive Schools*, Faculty of Education, University college,
    Cardiff.
HAMILTON, D. *et al.* (Eds) (1977) *Beyond the Numbers Game*, Basingstoke,
    Macmillan Educational.
HENDERSON, E.S. (1978) *The Evaluation of In-Service Teacher Training*,
    London, Croom Helm.
LEWIS, J. (1982) 'Helping schools change', *Education for Development*, 7, 2,
    pp. 49–62, Faculty of Education, University College, Cardiff.
MATTHEW, R. and TONG, S. (1982) *The Role of the Deputy Head in the
    Comprehensive School*, London, Ward Lock.
PARLETT, M. and HAMILTON , D. (1972) *Evaluation As Illumination: A New
    Approach to the Study of Innovatory Programmes*, Occasional Paper
    No. 9, Centre for Research in the Educational Sciences. University of
    Edinburgh.
PHILLIPS, D.D. and CALLELY, E.M. (1982) 'Evaluating an intervention

programme: The development of a methodology', *School Organization*, 2, 3, pp. 307–19.

POWDERMARKER, H. (1967) *Stranger and Friend,* London, Secker and Warburg.

SCHWARTZ, T.A. and KAPLAN, M.H. (1981) *Operationalizing Triangulation in Naturalistic Evaluation,* paper presented at the annual meeting of the American Education Research Association, Los Angeles, 1981.

WATTS, J. (1976) 'Sharing it out', in PETERS, R.S (Ed.) *The Role of the Head,* London, Routledge and Kegan Paul.

11 Schools Make a Difference: Implications for Management in Education

Pamela Young

The theme of this chapter is that research evidence and school practice suggest schools do make a difference to pupil development. The sources of these differences, together with the ideas and strategies thrown up by research and practice, are thought to be significant for management in education.

A school is a complex dynamic institution which is constantly responding to the needs of its members and to the world outside its gates. In the past fifteen years or so, the quality of some of a school's responses has been challenged from a number of directions. In essence, the challenge has been based on research into school outcomes which suggests that 'schools bring little influence to bear upon a child's achievement that is independent of his background and general social context' (Coleman *et al.*, 1966, p. 325). The credibility given to the notion that schools do not make a difference is understandable. In the early sixties the belief was widespread that schooling could make a major contribution to the attainment of equality of educational opportunity for all pupils. Through the sixties and into the seventies, however, traditional faith in school was eroded under a series of attacks. For example, evaluations of compensatory education led, in America, to a questioning of the ability of the school to teach basic cognitive and social skills. Echoes of a similar kind of questioning can be found in the UK in the so-called 'Black Papers' (1969; 1972). The Black Papers' doubts were directed towards all sectors of the maintained school system and, unlike the American work, were not founded upon large-scale research activity. At another level, a chorus of employers, and to a much lesser extent further and higher education teachers, voiced their concern at the inability of school leavers to perform basic reading, writing and computation tasks.

This plausible, but essentially unprovable, idea about the ineffectual nature of schooling is one which has influenced public debate, first in America where much of the research has been conducted, and latterly in this country. What school critics who have participated in the debate have tended to overlook is that little or no attention has been paid (at least in the Coleman work and the replication studies) to what is going on in schools. In ignoring the process of schooling, critics have actually misrepresented the work of schools and what they try to achieve. The outcome of this misrepresentation has been to produce a distorted picture of what schools do achieve, that has attained a certain notoriety. It has been suggested (Madaus *et al.*, 1980) that if the belief persists that educational performance is the outcome solely of social and economic conditions outside the school, and is left uncorrected, it will not be difficult to foresee it becoming a self-fulfilling prophesy.

Happily in many schools and in a large number of studies published in the past fifteen years there is a considerable body of evidence to suggest that schools do make a difference to the development of their pupils. The published sources also underline the major problem of determining what it is about schools which really has a significant effect on the learning of children: the teachers or the teaching? the curriculum? leadership and followership? the resources available? or is it a complex combination of these different characteristics of pupils, the teaching, the nature of what is taught to the children, the way in which resources are used? Unhappily we do not have access to a large, immediate body of evidence which could be of assistance in resolving these questions. Such evidence is located in the schools themselves, where the time given to the practice of managing teaching and learning leaves little opportunity for the widespread dissemination of the successful ideas and strategies which they have evolved. Instead, we have to rely upon research conducted with and in a number of schools for information about school differences. Fortunately, this body of research is eclectic in terms of size of sample, theoretical context, school form and many other features. Thus it offers to those interested in the theory as well as the practice of management in education a rich source of material which has a contribution to make to the state-of-the-art of education management, if only to confirm what is already known. Some of these ideas stand out: that a school's 'climate' or 'ethos' is much more within the control of those who teach and are taught than is sometimes realized;

that skilful leadership in this matter of climate is crucial; that there are strategies whereby it is possible and practicable to plan and manage school climate (ethos) purposefully; resources and their impact on schooling — as yet we know little about teachers and the resources they select and how they use them for teaching and learning; that schools are expected to be not only vehicles for social change but also to preserve and transmit traditional values: thus schools are faced with the integration of both stability and change; and that schools are expected to be skilful not only in managing stability and change but also in effectively evaluating what they are doing. Finally, the studies throw some light on a difficult area for education management: the participation of pupils and the development of interpersonal rather than impersonal relationships between teachers and pupils. Until recently the emphasis in education management has been on teaching and non-teaching staff rather than pupils, thus difficulties can arise in terms of interpretation and strategies for, say, decision-making in schools.

The number of studies which have appeared in the past fifteen years which contribute to our understanding of the differences schools make to pupil development are many. Some have received a wider exposure than others, for a variety of reasons, notably topicality of the subject matter and pertinence for education policy-making. No attempt is made here to achieve encyclopaedic coverage of the studies or to choose them for the degree of exposure they have received in the educational process. Rather, they are selected with a bias towards the writers' work with and knowledge of schools and the way they are managed.

Educational Management

Education management has in its short lifetime been primarily concerned with research and teaching focused on the internal organization of schools and other educational institutions. For its sustenance, education management has drawn upon concepts and frameworks developed in a number of social science disciplines, notably organization theory and social psychology. Such concepts and frameworks have been variously utilized as a means of examining 'the internal operation of educational institutions, and... their relationships with their environments, that is, the communities in which they are set, and... the governing structures to which they are formally responsible' (Glatter, 1979, para. 5.3). There is no intention

in the quotation, nor elsewhere in the education management literature, to perpetuate a perhaps widely held but mistaken idea that
education management is solely concerned with techniques largely
derived from industrial and commercial settings, that operate to the
disadvantage of the educational purposes which underlie the activities
of teachers. This idea of education management probably stems from
the early 1970s when managerial approaches to the running of schools
were overly influenced by non-educational models and techniques
(planning, programming budgetary systems, management by objectives and so on). Taylor (1976) has clearly emphasized the pitfalls
awaiting those who seek to effectively manage schools with these
models and techniques alone. This is not to say, however, that
education management does not make use of techniques: it does.
Some, like curriculum development and staff deployment analyses,
have arisen within the education service itself in response to specific
contexts in educational institutions and are widely used. They are not
the subject of discussion here; rather the concern is with reports of
research that are already utilized in a number of schools.

Education management's focus on the internal organization of
educational institutions, as pointed out above, has been much influenced by a number of social science disciplines, notably sociology,
whence social systems theory has been derived. The social systems
influence has led the school to be described as an institution which
interacts with its environment and has given rise to a linear input-
output model — or theory — which attempts to explain how things
can be described in the 'real world'. The input-output model has a
seemingly seductive attraction for the researcher and educational
administrator since it is appealingly logical, rational and orderly.
Thus it has proved to be very popular for analysis of the apparent
relative effectiveness of different programmes in various educational
institutions. However, by the late 1970s it became clear that this
theoretical approach contributed little to our understanding of the
ways in which a complex, dynamic institution like a school functions, the subtle ways, for example, in which teachers and pupils
work out means of accommodating to the rules, regulations and
'ethos' of the institution. At the very least schools are institutions
made up of people who, while they may share common roles and
expectations, may implement those roles in highly individualistic
ways (Getzels, 1969). Our understanding of this phenomenon is
limited, but our need for greater knowledge here is important for
developing ideas and strategies in order to manage teaching and
learning effectively. What we do have are several theoretical models

but rather fewer practical examples (Open University, 1981) that can act as a basis for discussions and workshop activities.

School Climate and Classroom Environments

What various research studies of teaching and in schools have contributed (for example, in the primary sector, Sharp and Green, 1975; King, 1978; Galton *et al.*, 1980; Galton and Simon 1980; Galton and Willcocks, 1983; and in the secondary sector, Lacey, 1970; Reynolds, 1976; Rutter, 1979; Ball, 1981; Turner, 1983) to education management's understanding of schools and the behaviour of people in them, is to focus and sharpen our attention on what actually goes on in them. Thus, our attention is directed towards on examination of the inner workings of that system we call a school organization. The studies require us to look carefully at school processes, to study afresh the relationships between human behaviour and the contexts characteristic of the organization. The last is what Rutter *et al.* (1979, p. 183) call the 'school's ethos',[1] culture or pattern, which tends to develop in any relatively self-contained organization. Rutter, in raising the issue of 'school ethos', highlights an issue of particular interest to practitioners of the art of education management — the realizable nature of school values and norms and the degree to which they are consistent throughout the school, and the extent to which children as well as staff accept them. Rutter is careful to point out that schools have a choice in the norms they select; they are neither random nor dictated from outside. He and his co-workers go beyond this significant statement about a school's ability to choose its norms to suggest what the chief mechanisms are likely to be:

1 teacher expectation about the children's work and behaviour;
2 the models provided by the teachers' own conduct in school, and by the behaviour of the other pupils; and
3 the feedback that the children receive on what is acceptable performance at the school. (Rutter *et al.*, 1979, p. 187)

Rutter's observations further suggest that it appears to be helpful for there to be some kind of consensus on how school life should be organized and for the accepted set of norms to be applied consistently throughout the school. These ideas of Rutter and his colleagues about a 'school's ethos', as presented in *Fifteen Thousand Hours*, are by no means new, as two North Americans, Halpin (1956) and Likert

(1961), have demonstrated, but they are none the worse for being restated by Rutter *et al.* Their importance perhaps lies in the attention they draw to a number of issues:

1   describing and defining what is meant by the term 'school ethos';
2   going some way to measuring the climate of a cohort of schools;
3   raising the issue of the relationship between school ethos and the effectiveness of schools; and
4   the vital issue: do we have the means by which we can deliberately create planned organizational ethos in our schools?

In raising the issue of school ethos, they add to our state-of-the-art concepts and knowledge and underline the importance of leadership style and motivation (coupled with organizational structure) as the basic building blocks of ethos. These, as Rutter *et al.* (1979) and Reynolds (1976) point out, are within our control. We can choose to coerce people, or we can choose to enthuse people through a sense of involvement.

In a rather different vein from Rutter *et al.*, but still with an emphasis on the activities of teachers and pupils, is the concern of a number of sociologists with exploring, describing and explaining school processes (Hargreaves, 1967; Lacey, 1970; Ball, 1981; Turner, 1983). Their work has focused attention on the sub-cultural polarization that exists in secondary schools. Lacey looked at a grammar school in the 1960s and suggested a model which described the passage of pupils through the school and how they are separated and ranked according to a multiple set of criteria which make up the normative, academically-orientated, value system. This differentiation of pupils by teachers was carried out in the course of their normal duties, thus creating unwittingly a polarization in the pupil body whereby the normative culture was opposed by an alternative outline, an anti-group. Hargreaves, as one of the same Manchester research team, focused broadly on the structure of informal groups of pupils in a secondary modern school and the influence of such groups on the educative process. The main consequence of Hargreaves' work has been to affirm the fundamental importance of the social system, especially the structure of peer groups in relation to the education process. Ball's (1981) study of a comprehensive, which is one of a third generation of studies emerging from the early initiative at Manchester, underlined the findings of Lacey and Hargreaves of a sub-cultural polarization. He was able to point up the differences in the more complex process of sub-culture formation and polarization within a comprehensive. He did this through an analysis of options and curriculum choices which revealed a mechanism that in many respects replaced the streaming of earlier time. 'Options', according to Ball (p. xiii), 'had apparently inherited the function of finely differentiating pupils beyond the coarse labelling of band.'

Leadership: The Crucial Factor

Whilst polarization within the school and the development of sub-cultures were not the main subjects for discussion in Sharp and Green (1975), and in King's (1978) studies in the primary sector, both highlighted the ways in which the differentiation of pupils can be carried out by teachers as part of their normal duties, which may be contrary to the schools' goals and to the critical role of the head-teacher as a leader. These two studies and the secondary studies confirm the significance of the dynamic features of leadership rather than the attributes of the leader: his ability, for example, to influence the way staff function internally — that is, how they interact, communicate and conduct their classroom business. As a leader and member of the staff group, it is one of his major functions to help the group to develop ways of interacting that promote rather than hinder the achievement of goals that individual members share. 'Leadership ... seeks to [promote] ... followers to act for certain goals that represent the values and the motivations, the wants and needs, aspirations and expectations of both leaders and followers — leadership too is inseparable from the followers' needs and goals' (Burns, 1978, p. 19).

Goal Displacement

A daunting finding, which confirms what we already know, has emerged from the various studies of the school process: people may share common roles and expectations, but they are likely to carry out those roles in highly personal ways that are not congruent with a school's stated objectives, for example, 'working cooperatively together via group work'. The various studies provide us with numerous examples of such dissonance which could well form the basis for, at the very least, a discussion about how similar goals can be variously managed so as to match together differing goals. In the ORACLE research it was found, for example, that open-ended or higher order questioning (a frequently cited objective in primary school schemes) was very little used by teachers. As a result pupils had only limited experience of using questioning in a problem-solving situation. 'Group work' is a strategy that is frequently employed to attain several objectives and yet, as the same piece of research revealed, two clear trends were observable that did not 'fit' with such objectives: the prevalence of 'grouping' (four or five children seated around a table usually working on an individual assignment); and the virtual absence of 'group work' whereby a small group of children work together collaboratively on the same problem or task. These two trends are confirmed by other research studies (Bealing, 1972; HMI, 1978). The ORACLE research has identified specific strategies (Simon and Willcocks, 1981, p. 53) as important to the success of group work, that are just as crucial in the secondary as the primary sector: questioning, listening and managing disputes.

An earlier study of a single primary school in a working-class area (Sharp and Green, 1975) revealed an individualistic implementation of common goals and expectations similar to that observed in the larger ORACLE sample. Sharp and Green (p. 115) claim that teachers do not distribute their time and other resources equally among children. The favourably categorized pupils were those who fit the teachers' ideal for children from a 'good area' or a 'middle-class district'. In their judgment classroom activities, including social control and the assessment of progress, contribute to the conservation of the social order, and on this account child-centred education (a major objective in the early years of schooling) is judged to have failed. The claim by Sharp and Green is a strong one and perhaps needs to be set against the study's lack of a measure of social class which is independent of the teachers' perception. Theoretical interpretations apart, their claim says something about the implicit and explicit interpretation of one of the schools' goals, that of child-centredness.

Using a different approach, King's (1978) examination of one infant school reveals not dissimilar individual interpretations by teachers that it is significant for a headteacher as a leader to manage a school and its occupants in order to achieve common goals. He makes a number of points about the way in which teachers assess and typify pupils. According to King's (p. 59) observation, the teachers drew mainly upon their own experience of the child in the classroom situation rather than consulting other teachers' records. In making their judgments, three aspects of each child's classroom behaviour were assessed and incorporated into the picture or typification: compliance with teacher's rules of behaviour, the relationship with other children, and their learning progress. King contends that infant teachers encounter and accept child-centred ideologies as part of their professional socialization in colleges and departments of education. These ideologies, according to Whitbread (1972), are institutionalized and then dispensed in a set of everyday recipes for doing things that are not subject to a critical analysis for their contribution to a school's goals.

What these studies and others cited elsewhere in this chapter underlined is the considerable autonomy that exists for the individual teacher that can in some instances deflect from the achievement of known and approved goals. They also point up the need for an effective headteacher to ensure that the school community as a group functions well and that known and agreed goals are reached to the satisfaction of all.

Managing Planned Change

Schools continue to face the need to adapt to changing educational and social circumstances. They are expected not only to be the means of achieving social change, but also to maintain and transmit traditional values. Thus schools have to cope with the integration of both stability and change, notably in curricular matters.

Given the current state of the art of education management there is a considerable body of theory based on empirical data which can and does provide people with models and strategies to assist with the difficult task of meshing together stability and change. The literature is read widely by those concerned with education management and adapted to the needs of individuals and their schools. For example, the three strategies of planned change — empirical rational, power-coercive and normative re-education — are probably too well known to require further description. We also have models which describe the change process and advise on how to proceed. Further, there are case studies of change and a number of action research reports on planned, managed change which stress school processes upon which to draw. The action-research-based reports on change may well prove to be a most fruitful source of data on school processes and the activities of teachers and pupils. As yet they are limited in number and are perhaps rightly treated with some caution in the search for illumination for management of change practices. Ball (1981), in his study of 'Beachside Comprehensive', asks the question: what is going on here? He seeks in part to describe and understand the social system in terms of those involved in the schools and their interpretation of the situation. At the same time, Ball describes a change from broad ability banding to mixed ability teaching. His study reveals the gradual way the change occurred with a democratic (on the lines advocated by Yukl, 1981) and open process of voting for change year by year, and the careful pioneering and implementation of change by the English department. Ball's study also looks at the different motives of staff for supporting the change and the growth of support as the staff become concerned that the benefits outweigh the cuts. Ball's linkage of change management processes with an understanding of the social system provides those concerned in education management with useful insights into a number of interesting topics — motivation, leadership, organizational climate, change and conflict in organization.

Resource Allocation

Research to date does not indicate clearly the precise contribution of resources to pupil achievement. It seems reasonable to say, however, that expenditure, books, staffing, buildings are prerequisites for learning, and that skilled allocation of such resources may be significant for the attainment of some goals. This is certainly the assumption made in the literature relating to desired skills for effective leadership. The assumption tends to reflect an economic approach where the deployment of resources is necessary to attain designated outcomes. Thus a desirable key management skill for a headteacher would be '... to use resources responsibly and to turn them to good account'. More specifically, managerial skills allied to those of an interpersonal nature, in forecasting and planning, finance and accounting, organizational techniques, the allocation of staff and children, are a requirement for headship in the 1980s. There is no quarrel with the rationality that underlies the importance of such skills, but it would seem that, until recently, another aspect of resources and their allocation has taken something of a back seat — the different ways in which teachers and pupils use allocated resources.

Some of the studies cited in this chapter illustrate this aspect very well and can sometimes offer explanations for individual resource usage. Furthermore, the studies observe that teachers and pupils interact among themselves as well as with physical facilities, thus creating social-psychological resources in the school which seem, according to research, to be more important than physical resources. Both the Reynolds (1976) and Rutter studies, for example, strongly suggest that encouraging children to participate in the running of schools seems to be conducive to good attainment, attendance and behaviour.

In a rather different vein, Sharp and Green (1975, p. 115) discuss the ways in which teachers distribute their time and other resources among children. It is their contention that the favourably categorized pupils who fitted the teachers' ideal for children from a 'good area' or a 'middle-class' district benefitted from the teachers' resource distribution. Again, King (1978, p. 41) discusses the teachers' distribution of time in listening to beginners read every day whilst engaged in numerous other activities like tying a shoe-lace, exhorting other children to work, and writing in a word-book. Both are specific examples taken from research into two single schools, but nevertheless illustrate the point that management is not concerned solely with the efficient allocation of resources but with the ways in which these resources are used and adapted at the classroom level.

Evaluation: A Management Skill

Evaluation is part of the management of effective schools and as such may be seen as a form of social research which draws on a lengthy tradition that goes beyond the technical to include a reflection on the ways schools work. By and large, until recently, teachers have tended to make extensive use of their ad hoc professional judgments (King, 1978, p. 59), coupled with some testing, in the evaluation of practices and their outcomes. The primary survey by HMI in 1978 has suggested that this is less than satisfactory for many judgments about effective learning on the part of children. Even before 1978 evaluation instruments which would be appropriate for both the process of school and product outcomes were sought. One stumbling block has been the restricted use of existing instruments by teachers who were aware of the limitations of such instruments. One of the outcomes of recent research in the classroom has been the development of additional means of evaluation. A recent primary school survey has a number of strategies which may be usefully added to a manager's repertoire.

The Observational Research and Classroom Learning Evaluation Project — ORACLE (1975–80) — was the first large-scale observational study of fifty-eight classrooms in nineteen primary schools in three LEAs to be undertaken in this country. It was concerned primarily with a study of the relative effectiveness of different teaching approaches across the main subject areas of the primary school. As the title indicates, classroom observation was the main research method used to provide description of current classroom practice against which teachers could evaluate aspects of their own teaching. What this project offers to education management, amongst other things is a 'glassbox' model (Galton *et al.*, 1980a) where the classroom is open to view and teaching behaviours that could well be adapted for individual needs. One of the current problems in a contracting primary school is to maintain a balanced curriculum. It might well be possible to do (in a modified way) what the ORACLE workers did, using both the Pupil and Teacher Record: to construct the curriculum as it is actually experienced both by pupils and teachers and to estimate what they called 'the real curriculum' (*ibid.*, p. 28). One of the interesting findings from use of this technique was a calling into question of an old belief that schools fail to concentrate on the basics; in practice many primary schools spend a good deal of time on the basics — too much on occasion, according to the HMI Primary Survey of 1978. The research team went on to suggest the need to deliberately develop the use of such strategies, particularly questioning if cooperative group work is to be effectively managed in the classroom.

What the ORACLE researchers and Rutter's work (to a lesser extent) note, when referring to evaluation, is the need for self-criticism on the part of teachers. Both pieces of work, in making this point, highlight the social scientific tradition of considered investigation combined with critical analysis. What is now required from those concerned with effective education management is a translation of such recommendations into strategies which can be practised by teachers in their schools: for example, ways in which questions about different aspects of school organization can be asked, and, perhaps more importantly, the political nature of evaluation and the questions that ought to be raised by this aspect.

Conclusions

It is clear from the limited number of studies considered in this chapter that they have something to contribute to our knowledge of school processes. Their concern with an explanatory framework, rather than a predictive one, adds to an understanding of the working of schools, what they actually accomplish and the manner in which they achieve their objectives. These sources have many ideas to offer education management from both practice and theory perspectives. What they also bring to our attention is the prime need for further investigation which will enlarge our understanding of the processes of schooling. We know, for example, relatively little about a school's environment, its nature, antecedents and consequences — a significant area of effective school management.

Note

1 He and his co-workers suggest that three aspects of their findings — that the style and quality of life at school was having a relatively pervasive effect on children's behaviour; that there was something about the way children were dealt with in general which influenced their behaviour; and the ways in which punishment is used and the frequency with which it is given will carry messages to *other* (their italics) children, and create an atmosphere which can run counter to the intended effect on the offending individual — suggest that the importance of the separate school process measures may lie in their contribution to the ethos or climate of the school.

References

BALL, S.J. (1981) *Beachside Comprehensive: A Case-Study of Secondary Schooling*, Cambridge, Cambridge University Press.

BEALING, D. (1972) 'The organization of junior school classrooms', *Educational Research,* 14, pp. 231–5.

BENNETT, N. (1976) *Teaching Styles and Pupil Progress*, London, Open Books.

BURNS, J. MACGREGOR (1978) *Leadership*, New York, Harper and Row.

COHEN, M.D. and MARCH, J.G. (1974) *Leadership and Ambiguity: The American College President*, New York, McGraw-Hill Book Company.

COLEMAN, J.S. *et al.* (1966) *Equality of Educational Opportunity*, Washington D.C., Office of Education, US Department of Health, Education and Welfare.

GALTON, M.J. and SIMON, B. (1980) *Progress and Performance in the Primary Classroom*, London, Routledge and Kegan Paul.

GALTON, M.J. and WILLCOCKS, J. (1983) *Moving from the Primary Classroom*, London, Routledge and Kegan Paul.

GALTON, M.J., SIMON, B. and CROLL P. (1980) *Inside the Primary Class-*

room, London, Routledge and Kegan Paul.

GETZELS, J.W. (1969) 'A social psychology of education' in LINDZEY, G. and ARONSON, E. (Eds) *The Handbook of Social Psychology*, Vol. 5, 2nd ed., Reading, Mass., Addison-Wesley.

GLATTER, R. (1978) 'Influence or control? A review of the course', *Unit 16 of Open University Course E222*, Milton Keynes, Open University Press.

HALPIN, A.W. (1958) 'The development of theory in educational administration', in HALPIN, A.W. (Ed.) *Administrative Theory in Education*, London, Macmillan.

HER MAJESTY'S INSPECTORATE (1978) *Primary Education in England*, London, HMSO.

KING, R. (1978) *All Things Bright and Beautiful?* London, John Wiley and Sons.

LACEY, C. (1970) *Hightown Grammar*, Manchester, Manchester University Press.

LEHMING, R. and KANE, M. (1981) *Improving Schools: Using What We Know*, Beverley Hills, Calif., Sage Publications.

LIKERT, R. (1961) *New Patterns of Management*, New York, McGraw-Hill Book Company.

MADAUS, G.E., AIRASIAN, P.W. and KELLAGHAN, T. (1980) *School Effectiveness: A Reassessment of the Evidence*, New York, McGraw-Hill Book Company.

OPEN UNIVERSITY (1981) *Management and the School*, E323 Block 1, 'Management in action: An introduction to school management', and Block 7, 'Shorefield Comprehensive School: A case study on the management of change', Milton Keynes, Open University Press.

REYNOLDS, D. (1976) The 'Delinquent School', in Woods, P. (Ed.) *The Process of Schooling*, London, Routledge and Kegan Paul.

RUTTER, M., MAUGHAN, B., MORTIMORE, P., OUSTON, J. and SMITH, A. (1979) *Fifteen Thousand Hours*, London, Open Books.

SCHULTZ, A. (1953) 'Concept and theory formation in the social sciences', *Journal of Philosophy*, 51.

SHARP, R. and GREEN, A. (1975) *Education and Social Control*, London, Routledge and Kegan Paul.

SIMON, B. and WILLCOCKS, J. (Eds) (1981) *Research and Practice in the Primary Classroom*, London, Routledge and Kegan Paul.

TAYLOR, W. (1976) 'The head as manager: Some criticisms', in PETERS, R. (Ed.), *The Role of the Head*, London, Routledge and Kegan Paul.

TURNER, G. (1983) *The Social World of the Comprehensive School*, London, Croom Helm.

WALKER, D.E. (1979) *The Effective Administrator: A Practical Approach to Problem Solving, Decision Making, and Campus Leadership*, San Francisco, Calif., Jossey-Bass.

WHITBREAD, N. (1972) *The Evolution of the Nursery-Infant School*, London, Routledge and Kegan Paul.

YUKL, G.A. (1981) *Leadership in Organizations*, Englewood Cliffs, N.J. Prentice-Hall.

12   The Second Stage: Towards a Reconceptualization of Theory and Methodology in School Effectiveness Research

David Reynolds and Ken Reid

Earlier chapters have presented reports of work in progress and outlined the state of thinking about particular areas within the general field of school effectiveness studies. Our aim in this concluding chapter is somewhat different. Whilst summaries of research conducted to date may be useful, they are available elsewhere (Rutter, 1983; Reynolds, 1982) and hardly need repetition. We are concerned instead to identify the principal problems — of theory and methodology — that the 'first stage' of work over the last seven or eight years has revealed. These gaps in our knowledge, inadequacies in our theoretical conceptualizations and deficiencies in our methodologies will all be explored in some detail. Before this, though, it is necessary to outline what insights the first stage of work has generated.

This work — by Rutter *et al.* (1979), Reynolds (1976, *etc.*), Gray (1981) and Galloway *et al.* (1983) — has begun to indicate that there are substantial differences in the effectiveness of different schools. Although the effects of the school seem to be small by comparison with those of the home, the difference of seven or eight points in verbal reasoning score which seems to be gained by attending an 'effective' rather than an 'ineffective' school is clearly not inconsiderable.

British studies in this field seem to indicate that variables such as pupil/teacher ratio, class size, quantity of resources spent per child and quantity/quality of physical plant in schools do not have major effects upon outcomes (see Rutter, 1983, and Reynolds, 1982, for more detailed reviews). Likewise, the formal organizational structure of the school appears to be less important in determining effectiveness than the informal, unstructured world or 'ethos' that the school possesses. High levels of pupil involvement in running the school, a balance between using alienating controls and weakly permissive use of minimal controls, a headteacher role that combines firm leadership with some teacher participation and a system of reinforcement that emphasizes rewards for good behaviour rather than punishments for bad seem to be associated with being an effective institution.

This first stage of work in Britain, although it has clearly brought us much interesting and useful information, now seems (perhaps inevitably) to have generated more questions than it has produced answers. Although schools have effects and although we are beginning to understand the processes that are responsible for those effects, the gaps in our knowledge that the early work has revealed indicate to us the need for a 'second stage' programme of work that focuses particularly upon ten discrete areas of work.

1   Sampling Strategy

It is axiomatic that existing samples of schools have been too small in number, since regression analysis of samples of eight (Reynolds) or twelve (Rutter) is likely to generate highly unreliable estimates of variance because of the effects of outlier or rogue schools upon overall relationships. We also need more representative samples of schools — the South Wales secondary modern schools in the Reynolds (1976, etc.) work are atypical compared with the national pattern of comprehensive schools. The Irish samples of schools utilized by Madaus *et al.* (1980) are also atypical (which is particularly unfortunate since this is the only study to show school effects as greater than home effects). Even the Rutter *et al.* (1979) London comprehensives are atypical in their resource availability, for example. Whilst it may well be likely that the Sheffield comprehensives used by Galloway *et al.* (1983) are the most 'representative' of all the samples, the limited range of information upon the processes of the schools collected in this study reduces its usefulness. Recent Scottish data (Gray *et al.*, 1983) must be viewed with the greatest caution since, as one study on ability grouping (Tibbenham *et al.*, 1978) reported, 'the outstanding feature to emerge is the difference between the situation in Scottish comprehensives and that in the rest of Britain.'

As well as ensuring 'representativeness' of sample composition, it is important not to miss the full *range* of school types, since only the full range of school factor differences can reveal the full power of the school variables. The relative homogeneity of the Rutter and Reynolds samples — which makes their reported school effects perhaps even more convincing — should be avoided in future work.

There is also a need for studies of primary schools to be conducted along the lines of the potentially impressive set of data collected in the ILEA study outlined earlier by Mortimore and his co-workers. There is, of course, greater accord between the findings of research on primary and secondary schools in the United States than in Britain. The lack of British research into the institutional effects of primary schools also hinders comparative study, hampers secondary school work and makes it impossible to test the important suggestion of Jencks *et al.* (1971) that ineffective primary schools served ineffective secondary schools, generating an additive disadvantage for some pupils. It should be remembered that this amounted to 5 or 6 per cent of the differences between individuals.

2   Concerning Intakes

In many ways we believe that second stage work must rediscover the importance of pupil intakes. The current emphasis upon the school as a determinant of pupil outcomes stands in danger of neglecting the important role played by intakes in determining outcome and the crucial interaction between school, child and family that determines school effectiveness. Whilst the current emphasis upon school factors is necessary to displace conventional psychological paradigms attributing causation to home and family factors, the assertion of the *independence* of the school may prove damaging if it prevents us from seeing the interaction between pupils from specific home backgrounds and certain specified features of their schools, as in the South Wales study where *working-class* pupils find school rules governing 'dress, manners and morals' irksome because of their essentially *middle-class* nature (Reynolds, 1975). Outcomes cannot merely be seen as being produced by effective or ineffective schools without an assessment of which pupils, from which families and for which communities they are held to be effective or ineffective. As well as being *independent* in their effects on pupils, schools (and their levels of effectiveness) must also be seen as *dependent*. That is, they must be seen as dependent upon outside school factors for the determination of their effectiveness as educational institutions.

The 'rediscovery' of intake importance needs to be pursued in other ways too. More intake variables than the two used by the

Rutter team are potentially important, a point frequently made over the last few years (Reynolds, 1981; Gray, 1981). Also, we need to discover a sense of the history of school institutions and of the complex interactive process between school and catchment area. Many expectations of, opinions of and attitudes to a school may exist in a community but not be tapped by any measurement of verbal reasoning score. These perceptions need to be measured and analyzed.

Two final problems concerned with intake factors have only recently emerged with the passing of the 1981 Education Act's regulations on the publication of examination results. First, it is possible that intakes are now being directly affected by apparent output quality. Whilst the number of parents choosing to send their children to one school or another on the basis of public examination performance probably remains small, since most parents continue to opt for their neighbourhood school, there are hints that it is a growing practice.

If and when this practice escalates and assuming that it is higher ability pupils who are being moved to apparently higher performance schools, it is bound to intensify differences between those schools situated in 'good' and 'bad' catchment areas. Whilst schools with poor catchment areas are not necessarily (adjusting for their intake quality) any less effective than others, it may well be that the changing academic and social balance of poor catchment area schools will have 'knock-on' group effects on academic performance greater than would be predicted merely by knowledge of these pupils' individual academic abilities. At sixth form level, for example, the removal of quite a small number of high ability pupils may have quite dramatic effects on the academic and social mix of the classes in certain subjects. Below certain levels of intake quality, then, it may be very difficult to be an 'effective' educational institution, and it may well be that the operation of the 1981 Education Act is making such schools more common by changing pupil intellectual balance *and* mean intake ability.

The second effect of the 1981 Act is to make largely redundant cross-sectional studies of the kind used by Reynolds, Brimer and others since, because of parental choice, intake quality at certain schools may be changing quite rapidly over time. Using intake scores as a surrogate for the intake scores of output cohorts that are not available may be unwise, since the former are no longer as valid a guide as they once were to the scores of the output cohorts when they were intakes.

3 Concerning Process

We still do not have a clear idea *which* school factors are associated with outcome, nor do we have any real idea as to *how* the process factors actually generate outputs, which may be through effects upon peer group processes or upon individual self-conception, for example. We still do not know what creates the factors themselves, whether they be personality factors, prior educational experience of the headteacher or more idiosyncratic factors concerned with the past biographies of school staff. Although there are hints that output quality in turn directly affects process (perhaps through affecting the expectations of teachers), the strength of this influence is unclear. If past school success or failure does perpetuate itself in this way, we need to know far more about the mechanisms through which the process may operate.

Some of the confusion about conceptualizing school outcomes that Strivens notes earlier seems to be self-inflicted damage, easily remediable by the adoption of a paradigm that sees school organizations as both objective reality and yet subjectively perceived. We are consequently still very weak in terms of our understanding of key areas of within-school life. Curriculum in both a formal sense (the knowledge 'quantity' and 'content') and an informal sense (the more covert verbal and non-verbal cues that accompany the formal curriculum) has not been a major focus, as Wilcox reminds us earlier. The pastoral care system has not received the same attention as has the academic system, as Galloway noted. The headteacher and his or her effect upon teachers, pupils and the school in general has also been neglected as a factor, as have teacher/teacher relations. All these areas seem urgently in need of further work to improve our meagre understanding of within-school life.

4 Concerning Outcomes

It is clear from the recent Scottish material that outcomes may not be so highly interrelated as both the Rutter and the Reynolds work had suggested. Intercorrelations of above 0.6 in the latter two studies between their three or four outcome measures (delinquency, academic attainment, attendance, behaviour) drop in the Scottish work (Gray *et al.*, 1983) to only 0.2 between attendance and O-level attainment for one sample of sixty-nine uncreamed comprehensives. The South Wales studies' averaging of school performance in different areas generating an 'overall' school position seems in the light of this evidence a somewhat undesirable practice.

As well as separating outcomes for independent analysis, the generation of further outcome measures is a major task. The British educational system has a multiplicity of social, moral, cultural, aesthetic and sporting goals that is probably unique amongst industrial societies. Explicitly, only two-thirds of school hours are actually used for academic purposes; the rest are spent on sport, religion and various cultural pursuits, all of which would be separate from normal school life in societies such as France or Germany. Although the 1981 Education Act only specifies that parents should be provided with information on 'cognitive' outcomes, information on the within-school social processes that will probably generate differential social outcomes is also published for parents. There are numerous hints that parents do in fact assess schools on their social processes and on such factors as 'tone' or social reputation as well as on academic results, and there is overwhelming evidence that schools themselves aim for social as well as cognitive outcomes (see, for example, Morton-Williams, 1968).

The generation of new outcome measures to tap 'affective' rather than cognitive outcomes is important because there are hints from some American studies (see the review in Reynolds, 1982) of substantial school effects upon social or affective outcomes, such as students' perception of their ability to master fate. Also, there is evidence of difference between the selective and non-selective systems of education in social outcomes, such as behaviour, truancy and attitudes to school in the recent Children's Bureau studies (Steedman, 1980). Social outcomes are also important because they are the only gains for those children — roughly 14 per cent in Britain — who attain no measurable cognitive outcomes through examination passes at CSE or at O-level. For the other 10 per cent of children who merely attain a grade 5 CSE pass and the large number of children who will attain the same 'points' score in calculations of examination passes, it is only *social* outcomes that will generate variation between individuals that cannot be shown on scales of mere academic attainment.

What exactly these social measures should be remains a matter of considerable speculation. No doubt some measures should attempt to tap those goals that schools have always aimed for — sporting achievement, job getting and holding, the possession of self-esteem, favourable locus of control and positive self-conceptions. Perhaps now racial tolerance, non-sexist attitudes, coping skills, survival skills and the other more recent goals that have been given to the educational system also need to be tapped. Since these goals will entail moving away from mere behavioural social outcomes (such as rates of delinquency and attendance), the complexity of the necessary attitudinal measures that can tap the deep structure of pupil attitudes and perceptions makes this whole area one of quite awesome difficulty.

One last point needs to be made about outcomes. The possible rise in their number only increases the need to conceptualize and measure more school process factors, since we have been very unsuccessful in finding school process items that are linked with social outcomes. In the Rutter *et al.* (1979) work, for example, only seven process items could be found that correlated with delinquency, whereas fourteen were correlated with academic attainment. Whatever within-school factors are associated with the social outcomes, we seem a long way from discovering them. The discovery of more *social* outcomes would merely increase the pressure on us in this area of work.

5   Disaggregating Pupils and Schools

One of the principal handicaps in the work on school differences and school effects has been the treatment of the pupils as unitary groups. The emphasis has been upon how whole cohorts of pupils are affected by their schools. In view of hints from American work that schools are differentially important for different groups of pupils (as in the case of the Coleman Report, 1966, and its findings of large school effects for low social class blacks), we need to analyze separately for boys and girls, older and younger pupils, higher and lower social class pupils, and ethnic minority and 'host culture' children.

Disaggregating the pupil group in this way also helps us to move towards the disaggregation of 'the school' as a unitary concept. All studies so far treat the school and its factors as being a common experience for all pupils, since school factor scores on, say, rate of physical punishment, or 'time on task' in the classroom are global averages of the experience of all pupils in the school, an experience that probably very few pupils will actually have gone through. Disaggregation of the school could in theory be taken as far as looking at the individual pupil's school, in terms of the actual classroom, year, departmental and school experience of each pupil, as in using, say, the individual's rate of corporal punishment or the individual pupil's time on task during an average school day.

There are, of course, major practical difficulties with the collection of pupil-specific school factors. It would be hugely time consuming, involving the collection of data on perhaps forty or fifty school factors that would be unique to each child. Secondly, it would be methodologically difficult to cope with analyses where there is such huge variation in pupil factors, pupil home background factors and pupil school factors, since large sample sizes would be required to generate more than a mere handful of cases in each 'cell'. Thirdly, the weighting of each pupil's classroom experience, 'year experience' and school experience that would be necessary — in view of the different time and importance of each level in the life of the pupil — would also be difficult. Fourthly, such work as this could have no direct educational policy implications, since pupils are always treated as members of collectivities and never as individuals in overall educational policy-making.

Perhaps the answer to these difficulties may be to move away from school-specific school factors to class-specific school factors, year-specific school factors or department-specific school factors, where each of these school sub-units would have its own rating on the usual thirty or forty school factors. However it may be done, breaking down the unit of the school is important because of:

1   the presence of more variance within the school than between schools means that with our present analyses we are explaining little of the variance on any dependent variable we use;

2   the need to dispose of the allegation that school process is merely the sum total of all within-school classroom processes — an allegation which, if it is true, renders redundant the use of the school as a unit of analysis;

3   the need to have more sensitive descriptions of within-school processes than those available at present;

4   the urgent need for school-based research to be linked with the bodies of knowledge on teacher effectiveness, classroom processes and the psycho-social structure of the classroom as a learning environment. There is a clear need for studies of classroom processes to look outside the classroom at the teacher in the wider world of the school (as attempted in Murgatroyd and Reynolds, 1984) and for school-based studies to look also at the classroom;

5 the need to integrate the work on primary school processes, most of which utilizes the classroom as the unit of analysis, with the work on secondary schools, most of which uses the school as its unit of analysis.

6 Concerning Change

In addition to our earlier points concerned with the epidemiology of schools as learning environments, we need experimental work to see how modifiable school regimes are in their processes and in their effects. We can gauge the effects of naturally occurring experiments such as the appointment of a new headteacher, a change of building or a change of streaming organization. We can also deliberately intervene with planned experiments, such as consultancy models of change, 'top down' models of change or approaches which lie mid-way between such extremes, such as the GRIDS project in institutional development at Bristol. Most important of all, we should try to understand which within-school factors hinder or potentiate the effects of these outside interventions. We have only a tenuous idea of the school factors important in affecting outcome — we have virtually no idea of the school factors associated with willingness or ability to change.

7 Concerning Methodology

We now need a methodology appropriate to these major tasks of description and explanation of school life outlined above. To use Bronfenbrenner's (1979) analogy, we have been caught in our methodology between a rock and a soft place — the rock being the rigour of conventional positivist empiricism and the soft place being some of the excesses of participant observation found in parts of the 'new' sociology of education.

A middle position that combines the strengths of both methods seems to be required. This could involve use of positivist methodology to *generate* relationships, combined with use of 'softer' data to *explain* relationships. Alternatively, the approach could involve moving towards hardening 'soft' data, through introducing more checks on participant observers, use of 'blind' observers or increased use of triangulation. Using the different approaches to bolster each other in a collaborative methodology seems more preferable than continued competition between them (see Evans, 1983, and Reynolds, 1981, for further discussion of this theme). The methodology necessary to understand *how* schools are as they are and *how* they have their effects is likely to be very different from that which has been necessary to show that they *have* effects.

8   Concerning Theory

We believe that we need to immerse ourselves more in theory. Much of the early work in this field has been highly atheoretical, as authorities such as Hargreaves (1981) have observed. The Rutter *et al.* (1979) work was atheoretical, as was the work of Brimer (1978), Madaus *et al.* (1980) and Gray *et al.* (1983), who can perhaps be excused from criticism since he possessed no process data to relate to theory in any case. The work of Reynolds (1976, etc.) seems distinctly eclectic in its use of theory.

The reasons for this are not difficult to understand. Much of the British work grew out of attempts to test the hypotheses of Jencks and Coleman and therefore tended to work within the same paradigm of traditional atheoretical empiricism as they. We have customarily lacked adequate process data to relate to theory in any case. Also, many of us have probably seen ourselves as *opposed* to any dominant theoretical paradigm, regarding them as grossly flawed in their emphasis upon family factors or socio-structural factors as determinants of school outcomes.

The problems caused by our atheoreticism, however, are now numerous. No piece of work is cumulative, either set against work from the past or against other work in the present; the field is, therefore, not integrated. Work is not testable in theoretic terms and does not generate any middle-range theory, which is the building block of any attempted construction of meta-theory. In the absence of such attempts to relate work to theory, the field of school differences is unrelated to any current theoretical position except that of 'grubby empiricism'. The marginality of the work within the British educational research community is clearly related to our theoretical marginality.

9   Concerning Analysis

Instead of current methods of analysis which give a snapshot of the intake/process/outcome interaction at a point *in* time, we urgently need dynamic models which show interaction *over* time. We need to be able to see the dynamic interaction between intake and process, outcomes and intakes (as above), and between outcomes and intakes as affected by the provisions of the 1981 Education Act. We need to see how decisions are made within the schools, how resources are distributed and how school factors are produced and reproduced by everyday decision-taking. Whilst it may be possible to generate 'nested' statistical models which can handle the mutual interaction and feedback between intake, process and outcome, it seems likely that quantitative analysis on its own is unlikely to generate the insight into these dynamic processes that is required. Only a more mixed methodological position as outlined above would seem to be adequate for fully dynamic analysis.

10 Concerning the Additive Nature of School and Family Effects

We have so far in the field been concerned to establish the independent nature of the school influence without establishing the directionality of influence. School influence may operate in the same directions as family influence (to depress working-class children's performance) or in different directions (to depress highly achieving middle-class children's performance, for example).

There are strong suggestions from a number of data bases (the Scottish Data Archive, the Sheffield schools study of Galloway *et al.*, 1983, and the ILEA data bases (Mortimore and Byford, 1979) that schools with poor catchment areas do worse than would be expected from a knowledge of their intakes and from knowledge of the overall relationship for all schools between intakes and outcomes. Ineffective schools, then, would seem to be serving more disadvantaged catchment areas in an *additive* relationship whereby initial disadvantage is confounded, confirmed and increased by school effects.

Aside from the importance of this thesis merely in its intellectual pay-off and furtherance of our understanding, it is the policy implications of the thesis that are of major importance. It has always been difficult to place evidence that schools have independent effects against other overwhelming evidence that suggests school reform as having had minimal effects upon the wider class structure (e.g., Halsey *et al.*, 1980). The notion that school influence is additive but *dependent* on the influence of wider social structures and ultimately reinforcing of them integrates at a stroke two apparently opposite bodies of findings.

Enabling the Strategy

Delivering programmes of work that attempt to move us forward and learn from the manifold defects of first stage work is clearly a difficult task; cut-backs in research funding intensify this problem. Three strategies seem to be practicable at present.

1   School change strategies and programmes of action research may generate more knowledge about school processes than they generate change, since in order to understand something fully it may be necessary to attempt to change it. Change attempts are likely to show the interrelationships between variables, the pathways that relate the levels of the school and the facilitators or inhibitors of change that are likely to be school factors of major importance (as in Phillips' work reported earlier).

2   Using existing data bases — on the lines of the Contexts Project reported earlier by Gray — may be fruitful also, since a large amount of information on school intakes and outcomes is already collected. Whilst there must remain doubts as to the representativeness of such data — since only certain LEAs collect them routinely — and whilst there must remain doubts as to their quality, use of these data seems a fruitful way forward.

3   Using 'teacher researchers', as in various centres within South Wales, would seem to be another useful initiative.

The teacher researcher concept is based upon the hope that the teacher, through conducting research into his or her own classroom or school, could both improve his or her own professional practice *and* generate useful research data that would be of wider interest. Lawrence Stenhouse (1975) argued vigorously in favour of teacher conducted research, viewing it as more concerned with developing professional practice than with the generation of 'objective' knowledge about schools. Since then, a considerable argument has developed over the merits and demerits of the concept (Hamilton and Delamont, 1974, Pring, 1978; Adelman and Alexander, 1982). There have been charges of bias, contamination of data, lack of rigour and subjectivity (see the collection of articles in *Interchange*, Vol. 11, No. 4, 1981), yet those in favour of the concept accepted these problems as the inevitable price of personal and professional growth.

More recently there have been attempts — most notably in South Wales — to develop the concept of the teacher researcher as *researcher,* not merely as teacher. The courses in behaviour and learning problems at University College, Cardiff and the various in-service courses at the West Glamorgan Institute have attempted to utilize teachers as data gatherers about within-school processes. In these courses, teachers undertake a school-based study of a certain issue or problem within their own school, taking the particular empirical material and relating it to the wider body of academic literature concerned. Whilst most of these studies contain a substantial amount of qualitative data on school factors, school processes and within-school life in general, many of these data (on whether schools stream, pastoral care provision, size, option arrangements, etc.) are likely to be specific enough to have reasonable validity. Data of a more quantitative nature on outputs, such as attendance, delinquency and examination success, are likely to be 'hard' enough to be other than observer-specific.

If such data — which in South Wales cover probably over 100 schools — can be utilized, perhaps with some additional checks on validity provided by the use of teachers as checks upon each other's observations, then a potentially large data base on processes and outputs is practicable, needing only the addition of data on intakes to make it more or less ready for systematic analysis. As a means of obtaining maximum data at minimum cost, the use of teachers in this way would seem to be another development to enable the strategy outlined in our earlier points, particularly since teachers may well be highly sensitive observers of within-school practices.

References

ADELMAN, C. and ALEXANDER, R. (1983) *The Self-Evaluating Institution,* London, Methuen.

BRONFENBRENNER, U. (1979) *The Ecology of Human Development,* Cambridge, Mass, Harvard University Press.

COLEMAN, J. (1966) *Equality of Educational Opportunity,* Washington, D.C. US Government Printing Office.

EVANS, J. (1983) 'Criteria of validity in social research: Exploring the relationship between ethnographic and quantitative approaches', in HAMMERSLEY, M. (Ed.). *The Ethnography of Schooling,* Driffield, Nafferton.

GALLOWAY, D. *et al.* (1983) *Schools and Disruptive Pupils,* London, Longmans.

GRAY, J. (1981) 'Towards effective schools: Problems and progress in British research', in *British Educational Research Journal,* 7, 1, pp. 59–69.

GRAY, J. McPHERSON, A. and RAFFE, D. (1983) *Reconstructions of Secon-*

dary Education, London, Routledge and Kegan Paul.

HALSEY, A.H. *et al.* (1980) *Origins and Destinations*, Oxford, Oxford University Press.

HAMILTON, D. and DELAMONT, S. (1974) 'Classroom research: A cautionary tale', in *Research in Education*, 11, 1, pp. 1–16.

HARGREAVES, D. (1981) 'Schooling for delinquency', in BARTON, L. and WALKER, S. (Eds), *Society, Schools and Teaching*, Lewes, Falmer Press.

JENCKS, C. *et al.* (1971) *Inequality*, London, Allen Lane.

MADAUS, G.F. *et al.* (1980) *School Effectiveness*, New York, McGraw Hill.

MORTIMORE, P. and BYFORD, D. (1979) *School Examination Results in ILEA., 1977 CRS 735/80)*, London, Inner London Education Authority.

MORTON-WILLIAMS, R. and FINCH, S. (1968) *Enquiry 1*, London, HMSO.

MURGATROYD, S.J. and REYNOLDS, D. (1984) 'Leadership and the teacher', in HARLING, P. (Ed.) *New Directions in Educational Leadership*, Lewes. Falmer Press.

PRING, R. (1978) 'Teacher as researcher', in LAWTON, D. *et al.*, *Theory and Practice of Curriculum Studies*, London, Routledge and Kegan Paul.

REYNOLDS, D. (1975) 'When pupils and teachers refuse a truce', in MUNGHAM, G. and PEARSON, G. (Eds), *Working Class Youth Culture*, London, Routledge and Kegan Paul.

REYNOLDS, D. (1976) 'The delinquent school', in WOODS, P. (Ed.), *The Process of Schooling*, London, Routledge and Kegan Paul.

REYNOLDS, D. (1981) Review of M. Rutter *et al. Fifteen Thousand Hours*, in *British Journal of Sociology of Education*, 1, 2, pp. 207–11.

REYNOLDS, D. (1981) 'The naturalist methods of educational and social research — A Marxist Critique', in *Interchange (Journal of the Ontario Institute for Studies in Education)*, 11, 4, pp. 77–89.

REYNOLDS, D. (1982) 'The search for effective schools', *School Organization*, 2, 3, pp. 215–37.

RUTTER, M. (1983) 'School effects on pupil progress — findings and policy implications', in *Child Development*, 54, 1, pp. 1–29.

RUTTER, M. *et al.* (1979) *Fifteen Thousand Hours*, London, Open Books.

STEEDMAN, J. (1980) *Progress in Secondary Schools*, London, National Children's Bureau.

STENHOUSE, L. (1975) *An Introduction to Curriculum Research and Development*, London, Heinemman.

TIBBENHAM, A., ESSEN, J. and FOGELMAN, K. (1978) 'Ability grouping and school characteristics', *British Journal of Educational Studies*, 26, 1.

13 *Studying School Effectiveness: A Postscript*

Anne Jones

I admire the authors of this book for allowing a practitioner to have the last word. This is a tribute both to their open-mindedness and to their recognition that they still somehow have not found 'the answer' despite years of pains-taking research and deep thinking. Somehow the sum of the parts does not equal the whole: the global view still has something missing, and the fine detail obscures the truth. None of this matters if nevertheless the research does in fact help practitioners to improve their effectiveness. I hope researchers do not regard it as impertinent or out of place for me to comment that the 'hidden agenda' of school effectiveness research should be to make schools more effective, not simply to make work for researchers. So what effects do these chapters have on the effective practice of a practitioner?

As a practitioner (who is, as it happens, also researching into this topic) I found the chapters both stimulating and illuminating. They made me think but they did not throw much *new* light on the path for a practitioner in search of a way forward. It was reassuring in a way to be reminded of the swings and fashions of research, sometimes looking at 'inputs' and denying the nature of the school itself; sometimes looking at the culture and organization of the school itself and ignoring the input variables; nearly always looking at the pupil as raw material and product rather than worker and contributor. These fashions are reflected too in teacher practice. So it was reassuring to find researchers reflecting our own tunnel vision, looking at schools through one end of a telescope or another, rarely seeing the whole picture. But it also makes us realize how distorted our vision is, either too detailed, or too long distance. Evaluation is now all the rage in schools and in research institutions, yet not only do we not know how to evaluate objectively, but very few people are able to devine what it is we are trying to evaluate.

Many of the contributors to this book are aware of this — they hint at the need for a dynamic approach to analysis — the model for this has not yet been found though it is certainly high on my own research agenda. The art of hitting a moving target — of seeing it long enough to measure, judge, and feel what it is like — is understandably difficult to master. Everything changes all the time: the school, the individual, the teacher, the class, the neighbourhood, the social and economic environment, the input and output variables, the goals of the school, society, the individual. Even if the researcher painstakingly follows an age cohort through a school, the outcomes change in nature and importance all the time. The question is, does the researcher realize this, or is the research based on assumptions which no longer apply?

Anyone who works closely with young people will realize that many of them no longer share the assumptions upon which most schools and research into schools are based. It could be that these assumptions no longer motivate pupils nor are appropriate for them in an age when academic achievement, individual success and paid 'work' as a means of gaining status and self esteem are gradually being supplemented or replaced by a new ethic which places more stress on cooperation, caring and coping and, in which, personal confidence and maturity are key factors in equipping people to be flexible and recitrent in enjoying a life which will not be all work and no play. And yet we still appear to judge both our pupils and our schools on the criteria of the past. So behind research techniques lies an even deeper question about basic assumptions. We thought we were working with caterpillars; at the moment they are in a stage of chrysallis; tomorrow they will be butterflies. Such a progression defies logical analysis yet it exists. What does that do to our techniques of teaching and analyzing? First, it forces us to look more at process than at content, at development rather than structure, at skills rather than knowledge, at the ability to move forward rather than the ability to mantain the *status quo* or 'a tight ship'. The very qualities we have been praising in schools and pupils may be the ones least useful to the pupils in later life: a too perfect school existence in terms of content and order may leave the pupils ill equipped for the life they have to lead. Second, it forces us to rethink our model both of schooling and of research into school effectiveness.

In searching for a new model for examining a dynamic situation, we need perhaps to reject a one-dimensional model (input and output or organization and culture) or even a two-dimensional model (input and output set against organization and culture). We probably need to devize a multi-dimensional molecular model, which itself has moving parts. To this model we may need to add some new dimensions which this present study hints at, but does not really explore. The obvious missing dimensions are the role of the pupil in the school and the nature of leadership and authority in the school. No doubt there are others.

First the role of the pupil: 'the ambiguous role of the pupil' (Bell) means that too often the pupil is treated as fodder, a 'given' rather than one of the determinants of the processes and outcomes. Further, as Reynolds says, the 'output' variables do not include such factors as the pupils' maturity (racial tolerance, non-sexist attitudes, coping skills etc.). They concentrate on the cognitive outputs and omit almost entirely the affective. Yet, in our society *affective* skills and *effective* skills are becoming more important; probably more impor-tant than cognitive skills: process not content. Schools may have adjusted to this fact more than researchers. Certainly from the studies quoted which touch on this, there is evidence that when pupils are counted as workers rather than raw materials, outcomes are different. For example, pupils involved in decision-making behave and mature in a different way from those who are not. This whole topic needs very serious investigation.

Equally important and barely discussed in this collection of papers, is the nature of leadership and authority in a school organiza-tion, and the effect this has on the learning outcomes for the pupils. Ron Davie's chapter touches on this when he describes the relative ineffectualness of Deputy Heads in introducing change strategies into their schools. Why is it that the Heads in his study were both more effective and effective in shorter a time than the Deputies? Power and status? Leadership and authority? How is it that some Heads share both their power and their leadership and others do not, and what effects does this have on schools? Very many Heads find the management of innovation and change very difficult. Many resist change altogether; others embark enthusiastically and then get into difficulties. Most Heads would admit that managing innovation and change in a constructive way, a way which mobilizes the energy of staff, pupils, and the local community is one of the most difficult tasks they ever face.

The point of this in the context of this chapter is not to solve the problem but to note how important this task is to the effectiveness of schools and the learning of pupils. Teachers will articulate very clearly the effects of impotent, misguided or headstrong leadership on the outcomes of schools. A school which has ineffectual leadership will feel paralyzed and immobilized. A school which feels its Head is leading it in the 'wrong' direction will 'split off' from its leader, dig in its heels and risk getting stuck. A school whose leader does not take the staff (or pupils) with him or her, for example, who does not consult properly or allow the staff and pupils to participate will again find itself in confused conflict. These dynamic situations will always effect the pupils' learning, both cognitive and affective.

In schools where there is deeply felt and unresolved conflict in the staff group, this conflict is likely to be acted out in various ways by the pupils. Staff apathy in pupil truancy; staff confusion in pupil confusion. All of this is likely to stem from the leadership (or non-leadership) given to the school by the Head. The extent to which and the way in which the Head exercises leadership and authority will have serious implications for the way the staff and ultimately the pupils are able to exercise their leadership and authority. This in turn will effect the amount of *real* learning which goes on. No matter what the structure, the curriculum, the degree of social deprivation, the sexual or racial or class balance, these other complex dynamic factors will be of crucial importance. So although several papers do hint at the importance of the dynamics of leadership in the dynamic situation we now have in schools, the nature of the complex and ever changing relationship between the Head, the individual, the culture of organization of the school, the local environment and the national scene is insufficiently explored. It is the *inter-relationship* of the parts and the *way* in which they relate which needs to be understood if humanly possible.

However, in the same way that the basic assumptions about what schools are for are now changing, so should the old criteria for judging the nature of leadership and authority be changed. Reynolds postulates that the criteria for evaluating pupil progress need to be expanded to include outcomes other than academic success. The same applies to the leadership of schools. The prevailing model seems to be content-based and two-dimensional: good input and good organization equals good learning for the pupil. The model needed now is infinitely more complex. The fact that *selectors* of Headteachers do not seem to have taken this into account may explain many of the mismatches (and ensuing breakdowns, whether they be institutional or personal) between Heads and schools which now occur, to the detriment of pupil learning.

It seems likely (but certainly needs researching further) that the Head's ability to handle complex dynamic situations will influence positively or negatively the ability of the *staff* to do the same, and of the pupils to learn these skills. The kind of skills I am postulating are all process skills. Mayhew (1974) defined them as:

1 *Peer skills:* the ability to build a network of contacts with one's equals;
2 *Leadership skills:* the ability to motivate subordinates, and cope with the complications of authority, power and dependence;
3 *Conflict resolution skills:* the ability to mediate conflict, handle disturbance, work under psychological stress;
4 *Information processing skills:* the ability to build networks, extract and validate information, to disseminate information effectively;
5 *Skills in unstructured decision-making:* the ability to redefine problems and find solutions which information and objectives are intriguous;
6 *Resource allocation skills:* the ability to decide on resource allocation, including the allocation of time;
7 *Entrepreneurial skills:* the ability to take sensible decisions and implement innovations;
8 *Skills of introspection:* the ability to understand the position of manager and its impact on the organisation.

If these skills are important, and there is growing evidence that they are, then they need to be included in the criteria for judging school effectiveness. They should be mirrored at levels of the organization. They are important in Headteachers, but they are also important in classroom teachers who are in positions of enormous power and leadership. Finally, they are skills which the pupils need to make their own and take with them into their life after school, if they are to cope with the demands of modern society.

My intention in writing this postscript has not been to detract from the merits of this extremely stimulating collection of papers but simply, as requested, to add some thoughts and comments of my own. I suspect that we shall never find out how to evaluate school effectiveness fully, but the impossible quest at least has the effect of helping practitioners and policy-makers to go on trying to improve what they do. All I ask is that those very improvements and criteria for success take account of the fundamental changes in our society, and include the pupils as real working partners in the enterprise.

Anne Jones

Reference

MAYHEW, L.B. (Ed.) (1974) *Educational Leadership and Declining Enrolments*, Berkeley, California, McCutchan.

List of Contributors

Eileen Callely, Faculty of Education, University College, Cardiff.
Jennifer Clark, Research and Statistics Unit, ILEA
Ronald Davie, National Children's Bureau, London.
Russell Ecob, Research and Statistics Unit, ILEA
David Galloway, Faculty of Education, University College, Cardiff.
John Gray, Division of Education, University of Sheffield.
Anne Hill, Research and Statistics Unit, ILEA
Audrey Hind, Research and Statistics Unit, ILEA
Mary Hunt, Research and Statistics Unit, ILEA
Anne Jones, Head of Cranford Community School, Hounslow
Ben Jones, Division of Education, University of Sheffield.
David Lewis, Research and Statistics Unit, ILEA
Jill Lewis, Faculty of Education, University College, Cardiff.
Barbara Maughan, Institute of Psychiatry, University of London.
Peter Mortimore, Research and Statistics Unit, ILEA
Janet Ouston, Institute of Psychiatry, University of London.
Derek Phillips, Faculty of Education, University College, Cardiff.
Ken Reid, Faculty of Education, West Glamorgan Institute of Higher Education.
David Reynolds, Faculty of Education, University College, Cardiff.
Pamela Sammons, Research and Statistics Unit, ILEA
Jane Steedman, Department of Statistics and Computing, University of London Institute of Education.
Louise Stoll, Research and Statistics Unit, ILEA
Janet Strivens, Faculty of Education, University of Liverpool.
Brian Wilcox, Education Department, Sheffield.
Pamela Young, Department of Educational Administration, University of London Institute of Education.

Author Index

Adelman, C. and Alexander, R., 202, 203
Ainsworth, M., 2, 11
Aitkin, M. *et al.*, 109, 110, 114, 126, 129, 131, 133
Alexander, K.L. and Griffin, L.J., 40, 43
Alexander, K.L. *et al.*, 16, 26
Alexander, R.
  see Adelman and Alexander
Anderson, C.S., 55, 56
APU
  see Assessment of Performance Unit
Armstrong, M., 118
Aronson, E.
  see Lindzey and Aronson
Assessment of Performance Unit (APU), 87, 101

Ball, S.J., 181, 182, 183, 186, 189
Banks, O. and Finlayson, D.S., 51, 56
Barnard, C.I., 48, 56
Barr, D. *et al.*, 146–7, 152
Barr, R. and Dreeben, R., 18, 19, 26
Barrett, C.
  see Galloway and Barrett
Barton, L., 11
Barton, L. and Walker, S., 204
Bealing, D., 184, 187
Bell, L.A., 52–3, 56, 207
Bennett, S.N., 103, 109, 110, 114, 118, 121, 126, 131, 133, 189
Bennett, S.N. *et al.*, 134

Berg, I.
  see Hersov and Berg
Bernstein, B., 1, 11
Best, R.E. *et al.*, 76, 84–5
Bidwell, C.E., 18, 26
Bidwell, C.E. and Kasarda, J.D., 18, 26, 27, 40, 43
Blackstone, T.
  see Mortimore and Blackstone
Bolam, R., 174 and 174n2
Bourdieu, P., 22, 27
Bowles, S. and Gintis, H., 4, 11, 22, 27
Brimer, 200, 204
Bronfenbrenner, U., 199, 203
Brookover, W.B. *et al.*, 5, 117, 134
Brown, R., 27
Burgess, S., 3
Burns, J.C. *et al.*, 152
Burns, J. MacG., 183, 189
Burstein, L., 127, 134
Button, L., 75–6, 85
Byford, D.
  see Mortimore and Byford
Bynner, J., 159, 174

Callely, E.M.
  see Phillips and Callely
Campbell, D.T.
  see Cook and Campbell
Carroll, H.C.M., 85, 86
Clarke, A.D.B. and Clarke, M., 4, 11
Coates, T.J. and Thoresen, C.E., 78, 85

Cohen, M.D. and March, J.G., 189
Cohen, M.D. *et al.*, 53, 56
Coleman, J.S., 2, 5, 11, 15, 27, 197, 200, 203
Coleman, J.S. *et al.*, 13, 30, 43, 177, 178, 189
Collins, R., 22, 27
Cook, T.D. and Campbell, D.T., 35, 43
Cooper, M.G., 2, 11
COPED, 139, 152
Corwin, R.G., 53, 56
Cowie, H., 121, 134
Croft, D.B.
    see Halpin and Croft
Cuttance, P., 6, 13–28

Dale, R.R., 90, 101
Davie, R., 167, 174, 208
Davie, R. *et al.*, 2, 11, 120, 134
Davies, T.I., 60–1, 73
De Long, J.T.
    see Derr and De Long
Delamont, S.
    see Hamilton and Delamont
Department of Education and
    Science (DES), 37, 43, 62, 73, 105, 114
Derr, B.C. and De Long, J.T.,
    143–4, 152
DES
    see Department of Education and
    Science
Donnison, D., 2–3, 11
Douglas, J.W.B., 30, 43, 120, 134
Dreeben, R., 18, 27
    see also Barr and Dreeben
Dreeben, R. and Thomas, J.A., 134
Dunham, J., 76, 78, 85

Edmonds, R.C. *et al.*, 117, 134
Edmunds, 5
Ekhohm, M., 153
EOC
    see Equal Opportunities
    Commission
Epstein, J.L., 49, 56
Epstein, J.L. and McPartland, J.M.,
    7, 49, 56

Equal Opportunities Commission
    (EOC), 87, 101
Erbring, L. and Young, A.A., 16, 17, 27
Essen, J. and Wedge, P., 120, 134
Eustace, P.J.
    see Wilcox and Eustace
Evans, J., 200, 203

Fairley, W.B. and Mosteller, F., 115
Fennessy, J.
    see Ralf and Fennessy
Finch, S.
    see Morton-Williams and Finch
Finlayson, D.S., 7, 49–50, 51, 56
    see also Banks and Finlayson
Finlayson, D.S. and Loughran, J.L.,
    51, 56
Fogleman, K., 26, 27
Ford, J., 30, 43
Fox, S. *et al.*, 149, 153
Freud, S., 140

Galloway, D., 7–8, 75–86, 195
Galloway, D. and Barrett, C., 77, 85
Galloway, D. *et al.*, 5, 11, 77, 78, 80, 82, 85, 191, 192, 201, 203
Galton, M.J. and Simon, B., 60, 73, 103, 118, 134, 181, 189
Galton, M.J. and Willcocks, J., 181, 189
Galton, M.J. *et al.*, 60, 73, 125, 131, 134, 181, 188, 189–90
Gath, D. *et al.*, 80, 85
Georgiades, N.J. and Phillimore, L., 147, 152, 153
Getzels, J.W., 180, 190
Gintis, H.
    see Bowles and Gintis
Glatter, R., 179, 190
Goacher, B., 36, 43
Gobell, A.
    see Upton and Gobell
Goldstein, H., 35, 43, 117, 134
Goodlad, J.I. *et al.*, 118, 134
Gray, H.L., 152
Gray, J., 73, 107, 108, 114, 117, 120, 134, 191, 194, 202, 203

Gray, J. and Jones, B., 8, 103–15,
   120, 134
Gray, J. and Satterly, D., 109, 110,
   114
Gray, J. *et al.*, 5, 11, 17, 25, 27,
   42–4, 70, 73, 195, 200, 203–4
Green, A.
   see Sharp and Green
Greenfield, T.B., 55, 56
Griffin, L.J.
   see Alexander and Griffin

Hall, G.
   see Klitzaard and Hall
Halpin, A.W., 7, 181–2, 190
Halpin, A.W. and Croft, D.B., 7,
   47–8, 49, 56
Halsey, A.H. *et al.*, 201, 204
Hamblin, D.H., 75, 76, 85
Hamilton, D.
   see Parlett and Hamilton
Hamilton, D. and Delamont, S.,
   202, 204
Hamilton, D. *et al.*, 158, 174
Hammersley, M., 203
Hannan, M.T. *et al.*, 40, 44
Hanushek, E.A., 15, 27
Hargreaves, D.H., 4, 11, 30, 32–3,
   44, 80–1, 85, 137, 152, 153,
   182–3, 200, 204
Harling, P., 204
Hauser, R.M., 16, 27
Henderson, E.S., 174 and 174n2
Her Majesty's Inspectorate (HMI),
   134, 184, 190
Hersov, L. and Berg, I., 85
Hewison, J. and Tizard, J., 125, 134
Hirst, P.H., 62, 73
HMI
   see Her Majesty's Inspectorate
Houghton, V.P. *et al.*, 56
Hurman, A., 62, 73

ILEA
   see Inner London Education
      Authority
Inner London Education Authority
   (ILEA), 36–7, 40, 44, 98, 101

Jencks, C. *et al.*, 2, 11, 30–1, 44,
   193, 200, 204
Jones, A. 82, 85, 205–10
Jones, B.
   see Gray and Jones

Kane, M.
   see Lehming and Kane
Kaplan, M.H.
   see Schwartz and Kaplan
Kasarda, J.D.
   see Bidwell and Kasarda
Kelley, E.A., 52, 56
King, R.A., 7, 51, 56, 70, 73, 181,
   183, 184–5, 187, 190
Klitgaard, R. and Hall, G., 106, 115
Klopf, G.J. *et al.*, 145–6
Kyriacou, C. and Sutcliffe, J., 78, 85
Kysel, F. and Varlaam, A., 122, 134

Lacey, C., 4, 11, 181, 182–3, 190
Lawton, D. *et al.*, 204
Lehming, R. and Kane, M., 190
Lewin, K., 139, 153
Lewis, J., 9, 137–53, 167, 174
Likert, R., 181–2, 190
Lindzey, G. and Aronson, E., 190
Loughran, J.L.
   see Finlayson and Loughran

McCullagh, P., 91
McDill, 5, 7
McPartland, J.M.
   see Epstein and McPartland
McPartland, J.M. *et al.*, 49, 56
Madaus, G.F. *et al.*, 25, 27, 178, 190,
   192, 200, 204
Madge, N.
   see Rutter and Madge
March, J.G.
   see Cohen and March
Marks, J. *et al.*, 40, 44, 120, 134
Mason, W.M. *et al.*, 128, 134
Matthew, R. and Tong, S., 173, 174
Maughan, B.
   see Ouston and Maughan
Mayhew, L.B., 209, 210
Meyer, J., 21, 26, 27
Meyer, J. and Rowan, B., 21, 27–8

Meyer, M. *et al.*, 28
Moos, R.H., 55, 56
Mortimore, J. and Blackstone, T., 125, 134
Mortimore, P., 26, 117, 134
Mortimore, P. and Byford, D., 201, 204
Mortimore, P. *et al.*, 17, 117–35, 193
Morton-Williams, M., 196
Morton-Williams, M. and Finch, S., 204
Mosteller, F.
 see Fairley and Mosteller
Mungham, G. and Pearson, G., 80, 204
Murgatroyd, S.J.
 see Reynolds and Murgatroyd
Murgatroyd, S.J. and Reynolds, D., 198, 204
Musgrove, F., 5, 11

Open University, 181, 190
Ouston, J. and Maughan, B., 6–7, 29–44
Parlett, M. and Hamilton, D., 158, 174
Pearson, G.
 see Mungham and Pearson
Peters, R.S., 175
Phenix, P.H., 62, 73
Phillimore, L.
 see Georgiades and Phillimore
Phillips, D.D. and Callely, E.M., 158, 174–5
Phillips, D.D. *et al.*, 9, 155–75, 202
Plewis, I. *et al.*, 37, 44, 126, 135
Powdermarker, H., 161, 175
Powell, J.L. and Scrimgour, M.N.G., 125, 135
Power, M., 4
Pratt, J., 78, 86
Pring, R., 202, 204
Purkey, S.C. and Smith, M.S., 24, 28, 54, 55, 56, 105, 106, 107, 115

Radical Statistics Education Group, 126, 135
Ralf, J.H. and Fennessy, J., 24, 28

Reid, K.
 see Reynolds and Reid
Reynolds, D., 1–11, 34, 55, 56, 86, 117, 122, 123–4, 135, 181, 182, 187, 190, 191, 192, 193, 194, 195, 196, 200, 204, 207, 208
 see also Murgatroyd and Reynolds
Reynolds, D. and Murgatroyd, S., 76, 86
Reynolds, D. and Reid, K., 10, 26, 106, 191–204
Reynolds, D. and Sullivan, M., 11
Reynolds, D. *et al.*, 20, 26, 28, 31, 44
Rowan, B.
 see Meyer and Rowan
Rudd, W.G.A. and Wiseman, S., 78, 86
Rutter, M., 4, 5, 11, 35, 44, 181, 187, 188, 191, 192, 193, 194, 195, 204
Rutter, M. and Madge, N., 120, 135
Rutter, M. *et al.*, 17, 20, 25, 28, 31, 34, 39, 40, 44, 60, 70, 73, 78, 83, 86, 103, 115, 117, 135, 181–2, 190, 191, 192, 196, 200, 204

Sagor, R., 54–5, 56–7
Sammons, P. *et al.*, 119–20, 135
Sarah, E.
 see Spender and Sarah
Sarah, E. *et al.*, 88
Satterly, D.
 see Gray and Satterly
Scheerer, H., 49, 57
Schmuck *et al.*, 139
Schonfeld, W.K., 55, 57
Schultz, A., 190
Schwartz, T.A. and Kaplan, M.H., 159, 175
Scottish Council for Research in Education, 36, 44
Scrimgour, M.N.G.
 see Powell and Scrimgour
Sewell, W.H. *et al.*, 28
Sharp, R. and Green, A., 181, 183, 184, 187, 190
Shipman, M., 37, 44
Simon, B.
 see Galton and Simon
Simon, B. and Willcocks, J., 184, 190

Simonite, V., 87, 91
Simpkins, T., 71, 73–4
Smith, M.S.
    see Purkey and Smith
Spender, D. and Sarah, E., 88, 101
Spooner, R., 76, 86
Steedman, J., 8, 25, 28, 35, 39, 40, 44,
    87–101, 196, 204
Stenhouse, L., 72–3, 74, 202, 204
Strivens, J., 6–7, 45–57, 195
Sullivan, M.
    see Reynolds and Sullivan
Summers, A.A. and Wolfe, B.L.,
    117–18, 135
Sutcliffe, J.
    see Kyriacou and Sutcliffe
Swedish Leadership Programme,
    145

Taylor, W., 180, 190
Thomas, J.A.
    see Dreeben and Thomas
Thomas, J.B., 4, 11
Thomas, R.A., 48, 57
Thoresen, C.E.
    see Coates and Thoresen
Tibbenham, A. *et al.*, 192, 204
Tizard, B. *et al.*, 117, 126, 135
Tizard, J.
    see Hewison and Tizard
Tong, S.
    see Matthew and Tong
Turner, G., 181, 182, 190
Tyerman, M.J., 2, 11, 86

Upton, G. and Gobell, A., 174

Vanderslice, G., 142, 153
Varlaam, A.
    see Kysel and Varlaam

Walker, D.E., 190
Walker, S.
    see Barton and Walker
Warnock, 142
Watson, G., 153
Watts, J., 173, 175
Weber, G., 117, 135
Wedge, P.
    see Essen and Wedge
Weick, K.E., 53, 57
Whitbread, N., 185, 190
Wilcox, B., 7, 59–74, 195
Wilcox, B. and Eustace, P.J., 61, 74
Wiley, D.E., 15, 28
Willcocks, J.
    see Galton and Willcocks; Simon
        and Willcocks
Wiseman, S.
    see Rudd and Wiseman
Wolfe, B.L.
    see Summers and Wolfe
Woods, P., 204

Young, A.A.
    see Erbring and Young
Young, P., 9–10, 177–90
Yukl, G.A., 186, 190

Subject Index

ability
of pupils, 15–17, 22, 23, 24, 30, 37
academic attainment, 68–71, 81–3,
87–101, 194, 197, 208
academic goals
and schooling, 50–1
access
to secondary schooling, 30
accountability, 31, 42, 51, 143, 144
American Programme [in New York
city], 9, 145–6
content of, 146
objectives of, 145–6
APU
see Assessment of Performance
Unit
Aspects of Secondary Education, 105
Assessment of Performance Unit
(APU), 87, 122
Language Survey team of, 122
attendance rates, 34
authority
in schools, 207–8
see also headteachers; leadership

Basic Mathematics Test (BMT), 120,
121, 128
'Beachside Comprehensive'
[school], 186
behaviour problems
in Cardiff secondary schools,
155–74
BERA [British Educational
Research Association], 118
Bethel (Maine, USA), 139

Black Papers, 177
BMT
see Basic Mathematics Test
boys
and examination results, 87–101
Bristol
GRIDS project in, 199
British Psychological Society, 4
bussing, 16

Cardiff Programme, 9, 146, 147–52,
155–74
basic assumptions of, 157–8
and changes in colleagues'
behaviour, 169–70
course content of, 155–6
and deputy heads, 172–4
evaluation of, 156, 171–4
and headteachers, 171–2, 173–4
and institutional change, 156–74
methodology of, 158–9
and 'pathways to development',
160–3
results of, 160–74
and School-Based Study, 147–52,
156, 160, 167–9, 172
schools in, 159
teachers in, 159–60
Cardiff, University College
see University College, Cardiff
case studies, 10, 13, 24
catchment areas
see schools, catchment areas of
'Checkpoints', 121
child-centred approach, 184, 185

219

'Child at School' schedule, 122, 123, 128
City and Guilds examinations, 39
'climate'
    see school ethos
co-educational schooling, 87–101
cognitive development, 120–2
cognitive outcomes, 196
Coleman Report, 197
compositional effects, 16–17, 20
comprehensive schools, 31, 50, 75–6, 80–1, 82, 84, 89–91, 96, 100
Comprehensive Schools Feasibility Study, 50
Contemporary Educational Records Archive
    proposal for, 72–3
Contexts Project, 109–12, 202
correspondence theories, 22
COSMOS [Committee for the Organization, Staffing and Management of Schools], 61
counsellors, 75
    see also pastoral care
Countesthorpe system, 173
CSE [Certificate of Secondary Education] examinations, 36, 38–9, 87, 91, 97, 100, 109–12, 196
curriculum, 7, 59–74, 195
    and balance, 61–4, 72
    content of, 59, 60
    and learning environment, 59–60
    notation system for, 7, 60–8, 71–2
    organization of, 59, 60–73
    in primary schools, 188
    and school effectiveness, 7, 59–74, 195
    and subject groupings, 62–4
    and teaching, 59–60

delinquency, 34, 197
Department of Education and Science (DES), 26, 39, 59, 87
deputy heads
    and institutional change, 9, 172–4, 207
DES

see Department of Education and Science
disruptive behaviour, 78–83

Edinburgh Reading Test (ERT), 120–1, 128
Education Act (1981), 194, 196, 201
ERT
    see Edinburgh Reading Test
ethnic minorities, 36, 37, 39
ethnography, 8, 23, 54, 55, 158
examination results, 6–7, 8, 34, 36, 37, 38–41, 42, 43, 45, 68–71, 87–101, 109–12, 194, 195, 196
    in mixed schools, 87–101
    publication of, 194
    in single-sex secondary schools, 87–101
exemplary schools framework, 6, 13, 23–5
experiential training programme, 146–7

family background
    see home background
Fifteen Thousand Hours, 103, 181
From Birth to Seven, 2
Functions of the Executive, The, 48

gender, 87–99
girls
    and examination results, 87–101
    and performance at school, 36
    and single-sex schools, 87–8
    and type of school attended, 90
grammar schools, 89–91, 96, 100
GRIDS project, 199

Harnischfeger-Wiley model, 15
headteachers, 9, 171–2, 173–4, 185, 195, 207–9
    and institutional development, 9, 171–2, 173–4
    and leadership, 207–9
    role of, 185, 195
Her Majesty's Inspectorate (HMI), 37, 42, 61, 62, 105, 118, 187
'hidden curriculum', 33, 37, 77–8
HMI

see Her Majesty's Inspectorate
home background, 1–4, 15, 22, 23, 24, 30, 89–90, 100, 106, 125, 201–2

IEA, 5
ILEA
  see Inner London Education Authority
independent schools, 90–1, 96, 100
individualistic paradigm, 1–5, 6
inner cities
  see Inner London Education Authority, Junior School Project
Inner London Education Authority (ILEA) comprehensive
  schools in, 60
  and examinations, 39, 40–1
  Junior School Project of, 8–9, 26, 117–35, 193
    aims of, 118–19
    analysis strategies used in, 129–32
    and background variables, 130
    fixed effects in, 128–9
    and measurement of progress, 129–30
    measures used in, 119–26
    methods of, 119–32
    and observational data, 130–1
    and predictor variables, 128
    and pupil outcomes, 131–2
    and random effects, 128–9
    reporting of, 132
    sampling in, 126–7
    and school variables, 131–2
    statistical problems of, 126–9
    units of analysis in, 127–8
  Research and Statistics Group of, 98
input-output framework, 6, 10, 13–19, 20, 23, 25, 180
inputs model, 33
in-service courses, 155–74
institutional change, 9, 155–74
  and deputy heads, 172–4
  and headteachers, 171–2, 173–4

in secondary schools, 155–74
institutional framework, 6, 13–14, 21–2, 23, 24–5
  see also institutional change
intake differences, 5, 6, 8, 15–17, 34–5, 38, 40–1, 81–3, 88–9, 91, 98–9, 109–12, 119–20, 193–4, 201, 202, 203
  and examination performance, 88–9, 91, 98–9
Interchange, 202
Ireland
  school samples from, 192

Junior School Study
  see Inner London Education Authority, Junior School Project of
junior schools, 117–33
  background of pupils in, 120
  classrooms in, 124–5
  cognitive development of pupils in, 120–2
  non-cognitive development of pupils in, 122–4
  teachers in, 124–6

Keeping the School under Review, 36–7

leadership, 9, 10, 183
  in Nebraska schools, 146–7
  in New Zealand elementary schools, 145–6
  and organizational climate, 48
  in schools, 145–7, 207–8
  in Sweden, 144–5, 146
  see also management
learning difficulties
  in Cardiff secondary schools, 155–74
LEAs
  see local education authorities
Leicester, University of, 103
Leverhulme Foundation, 125
local education authorities (LEAs), 29, 31, 34, 36, 37, 38, 40, 42, 61, 73, 80, 202

see also Inner London Education
  Authority
London
  behaviour in schools in, 83
  comprehensive schools in, 192
  examinations in schools in, 38
  outcomes in schools in, 40
  primary schools in, 26
  see also Inner London Education
    Authority
longitudinal research, 87–101,
  117–35
Lumley School, 137

Machiavellian approach, 138
management
  and classroom environments,
    181–3
  in education, 9–10, 177–90
  evaluation of, 10, 187–8
  and internal organization of
    educational institutions,
    179–89
  and school climate, 181–3
  see also leadership
Manchester
  researchers in, 182
Marxism
  see neo-Marxism
'Me at School' instrument, 123
Michigan [USA]
  elementary schools in, 106
mixed schools, 8, 87–101
  intakes of, 88–9, 91, 98–9
mode 3 CSE examinations, 36
multi-ethnic education, 26

National Child Development Study
  (NCDS) data, 40, 87, 89–101
National Children's Bureau, 2, 8,
  25–6, 196
National Training Laboratories
  (USA), 139
Nebraska, University of, 9, 138,
  146–7
  Centre for Urban Education of, 9,
    146–7
neo-Marxism, 4
New York

institutional change in, 138,
  145–6

New Zealand
  behaviour in schools in, 82–3
  pastoral care in schools in, 78, 79
  primary teachers in, 78
NFER [National Foundation for
  Educational Research] Basic
  Mathematics Test (BMT), 120–1,
  128

Observational Research and
  Classroom Learning Evaluation
  (ORACLE) project, 103, 125, 130,
  184, 187–8
O-level examinations, 38–9, 87, 91,
  92–8, 100, 109–12, 195, 196
ORACLE project
  see Observational Research and
    Classroom Learning Evaluation
    project
organization theory, 47–8, 50,
  52–3, 180
  see also school organization
Organizational Climate
  Development Questionnaire
  (OCDG), 48–50, 51
Organizational Development, 9,
  138–44, 151
  and communication, 142
  and conflict, 142
  and decision-making, 143
  and education, 9, 138–44, 151
  and goals, 142
  and groups, 142–3
  and industry, 139
  and knowledge, 140
  and power, 140–2
  and problem-solving, 143
  and self-awareness, 140
organizational framework, 6, 13–14,
  18–20, 23, 24–5
  see also Organizational
    Development; school
    organization
outcomes
  assessment of, 29–43
  cognitive, 196

definitions of, 29–30, 32–4
evaluation of, 31–2
measures of, 32, 34, 35, 36–8,
   42–3, 196
non-cognitive, 196
and pastoral care, 81–3
and school differences, 4, 5,
   6–7, 13–26, 29–43, 46–8,
   81–3, 84, 191–4, 195–7, 201,
   202, 203, 207
social, 122–4, 196, 197
variables relevant to, 84, 103–4;
   see also outcomes, measures of
outlier schools, 23–4

pastoral care, 7–8, 75–86, 156, 195
aims of, 75–8
and attendance, 82
and behaviour at school, 82
definition of, 76–7
evaluation of, 81–4
function of, 75–8
models of, 78–81
organization of, 78–81, 82, 84

Plowden Committee, 11
Plowden Report, 2
primary schools
and pastoral care, 83–4
and school differences, 8–9, 26,
   117–35, 192–3, 199
see also Inner London Education
   Authority, Junior School
   Project of
Primary Survey [by HMI], 188
process
in schools, 5, 6, 33, 157–74, 178,
   182, 189, 195, 197, 198, 200,
   201, 203, 206–9
Programme for Principals of
   Elementary Schools, 9
Programme of School Leader
   Education, 9
pupils
and attendance, 123–4
attitudes of, 49–51, 122–3
behaviour of, 78–83, 122
backgrounds of, 2–4, 120
and educational management, 179

and examinations, *see* examination
   results
and home background, *see* home
   background
individual characteristics of, 1–5
role of, 207
self-concepts of, 123
status of, 49–51

QSL
   see Quality of School Life Scales
qualitative approaches
and school effectiveness studies, 8,
   9, 22, 103–15
Quality of School Life (QSL) Scales,
   49
quantitative approaches
and school effectiveness studies, 8,
   9, 22, 103–15

racial background, 14–17
Raven's Coloured Progressive
   Mastrices test, 120–1, 128, 129
reading, 107–9, 121
resources
and school effectiveness, 6, 13, 15,
   17, 19–20, 30, 179, 186–8
ROSLA [raising of the school
   leaving age], 31
RSA [Royal Society for the Arts]
   examinations, 39

sampling
in Junior School Project, 126–7
and school effectiveness research,
   192–3
School-Based Study
   see Cardiff Programme, and
   School-Based Study
school climate
concept of, 7, 45–55
   see also school ethos
School Climate Scales, 51
school effectiveness
analysis in research on, 200–1
and change in schools, 137–53,
   185–6, 199–200
compared with school climate, 46

and contextual effects, 15–17, 20
and curriculum differences, 7, 59–74, 195
definitions of, 13–14
and disaggregation of pupils, 197–9
and disaggregation of schools, 197–9
and examination performance, 89–101, 109–12, *see also* examination results
frameworks for research on, 13–26
and home background, *see* home background
and intakes, *see* intake differences
and management in education, 177–90
methodology for research on, 199–200
model for research on, 205–10
and outcomes, *see* outcomes
and pastoral care, *see* pastoral care
and pupils' prior attainments, 99, 106–7
and qualitative approaches, *see* qualitative approaches
and quantitative approaches, *see* quantitive approaches
review of research on, 1–11
sampling in research on, 192–3
and skills, 209
social, 122–4
theory in research on, 200
see also 'school effects'
'school effects', 13–26
see also school effectiveness
school ethos, 7, 8, 10, 25, 45–55, 178–9, 180, 181–3, 191–2
school leader education programme [Sweden], 144–5, 146
components of, 144–5
objectives of, 146
school organization, 18–20, 25, 30, 45–55, 81–3, 124–5, 181–3, 191–2, 205, 208
School Organization and Pupil Involvement, 51
school outcomes
see outcomes

school subjects
and examination performance, 91–8
schooling
aims of, 32
as ineffectual, 177–8
see also school effectiveness; schools
schools
and between school comparisons, 37–8, 59–74
catchment areas of, *see* intake differences
and change, 9, 185–6, 199–200
and change strategies, 137–53, 185–6
compared with business, 143–4
and curriculum differences, 59–74
and home background, *see* home background
and in-school evaluation, 36–7, 40, 43
and institutional change, 155–74
and pupil behaviour, 78–83
and pupil characteristics, 1–5, *see also* home background
social context of, 4

Scotland
ability grouping in, 192
SCOTS schedule, 125, 130
Scottish Data Archive
see Scottish Education Data Archive
Scottish Education Data Archive, 25, 201
secondary modern schools, 89–91, 96, 100
segregated schooling, 87–101
sex differences
and education attainment, 88–99
and examinations, 92–9
Sheffield
behaviour in schools in, 82–3
comprehensive schools in, 82–3, 192, 201
pastoral care in schools in, 78–9
suspension rates in schools in, 82
Sheffield local education authority, 60–8, 72

single-sex schools, 8, 87–101
  intakes of, 88–9, 91, 98–9
'Smiley' instrument, 122–3
social background, 14–17, 21–2, 23,
  24, 25
  see also home background
social class, 4, 17, 22, 30, 31, 89, 100,
  184, 187, 193, 201
social-emotional goals
  of schooling, 50–1
social system
  and change in schools, 186
  and education, 182
social systems theory, 180
SPSS package, 127, 129
sub-cultures
  in schools, 182–3
Sweden
  institutional change in, 9, 138,
    144–5
  school leader education in, 9,
    144–5

teachers
  autonomy of, 185
  backgrounds of, 124–5
  and categorization of pupils,
    184–5, 187
  and change in schools, 9, 151–2
  and collection of research data, 203
  and differentiation of pupils,
    182–3
  and examinations, 109–12
  and goal displacement, 183–5
  inputs of, 19–20
  and institutional development,
    157, 159–74
  in junior schools, 124–6
  and mathematics, 109
  and pastoral care, 78–81
  and projects on institutional
    change, 144–52
  and qualitative approaches,
    103–15
  and quantitative approaches,
    103–15
  and reading, 107–9
  as researchers, 202
  and resource allocation, 187
  and school ethos, 181

  and self-criticism, 188
  and skills, 209
  sources of satisfaction for, 78
  sources of stress for, 78
teaching methods, 187–8
teaching resources
  allocation of, 63–8, 69
teaching styles, 131
Teaching Styles and Pupil Progress,
  103, 109
Ten Good Schools, 105
Tower Hamlets, 4
truancy, 2, 3, 33

University College, Cardiff,
  155–74, 203
  Department of Education of,
    155–74
United States of America (USA)
  determinants of pupil learning in,
    1–2
  groups of pupils in, 197
  influence of schools in, 177, 178
  'outlier' studies in, 106
  qualitative and quantitative
    research approaches in, 105
  research on 'effective schools' in, 8
  school differences research in, 5
  school outcomes in, 30–1, 196
  social policies in, 16
  studies of elementary schools in,
    117–18
  studies of high schools in, 118
  work on school climate in, 47–8,
    51–2, 55

Wales, South
  behaviour in schools in, 83
  school positions in, 195–6
  secondary schools in, 138, 192
  social class and schooling in, 193
  teachers as researchers in, 202–3
Welsh Office, 156, 157, 159
West Glamorgan Institute, 203
writing
  creative, 121

Youth Training Scheme (YTS), 42

zoning, 16